2009 Saint Paul

ALMANAC

Assistant copy editors: Brie Goellner, Nancy Yang, Emily Ojanen, Marissa Papatola

Community editors: Andreesa Wright, Diego Vázquez, Jane Cagle-Kemp, Donna Legato, Tou SaiKo Lee, and Michelle Bierman

Copy editor: Jan Zita Grover

Cover designer: Kevin R. Brown

Designer and typesetter: Donna Burch

History facts researcher: Steve Trimble and Brie Goellner

Proofreader: Laura Beaudoin

Publisher and managing editor: Kimberly Nightingale

ISBN 978-0-9772651-4-5

Manufactured in Canada by Friesens

Saint Paul Almanac
PO Box 16243
Saint Paul, MN 55116
saintpaulalmanac.com

Saint Paul Almanac is a subsidiary of Arcata Press, a nonprofit publisher.

ACKNOWLEDGMENTS

This year, like each year, the *Saint Paul Almanac* came into being because many people and organizations assisted in its birth. Carol Connolly, poet laureate of Saint Paul, and Denise Fosse, Saint Paul Almanac board chair—both human beings of extraordinary measure—kept belief in the *Saint Paul Almanac* and pushed us on to new heights. Over eighty authors are represented in this year's *Saint Paul Almanac.*

We started a Community Editors Program for this year's edition. Six Saint Paulites from different neighborhoods, backgrounds, and ages became editors, reaching into their own communities to find stories of our city. Donna Legato, Diego Vázquez, Andreesa Wright, Jane Cagle-Kemp, Tou SaiKo Lee, and Michele Bierman did a tremendous job of organizing to bring you the stories of their Saint Paul communities. A special thank-you goes to writer and teacher May Lee, who was not an "official" community editor but brought many writers and stories our way. Thank you to Sue Zumberge at Common Good Books and Kathy Mouacheupao at the Center for Hmong Arts and Talent (CHAT) for all their help too.

Our production team worked long and hard. Jan Zita Grover copyedited all the stories with great respect for each of them. Thank you to Kevin R. Brown for a dynamic cover and to Donna Burch for beautiful interior design and typesetting work. Deep appreciation goes to Nigel Parry, our Webmaster, for his fine work, great prices, and easygoing way. We had a host of young assistant copy editors: Brie Goellner, Emily Ojanen, Nancy Yang, and Marissa Papatola fact-checked to be certain our listings were as accurate as possible. Thank you to our proofreader, Laura Beaudoin, for her eagle eyes. Steve Trimble researched interesting facts and quotes related to Saint Paul, and Brie Goellner added a few extras. It's always fun to see what they come up with.

Thank you to photographers Patricia Bour-Schilla, Lou Michaels, and Tom Conlon. They ran all over town finding those special photos of our city and its people. Thank you to Tobechi Tobechukwu for his photos of the Golden Thyme and Brian Macke for his RollerGirls photo. Eric Mortensen and Bridget White at the Minnesota Historical Society photograph collections helped us locate hard-to-find photos; Rod Eaton and Aaron Isaacs at the Minnesota Streetcar Museum and Susan Hoffman at the Jewish Historical Society of the Upper Midwest assisted with the elusive photo search as well.

Also thank you to Sara Remke, Ilka Bird, Kalue Her, Dan Tilsen, Chris Crutchfield, Bernie Brodkorb, and Dawn Trexel for keeping the *Saint Paul Almanac* operating in fine shape.

Thank you to Traveler's Arts & Diversity Employee Committee, the City of Saint Paul Cultural STAR Program, Friends of the Saint Paul Public Library, KFAI Radio, the Black Dog Café, Twin Cities Daily Planet and all of our individual donors for your kind support and generous contributions.

It's the writers who truly make the *Saint Paul Almanac* sing. Without your words, we don't exist. Thank you for the courage to send in your writing and for working collaboratively with us to make this little book happen.

TABLE OF CONTENTS

INTRODUCTION

Find your place on the planet. Dig in, and take responsibility from there.
—Gary Snyder

When I was six years old, I spent many weeks in the burn ward of Ramsey Hospital, now Regions. Even when you're six, you learn that surviving a catastrophe splits you off from the world, and it takes some time to re-enter it. For some people and their tragedies, it takes a whole life to root oneself back into community. One thing that helped me re-enter life was reading, specifically poems. I had a poetry book, *Wynken, Blynken, and Nod*, by Eugene Field. I'd sit up in my hospital bed and read that poem over and over and stare out the window at all that Saint Paul snow.

Each one of us suffers great difficulties. Most of us will have several catastrophes in one lifetime. We move in and out of feeling we belong. We step out into wild frontiers that challenge and terrify us. Whatever you may personally be experiencing, we hope the stories in the *Saint Paul Almanac* offer a small place of refuge. It's true: Saint Paul is often thought of as a quiet town where things change slowly. But that's a deliberate disguise—hiding all the city's newness and difficulties under a practiced stodginess. Helping each other through new times and tough times strengthens us all. This year the *Saint Paul Almanac* enlisted the support of six Saint Paul residents as community editors. These editors reached into their communities to help bring together the diverse writers you read in this year's *Almanac*. Whether you're here for one day or for over 100 years, we hope reading the *Saint Paul Almanac* helps you feel welcome and at home. You really do belong—right here in Saint Paul. —Kimberly Nightingale

Photo © Patricia Bour-Schilla

CITY OF

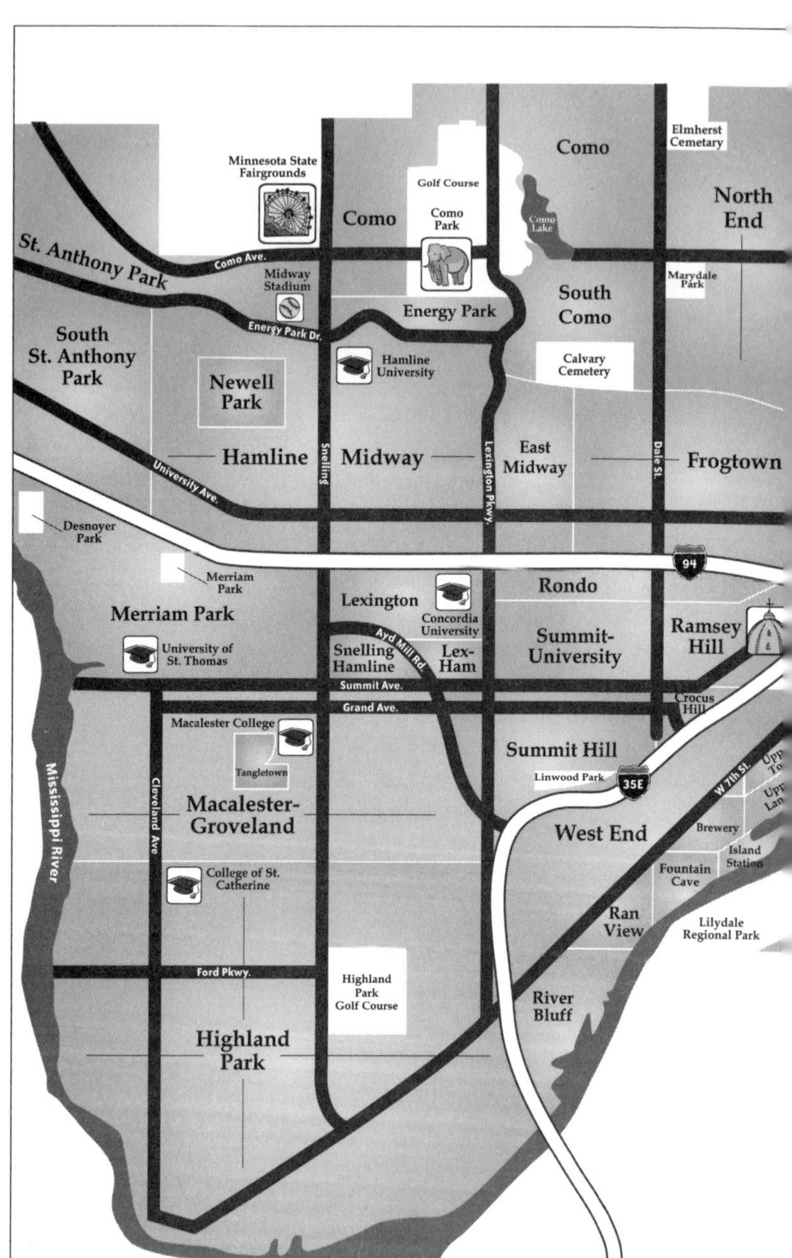

Illustration © Ellen Dahl

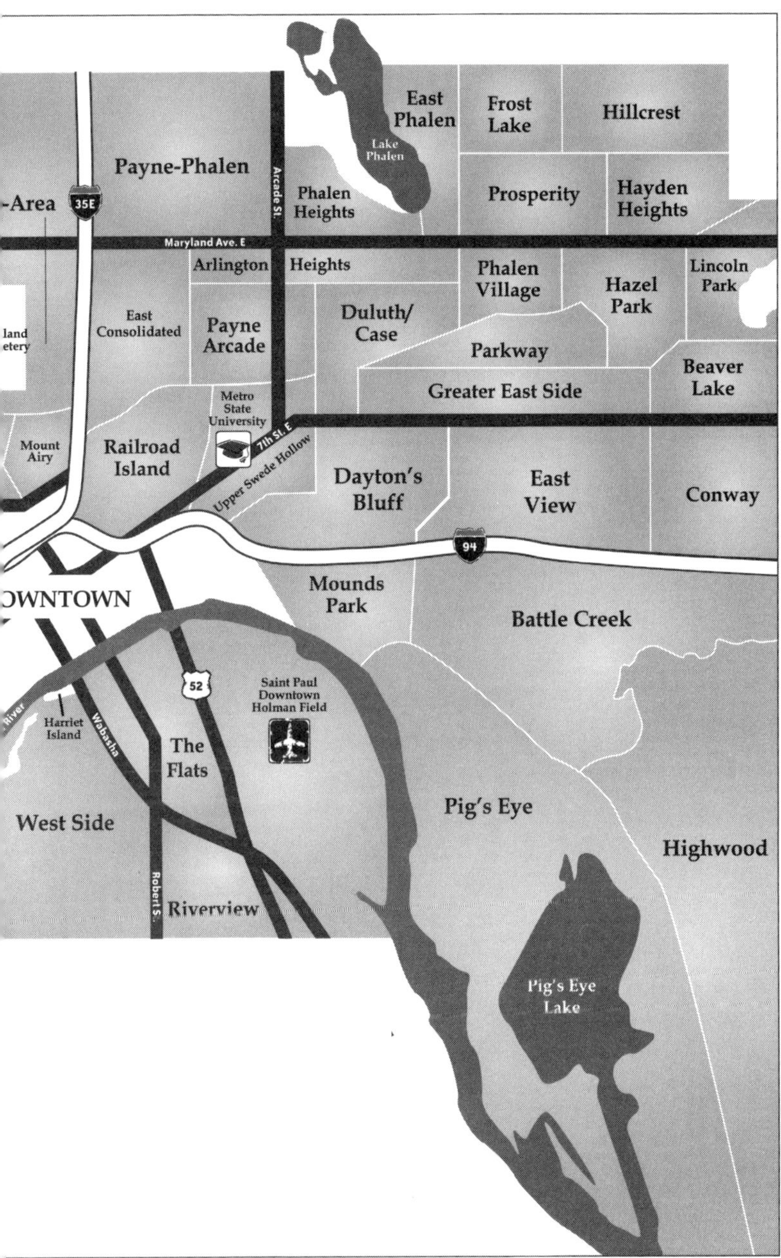
East Phalen
Frost Lake
Hillcrest
Lake Phalen
Payne-Phalen
Arcade St.
Phalen Heights
Prosperity
Hayden Heights
-Area
35E
Maryland Ave. E
Arlington
Heights
Phalen Village
Hazel Park
Lincoln Park
East Consolidated
Payne Arcade
Duluth/ Case
Parkway
Beaver Lake
land
etery
Greater East Side
Metro State University
Mount Airy
Railroad Island
7th St. E
Upper Swede Hollow
Dayton's Bluff
East View
Conway
94
OWNTOWN
Mounds Park
Battle Creek
52
Saint Paul Downtown Holman Field
River
Harriet Island
Wabasha
The Flats
West Side
Pig's Eye
Highwood
Robert S.
Riverview
Pig's Eye Lake

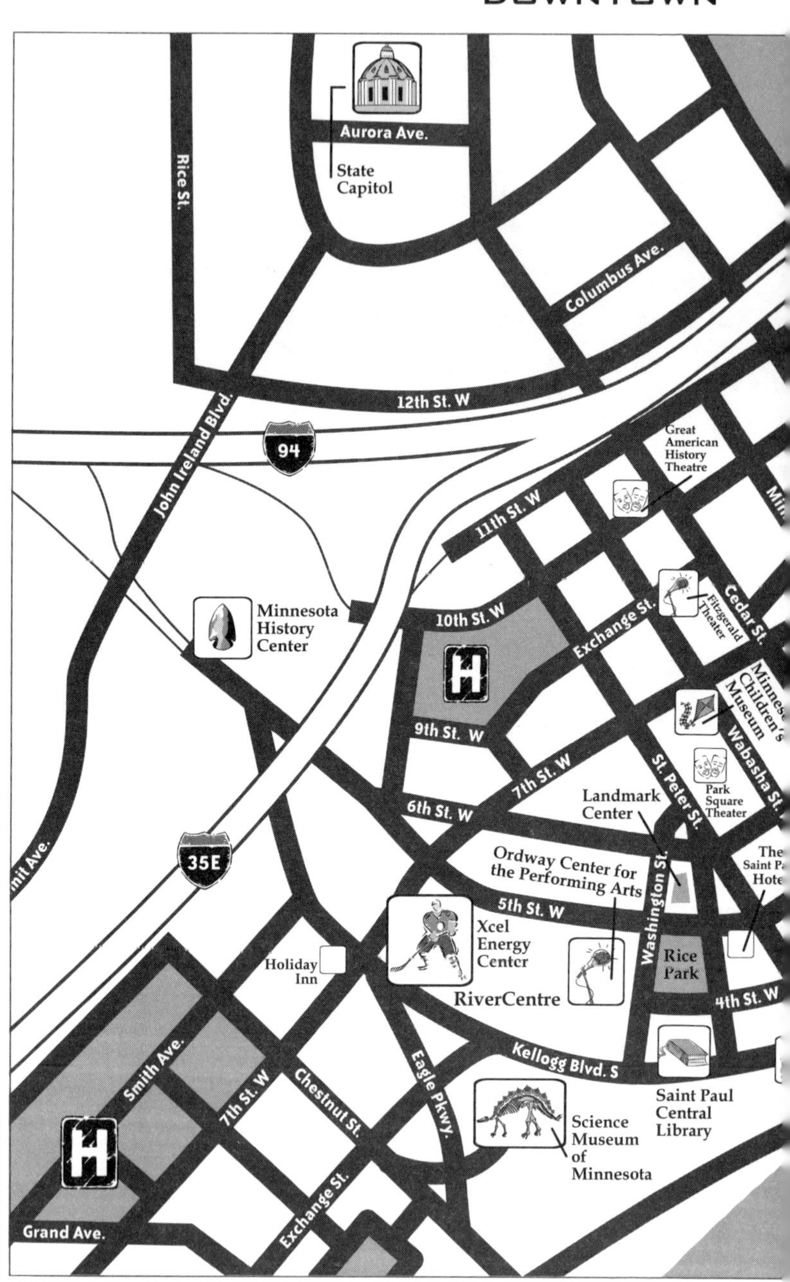

Aurora Ave.
State
Capitol
Rice St.
Columbus Ave.
12th St. W
John Ireland Blvd.
94
Great
American
History
Theatre
11th St. W
Minnesota
History
Center
10th St. W
Exchange St.
Fitzgerald
Theater
Cedar St.
Children's
Museum
9th St. W
7th St. W
Wabasha St.
St. Peter St.
Park
Square
Theater
Landmark
Center
6th St. W
35E
Ordway Center for
the Performing Arts
Washington St.
5th St. W
Xcel
Energy
Center
Holiday
Inn
RiverCentre
Rice
Park
4th St. W
Kellogg Blvd. S
Eagle Pkwy.
Smith Ave.
7th St. W
Chestnut St.
Saint Paul
Central
Library
Science
Museum
of
Minnesota
Exchange St.
Grand Ave.

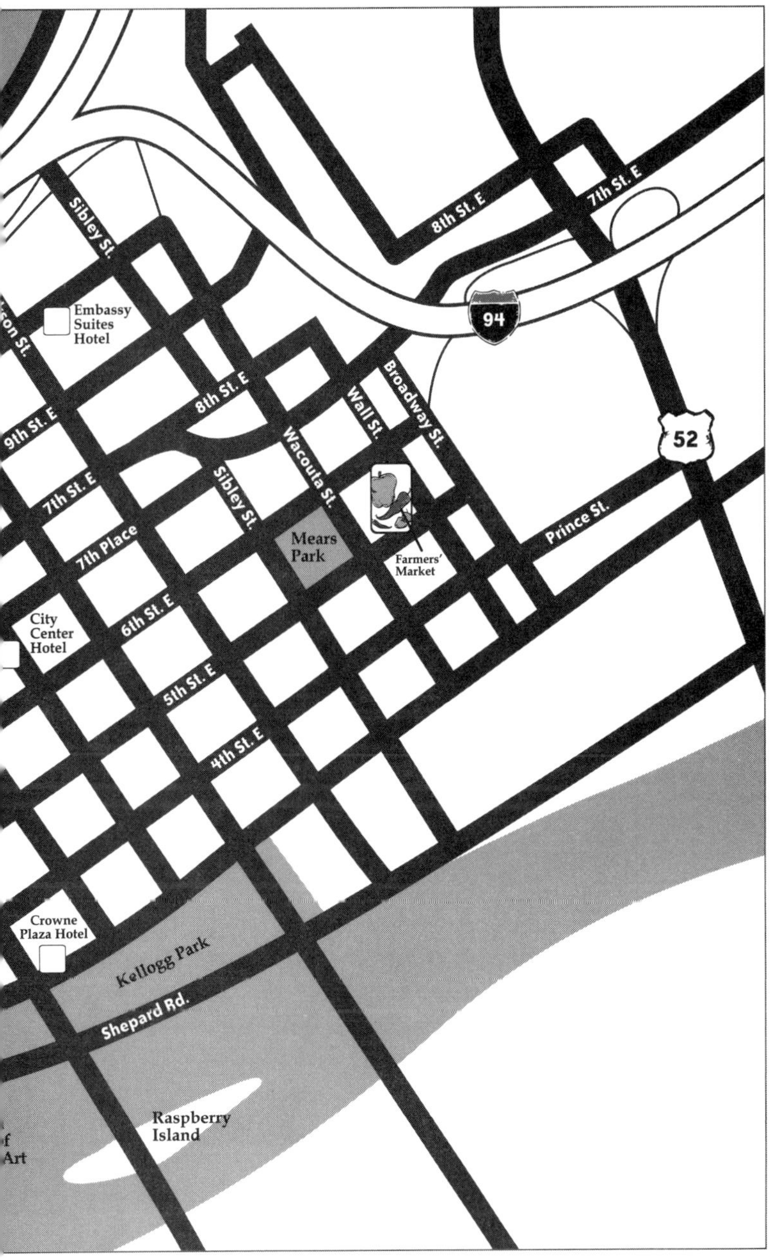

Sibley St.
8th St. E
7th St. E
Embassy Suites Hotel
94
Broadway St.
Wall St.
8th St. E
9th St. E
Wacouta St.
52
7th St. E
Sibley St.
7th Place
Mears Park
Farmers' Market
Prince St.
City Center Hotel
6th St. E
5th St. E
4th St. E
Crowne Plaza Hotel
Kellogg Park
Shepard Rd.
Raspberry Island
Art

2009

JANUARY

S	M	T	W	T	F	S
28	29	30	31	1	2	3
4	5	6	7	8	9	10
11	12	13	14	15	16	17
18	19	20	21	22	23	24
25	26	27	28	29	30	31

FEBRUARY

S	M	T	W	T	F	S
1	2	3	4	5	6	7
8	9	10	11	12	13	14
15	16	17	18	19	20	21
22	23	24	25	26	27	28
1	2	3	4	5	6	7

MARCH

S	M	T	W	T	F	S
1	2	3	4	5	6	7
8	9	10	11	12	13	14
15	16	17	18	19	20	21
22	23	24	25	26	27	28
29	30	31	1	2	3	4

APRIL

S	M	T	W	T	F	S
29	30	31	1	2	3	4
5	6	7	8	9	10	11
12	13	14	15	16	17	18
19	20	21	22	23	24	25
26	27	28	29	30	1	2

MAY

S	M	T	W	T	F	S
26	27	28	29	30	1	2
3	4	5	6	7	8	9
10	11	12	13	14	15	16
17	18	19	20	21	22	23
24	25	26	27	28	29	30
31	1	2	3	4	5	6

JUNE

S	M	T	W	T	F	S
31	1	2	3	4	5	6
7	8	9	10	11	12	13
14	15	16	17	18	19	20
21	22	23	24	25	26	27
28	29	30	1	2	3	4

JULY

S	M	T	W	T	F	S
28	29	30	1	2	3	4
5	6	7	8	9	10	11
12	13	14	15	16	17	18
19	20	21	22	23	24	25
26	27	28	29	30	31	1

AUGUST

S	M	T	W	T	F	S
26	27	28	29	30	31	1
2	3	4	5	6	7	8
9	10	11	12	13	14	15
16	17	18	19	20	21	22
23	24	25	26	27	28	29
30	31	1	2	3	4	5

SEPTEMBER

S	M	T	W	T	F	S
30	31	1	2	3	4	5
6	7	8	9	10	11	12
13	14	15	16	17	18	19
20	21	22	23	24	25	26
27	28	29	30	1	2	3

OCTOBER

S	M	T	W	T	F	S
27	28	29	30	1	2	3
4	5	6	7	8	9	10
11	12	13	14	15	16	17
18	19	20	21	22	23	24
25	26	27	28	29	30	31

NOVEMBER

S	M	T	W	T	F	S
1	2	3	4	5	6	7
8	9	10	11	12	13	14
15	16	17	18	19	20	21
22	23	24	25	26	27	28
29	30	1	2	3	4	5

DECEMBER

S	M	T	W	T	F	S
29	30	1	2	3	4	5
6	7	8	9	10	11	12
13	14	15	16	17	18	19
20	21	22	23	24	25	26
27	28	29	30	31	1	2

CALENDAR

Plus Saint Paul

Stories,

Articles,

and Poems

JANUARY

Photo © Patricia Bour-Schilla

O lovely, serene January
When at last we are done being merry
And can brood and feed birds
And look up odd words
In Webster's abridged dictionary.
—Garrison Keillor

Downtown Saint Paul Winter Farmers' Market: Saturdays through March

Land O' Lakes Kennel Club Dog Show: January 2–4

Orchid Show: January 2–25

International Chamber Orchestra Festival: January 8–30

Saint Paul Chamber Orchestra: January 8, 9, 10, 16, 17, 1

Minnesota Boychoir Winter Concert: January 11

Saint Paul Winter Carnival: January 22–February 1

Fourth Friday at the Movies: January 23

Minnesota Opera, *Faust*: January 24, 27, 29, 31, February 1

Historic Saint Paul Concert with the SPCO: January 24

Saintly City Cat Show: January 31–February 1

See pages 288–310 for more information and more events

➪ Thomas R. Potts, a physician, came to Saint Paul in 1849, practiced medicine for twenty-six years, and became the city's first mayor, serving from 1850 to 1851.

JANUARY

S	M	T	W	T	F	S
28	29	30	31	1	2	3
4	5	6	7	8	9	10
11	12	13	14	15	16	17
18	19	20	21	22	23	24
25	26	27	28	29	30	31

29 MONDAY

30 TUESDAY

31 WEDNESDAY

1 THURSDAY

New Year's Day

Photo © Tom Conlon

Eternal summer in the Sunken Garden at the Marjorie McNeeley Conservatory, Como Park

2 FRIDAY	Land O' Lakes Kennel Club Dog Show Orchid Show
3 SATURDAY	Saint Paul Farmers' Market Land O' Lakes Kennel Club Dog Show Orchid Show
4 SUNDAY	Land O' Lakes Kennel Club Dog Show Orchid Show

Cafesjian's Carousel, now located in Como Park, was built in 1914 by the Philadelphia Toboggan Company.

MINNESOTA ROLLERGIRLS

Drew Johnson

The door to the legendary Roy Wilkins Auditorium doesn't even open for an hour, yet eighty people are waiting as my wife and I step into line. In another half hour, the line will double and then double again, until the RiverCentre staff will ask the RollerGirls to open the doors early. A line of over three hundred people messes up the flow of the public through Saint Paul's convention center and to the Xcel.

One ticket check later, the missus and I are through the line and into the swirl of the Roy ("The exact geographical center of derby") on Minnesota RollerGirl night. My wife nabs a pom-pom from a dark-haired woman in an orange lab coat cut for speed, and we almost stumble over a player wearing sparkly red, and thickly draped with promotional tee shirts ("Free tee shirts to the first two hundred!"). We ask for a small, and she points us to Frau, a short-haired women in sparkly red athletic gear standing in a whirlwind of people, breezily fending off fans with a smile and a tee shirt. Shirt in hand and a check of the merchandise table later, we head into the auditorium to beat the crowds. By 7:30, the Roy will be packed with four thousand paying derby fans, so it's good to not be in the lobby when the rush begins.

Out come the announcers, the pre-show, the explanations, the rules ("Don't spill your beer!"), and the tee shirt gun. The edges of derby, with friends and family volunteering to take care of things while the players get ready, make derby feel like a mixture of performance art and a caricature of twentieth-century sporting life. Each team's gear is a mixture of glam and function, punk woman and safety. Hard-shell helmets and fishnet, tats and kneepads. Then the game begins, and all thoughts of camp are thrown to the river.

The hits, the falls, the brilliance are real. The players of the Minnesota RollerGirls have resurrected a dead sport and redeem it—game by game—from the depths of 1970s late-night television hell. Jammers speed around the oval track at dizzying speeds, while blockers make it their duty to send them into the crowd. Every time a jammer laps a player on the opposing side, her team gets a point. Most points win. The ball—in this sport—is the jammer herself. The game is dangerous—no middlema—and players frequently pull muscles and sprain ankles. Even the audience can get hit by a blocker shoving an uncertain jammer off-course, but those sitting at trackside see those moments as opportunities to become the

Photo © Brian Macke

Angelfire trying to break the pack on the derby track at Roy Wilkins Auditorium

playing field as they bend to take the rush of skates and skirt coming at them, cushioning their fall.

After a brief half-time show from a local band, the RollerGirls return to finish the game. Forty minutes of hard-fought roller derby are exhausting. As we sit at trackside, we see the fatigue and adrenaline wash through the players. Bench coaches frantically try to keep a lid on a lead or work out how to come back from a deficit. And as in any sport, the crowd calls out to their favorite players in support. The players call right back with a wink, or a gesture, or a scream to the back seats—and then they're off again, recharged by their fans, ready for that last push. The final whistle blows and the teams—so ready to attack each other on the track moments before—suddenly slap hands and cheer each other on.

The fans stream out of the Roy, leaving the volunteers to take down the track, the advertisement from local businesses, and the bleachers. My wife and I get on our bikes and head up the hill to home and son. As we ride, my wife favors her left leg as she massages the bruise left from an incoming jammer. She tells me how Mary Tyler Roar apologized after the match for plowing into her, and we laugh. We both know she's the lucky one tonight.

"You know, I'm sick of following my dreams, man. I'm just going to ask where they're going and hook up with 'em later."—Mitch Hedberg, Saint Paul comedian

JANUARY

S	M	T	W	T	F	S
28	29	30	31	1	2	3
4	5	6	7	8	9	10
11	12	13	14	15	16	17
18	19	20	21	22	23	24
25	26	27	28	29	30	31

5 MONDAY

Orchid Show

6 TUESDAY

Orchid Show

7 WEDNESDAY

Orchid Show

8 THURSDAY

Orchid Show

International Chamber Orchestra Festival

Saint Paul Chamber Orchestra

Photo © Tom Conlon

Looking eastward on Kellogg Street near Saint Paul Central Library

9 FRIDAY	Orchid Show International Chamber Orchestra Festival Saint Paul Chamber Orchestra
10 SATURDAY	Saint Paul Farmers' Market Orchid Show International Chamber Orchestra Festival Saint Paul Chamber Orchestra
11 SUNDAY	Orchid Show International Chamber Orchestra Festival Minnesota Boychoir Winter Concert

William Demarest, who played Uncle Charlie on *My Three Sons*, was born in Saint Paul.

Photo © Patricia Bour-Schilla

Old Capitol Winchester

CAPITOL WINCHESTER

Sasha Aslanian

My furnace was a young pup in 1936 when Saint Paul hit its all-time low temperature of -34°. Capitol Winchester sits like Santa Claus in my basement. He's entering his eightieth winter.

The raised letters of his name, Capitol Winchester, stretch across his chest like a workman's name embroidered on a pocket. He stands a sturdy four feet tall, with spider webs encircling his seventy-five-inch waist. Someone once tried to spiff him up by painting him white.

Capitol Winchester chugged along during a sixty-six-day stretch when it stayed below freezing from December 18, 1977, until February 23, 1978. He purred at age sixty when national TV crews came to town to film the tallest-ever Winter Carnival Ice Palace in 1986. Each October, he clocks in and runs until April. An old man who comes just for winter.

When I bought the house eight years ago, I nervously signed up for the utility company's appliance insurance program. They sent a guy over to check things out. I was sure my Capitol Winchester was a goner.

"Naw," the guy said, affectionately tapping the furnace with his clipboard. "These things can go for one hundred years. They're much better than the new ones."

The lady from the insurance company wasn't so impressed.

"You've got an old furnace," she droned as she declined my homeowner's policy.

"Yes, I know," I said politely, but she wasn't going to budge. It was like she wanted to take Old Shep out behind the barn and shoot him. American Express and I haven't spoken since.

Capitol Winchester may retire on me one of these days. I wonder each October as I swivel the thermostat knob whether I'm going to lose him during a -30° cold snap. But each April arrives, and he's still on the job.

I know the new models are the size of makeup cases. Those gaunt supermodels probably consume less energy. But could they work as uncomplainingly as Capitol Winchester?

He's so old that you can't Google him. The average furnace today lasts twenty years. I guess Capitol Winchester didn't get the memo about planned obsolescence. It's true he can't double as an iPod or text message me at work while he's breaking down. But Capitol Winchester is my true hero of winter.

➪ In 1848 William Finn, a Mexican American War veteran, was the first person to permanently settle in what is now Highland Park.

JANUARY

S	M	T	W	T	F	S
28	29	30	31	1	2	3
4	5	6	7	8	9	10
11	12	13	14	15	16	17
18	19	20	21	22	23	24
25	26	27	28	29	30	31

12 Monday

Orchid Show

International Chamber Orchestra Festival

13 Tuesday

Orchid Show

International Chamber Orchestra Festival

14 Wednesday

Orchid Show

International Chamber Orchestra Festival

15 Thursday

International Chamber Orchestra Festival

Orchid Show

Photo © Patricia Bour-Schilla

January thaw on Pike Island

16 FRIDAY	Orchid Show International Chamber Orchestra Festival Saint Paul Chamber Orchestra
17 SATURDAY	Saint Paul Farmers' Market Orchid Show International Chamber Orchestra Festival Saint Paul Chamber Orchestra
18 SUNDAY	Orchid Show International Chamber Orchestra Festival

August Wilson's first produced play was *Black Bart and the Sacred Hills*, staged at Saint Paul's Penumbra Theatre in 1981.

WOMAN ON LAUREL STREET REPORTS THAT HER NEIGHBOR HAS STOLEN NINE PAIRS OF HER SHOES AND LEFT A PILE OF HONEY AND FLOUR BY HER CAR

Deborah Keenan

Her husband gave her a book: photos of concrete angels hidden in churches. The one she loves wears a wreath of primroses, has a perfect, naked foot showing, kneels on one knee, holds a giant basin chiseled into the shape of a scallop shell. The shell/basin is two feet across, so you can imagine the work of the wings when she wants to take off. Her foot is erotic, narrow and strong. She looks a lot like an angel from the summer of love—hair hanging down, the calm look of hope on her face. She assumes the creator is a woman, then a man—what kind of artist would want an angel like this? She would.

The local paper reports that a woman has received a photograph in the mail—her snowman, stolen two nights before, with a machete in its throat and a knife in its eye. Police believe neighborhood children are responsible. It's summer, so now's a good time to think of this winter crime. A few months ago she told her youngest daughter that the next time there was a huge winter storm on a mild enough day, she would gather all her daughter's friends and drop them on the center land of the divided avenue—she told her that only a few years ago young people took the time to make extraordinary snow sculptures on the avenue: ten-foot rabbits holding snow baskets; a giant snow person with no gender, wearing a black velvet cape; a snow house big enough for a first-grade class to hide inside of. She is trying to inspire her daughter. She thinks some of her daughter's friends would put up with her wanting this. She thinks Francie would give her a loving smile, say yes. Maybe some others. She is full of dread too often about the future. Twenty-four Iraqi children blown up yesterday, with one American soldier, as he was handing them candy. She wants her daughter to go to the middle of the avenue and build something that cannot last.

Illustration © Andy Singer

Superplow

SNOW KING

Julian Welna

I love the snow. Not because it marks Christmas but because I love snow blowing. So when some people stay inside, I put on my coat and gloves and trek out with my snow blower, and I walk around knocking on doors seeing if anyone will pay me to snow blow. Most often they won't, but sometimes they do. It's all luck.

I'll go out in the morning and come home right before dinner. It's cold, sometimes frigid, but I'm a Minnesotan, so it doesn't bother me that much. I love being out there cold but somehow content, as if the world would wait for me. As if time itself will let me walk by unnoticed. If you have never snow blowed, I suggest that you do. You won't feel cold after a while, and you'll see that the world, if only for a second, seems to be right. Everyone has something that makes you feel like that—if you don't, I suggest you find yours or you'll be a very grumpy person. The snow blower is really loud, but it gives you all the time you need to think. It's a magical sort of peace that I get nowhere else. My parents get scared a little bit each time I go out because it's just me.

There are other people like me who love to snow blow as much or more than I do. It is the greatest thing I've ever done. Well, some people are very lucky: they get to do this on a very nice ATV, which is my dream. For all of you Minnesotans who flatter yourselves by thinking you're hardy, I suggest you snow blow for a while. That'll take you down a notch. I love the winter, plain and simple.

➪ "I think it is generally admitted that Saint Paul among Midwestern cities was not quite like other girls, but that she had a definite personality and flavor of her own."
—Grace Flandrau, Saint Paul writer

JANUARY

S	M	T	W	T	F	S
28	29	30	31	1	2	3
4	5	6	7	8	9	10
11	12	13	14	15	16	17
18	19	20	21	22	23	24
25	26	27	28	29	30	31

19 MONDAY

Orchid Show

Martin L. King Jr. Day

International Chamber Orchestra Festival

20 TUESDAY

International Chamber Orchestra Festival

21 WEDNESDAY

Orchid Show

International Chamber Orchestra Festival

22 THURSDAY

Orchid Show

International Chamber Orchestra Festival

Saint Paul Winter Carnival

Photo © Patricia Bour-Schilla

Fresh snow

23 FRIDAY	Orchid Show International Chamber Orchestra Festival Saint Paul Winter Carnival Fourth Friday at the Movies
24 SATURDAY	Saint Paul Farmers' Market Orchid Show International Chamber Orchestra Festival Saint Paul Winter Carnival Minnesota Opera, *Faust* Historic Saint Paul Concert with The SPCO
25 SUNDAY	Orchid Show International Chamber Orchestra Festival Saint Paul Winter Carnival

German-Jewish pioneers formed Saint Paul's first synagogue in 1856.

ART TO HEART

Jennifer Holder

Living in Sisseton, South Dakota, Terry Wilson, a Native American artist, part Dakota and part Blackfoot, had heard about Saint Paul's winter carnival but had never given it much thought until January 2008, when his sister, a New Hope resident, invited him to come and live with her. Wilson, a wood and pipestone carver, chainsawer, and bead worker, had the opportunity to participate in the 2008 Saint Paul Winter Carnival exhibition at the historic Como Lakeside Pavilion.

Although carnival organizers did not schedule the exhibition at Como Park, David Glass, owner of Black Bear Crossings on the Lake, expects that the wood carving demonstration that he sponsored in 2008 will become an official winter carnival event starting this year. "Small businesses have a responsibility to the community to step up and sponsor winter activities too," says Glass.

Outside the Black Bear Crossings coffee shop, Joe Semler and his family demonstrated their chainsaw carving skills to curious onlookers who happened on the exhibition by chance, as I had done. In the shelter of the coffee shop, Wilson showed some of his smaller works, such as his wooden canes, beaded jewelry, and antler and pipestone carvings. For a few minutes, I basked in the warmth of Wilson's story and his relationship with his art.

When he was ten, Wilson learned to carve from his foster grandfather, and he has been doing it ever since, about forty years. He likes to do carvings of animals—bears, wolves, turtles, owls, and eagles—that have a lot to do with his culture. "Those animals are sacred to us," he says. He carves in wood, deer antler, and red pipestone. Historically, Native Americans have used pipestone, also known as catlinite, to make the ceremonial pipes that are an integral part of their religious and civic ceremonies. Since 1937, only American Indians are legally permitted to quarry the soft red stone.

Reflecting on his success at the exhibit, Wilson tells me, "This week was very successful—I made many connections, sold a few pieces, and even got a couple of jobs." He was very excited to be hired to carve a dead tree at someone's house. "It's nice to be able to create something beautiful from something that is nothing. It gives me a sense of accomplishment."

Photo © Jennifer Holder

Artist Terry Wilson

Wilson has worked as an auto mechanic, construction worker, landscaper, and bus driver. But art, he says, is what he really likes to do; and everywhere he goes, he carves. The Twin Cities will be his home for a while. He enjoys being with family, but mostly, he says, "It's just me and my art. Art is a way for me to express myself. I put myself into art totally. I express my inner feelings and my spirit comes out in my carvings."

The process of creating gives Wilson comfort when he is down and immense joy when he is up. "When I'm sad and depressed, I turn those feelings into happy ones. There have been times when I've been angry about things and I turn that anger into love. People have said to me, 'Terry, you'll never amount to anything with art.' But it's been there for me through tough times, financially and emotionally. I sell everything I make.

"A lot of prejudice has been thrown at me, but I manage to deal with it. People think that Native Americans are all rich just because we have casinos, but we're not. Some of us are still struggling. We have to make it just like everybody else. So I use my artwork to make it through life."

Wilson's message to the young art student is "Don't stop what you're doing. Keep on creating. It's a healing thing for people. It will help some through hard times. Art says a lot of positive things to people. That's what I see."

➩ The Riverview Economic Development Association was founded in 1983 by a group of West Side business owners.

JANUARY

S	M	T	W	T	F	S
28	29	30	31	1	2	3
4	5	6	7	8	9	10
11	12	13	14	15	16	17
18	19	20	21	22	23	24
25	26	27	28	29	30	31

26 MONDAY

Chinese New Year

International Chamber Orchestra Festival

Saint Paul Winter Carnival

27 TUESDAY

International Chamber Orchestra Festival

Saint Paul Winter Carnival

Minnesota Opera, *Faust*

28 WEDNESDAY

International Chamber Orchestra Festival

Saint Paul Winter Carnival

29 THURSDAY

International Chamber Orchestra Festival

Saint Paul Winter Carnival

Minnesota Opera, *Faust*

Photo © Patricia Bour-Schilla

Beer gone bye

30 FRIDAY	International Chamber Orchestra Festival Saint Paul Winter Carnival Winter Flower Show begins
31 SATURDAY	Saint Paul Farmers' Market Saint Paul Winter Carnival Minnesota Opera, *Faust* Saintly City Cat Show
1 SUNDAY	Saint Paul Winter Carnival Minnesota Opera, *Faust* Saintly City Cat Show

Assumption Church's twin towers, built with local limestone in the early 1870s, are 210 feet high.

THE SAINT PAUL HOTEL IN THE LATE 1970s

Tom Conlon

I recently learned that the Saint Paul Hotel will celebrate its one hundredth anniversary in 2010. I wanted to make sure its role in our city's history was acknowledged in some manner. Perhaps my own personal reflections as a former employee and later a guest can contribute.

In my senior year at Highland Park Senior High School in 1977–1978, I had the privilege to work as a part-time weekend houseman at the hotel, which fascinated me, particularly since it had seen most of its former glory days pass.

Like many downtowns in U.S. cities, Saint Paul's was killed off by the decline of the passenger railroads, the development of new suburban shopping malls, and changing housing patterns; the once vibrant social, entertainment, and commercial activities downtowns were known for disappeared. With them, the old, aging luxury hotels deteriorated, and business travelers headed to newer hotels such as the Radisson on the riverfront.

The Saint Paul Hotel was no exception to this trend. Built around 1910, the twelve-story hotel was an imposing structure on the corner of St. Peter and Fifth streets. Its light tan façade had become faded and dirty, and the lobby floor and pillars had been tiled and wallpapered over in a 1950s-era modernizing effort that destroyed much of its original charm.

I remember once being in the old coffee shop as a child and even getting a haircut in the basement barbershop (sometime in the late 1960s), but by the late 1970s, both had been closed. A vacant old cigar stand and shoeshine chair stood at the entrance to the old coffee shop, which was dark but still had its old furnishings, as well as some in storage.

As a houseman, I had a master key to all parts of the building. My job required me to clean up public areas, such as the lobby, hallways, restrooms, and meeting rooms, repair a broken drape in a room, move a trash compactor up to ground level, and other odds and ends. Once in a rare while, I got to play the role of bellman. As a union job, it paid $3.11 an hour (with a 10-cent raise during my time there); the minimum wage was around $2.75 an hour at that time.

Our housekeeper, Evelyn Boykin, was a great boss, and we kept in touch for a few years after the hotel closed and even had a housekeeping

Photo © Tom Conlon

The Saint Paul Hotel

reunion at her home. For a time, she had gone over to the old Capp Towers (Best Western Hotel) a few blocks away until that closed and became the Naomi Family Center. Bob Johnson was the general manager when I was there (replacing Curt Walker), and Robin Smith was our catering manager.

I usually worked two five-hour weekend shifts from 4 to 9 p.m. By the end of my shift, the maids and housekeepers had gone home, and the only other employees in the whole building (besides myself) were the front desk clerk/night auditor, the custodial engineer, and on occasion, a private security guard, if there was a hotel function. I often completed my assigned work early, so the down time often allowed me to explore the bowels of the building.

Those who celebrated large events at the hotel in the 1970s probably walked through the old Hall of Queens (which held portraits of Saint Paul Winter Carnival queens) and into the chandeliered ballroom with the marble floor (now modernized). No one seems to know where the queen portraits went. If it was a smaller party, you probably went down the winding basement staircase to the old round casino room (now roughly where the café is).

The custodial engineers took me under their wing and showed me parts of the building and told me old stories. "Grizzly" Ed Adams (with his crewcut) would complain about one particular permanent resident who would call down for the most trivial reasons, such as hot pipes or staff's failure to turn on a small light in the elevator.

A front desk clerk, a young beautiful blonde named Shelley, used to gossip about all the hotel happenings and people, and we kept in touch years later, still laughing about our memories. Later, we even went to visit the high-maintenance resident, who had by then moved to Kellogg Square downtown.

Most evenings, the lobby was pretty quiet except for the occasional permanent resident entering or leaving the elevator (the hotel offered monthly rentals and contract rooms for Jefferson Bus Lines). The only time you could eat at the hotel was breakfast and lunch during the week at the old Gopher Grill, which was closed on the weekends. Occasionally there was a banquet in the marble-floored ballroom with its beautiful chandeliers.

Ken Casper, a contract security guard, had keys to the freezer in the grill and would make sandwiches for us late at night. An unexpected visit by the general manager one quiet night caused Shelley to sit down on her sandwich behind the front desk for fear of being fired. She didn't have time to hide the big bowl of potato chips, but no one said anything, and life went on as usual. We had many a laugh over that memory years later.

During the winter high school state tournaments, the place was alive with kids from all over Minnesota, and housekeeping told tales of pillows being thrown out from upper floor windows and older residents complaining of noise. I also remember occasional youth dances held in the casino room and often attended them when I got off duty.

Many of the rooms had old carpeting, black-and-white TVs, and were quite small. Rates started at $18/night. While working extra one night during a busy state tournament period, I encountered a girl in the hallway close to my age who said she'd forgotten her room key. She asked if I could let her in her room, which I did. We got talking, and I ended up giving her a tour of the normally vacant rooftop penthouses—only to unexpectedly crash a general manager's private party. We also went up on the roof, where you had a fantastic view of the state capitol, Mississippi River, and downtown Saint Paul. Years before, a radio station had broadcasted from there, but it was all vacant now.

Bob Short, then a U.S. Senate candidate, had owned the hotel, along with the old Leamington Hotel in downtown Minneapolis. When he sold it in the summer of 1979, the old hotel finally closed its doors. To my knowledge, this was the only time the hotel closed in its history. I had left my job in August 1978 when I entered the Marines, but while home on leave the summer after its closure, I visited the old hotel one last time.

One of the remaining custodial engineer friends of mine (Ed Findlay, who a few years ago was working as a security guard at the US Trust

Photo © Minnesota Historical Society

Bedroom in the Saint Paul Hotel in the 1940s

Building, formerly Burlington Railroad Building across from Galtier Plaza) was responsible for keeping the building heated and cared for during an uncertain transition that might have ended in demolition. He let me in for one last tour. It was sad to see the stacks of sheets and old plates on tables in the old ballroom and the place in general disrepair.

During another visit home in 1981, I had the pleasure to see the hotel reopened and brought back to elegance, as it remains today. There were now fewer but larger rooms, and none of the old employees that I knew of came back. The lobby, entrances, and restaurants had been rearranged, with the elegant Saint Paul Grill replacing the old Hall of Queens meeting rooms.

The old garage, where Landmark Towers now stands, was torn down. The main entrance is now on Market Street rather than St. Peter. And of course, no skyway connection existed in the 1970s.

I always remembered the old employee locker room in the always-overheated bathrooms, as well as the near-empty screened areas in the basement that once held more liquor, kitchen supplies, and canned food than in the final years. In 1990, that had all been replaced and modernized. While I was pleased that the hotel once again had life, color, and beauty, serving upscale clientele and social functions, I still had a bit of sadness that old memories, people, and icons of the old hotel were lost.

Today, I still find myself taking the occasional three-minute walk-through when I am downtown, and I always look forward to attending functions in the hotel. Unlike the many sterile modern hotel buildings that look alike, the Saint Paul still has a distinct architecture and character of its own. I had a fundraiser there during my first school board campaign in 1991, and occasionally I do a photography shoot for a high school reunion in the ballroom. The Sunday brunches are back too!

I also had an opportunity to stay in the hotel for two nights in 2004 and enjoyed the large, comfortable pillows, elegant surroundings and amenities, and great view over Rice Park and the Ordway Center. No hotel in Saint Paul can match its charm.

The Saint Paul Hotel has been a survivor and a reminder that we must preserve not only our architectural and cultural history but the memories such institutions play in people's lives. I hope future generations will have the opportunity to enjoy the hotel as I have through the years.

MY FIRST WINTER IN SAINT PAUL

Badeh Dualeh

I was born and raised in Somalia, then lived many years in Dallas. After I graduated from the University of North Texas, I moved to Saint Paul in search of a job and a wife. It was January 2004, and the temperature, with windchill had dropped to -40°. I thought my heart would freeze before I found work, not to mention a wife. My car would not start my first morning. I asked my friend who lived in Saint Paul, "Hey, why won't my car start?"

He said, "Your battery is dead. You need a new battery, and you better put anti-freeze in your radiator. This is not Dallas. And you will need new tires for driving in the snow."

I tried to open the hood of my car so my friend could charge my battery. He just watched me as my mustache frosted over. My ears were going to fall off. I thought I was turning into a snowman. Once we got a new battery, my windshield wipers broke from trying to clear away all the ice on my windshield.

Wherever I went, people started the conversation by asking, "Is this your first winter here?"

When I said that it was, then they told me, "This winter is not that bad; the one last year was worse."

They asked, "Why did you move to Saint Paul?"

"Because I love the weather."

They always replied, "Are you insane? Why did you move to Minnesota in the middle of winter?"

"I love the weather here, just as many Somalis love Minnesota weather."

I never wore gloves in my life before moving to Saint Paul. This was a mystery to me—how do I keep my gloves? I kept losing one pair of gloves after another.

In my geography class when I was in high school in Somalia, I learned about the Mississippi River. I never thought one day I would see it with my own eyes. The first time I saw it was when I drove over Highway 52 near downtown Saint Paul. The sad thing was, the river too was frozen. I could not wait until summer.

HERE, THERE AND BACK AGAIN

Tiffany Lee

I come from the many places
Of
The scary house in Frog Town
To the gang banging
Area
Of the crazy east
Then straight onto the
one
neighborhood we never did a thing
in;
Mounds area
From there, I go back to the east side
Where I lived next to one of my
Cousins who I'd never met and became
Close to
Then I moved again and
Remained
In the same block range of the
East side
Then straight on to the one
Neighborhood
My family & I, knew our
Neighbors
And somewhat hung out with
Them
From there, it's back to the
East side
And as usual, we're back
To staying
Inside the house
& doing nothing
Crazy aint it ?
No matter where we move,
it's always here, there and
Back
Again

FEBRUARY

Photo © Tom Conlon

Downtown Saint Paul Winter Farmers' Market: Saturdays through March

Saint Paul Winter Carnival: Through February 1

Saintly City Cat Show: January 31–February 1

Minnesota Opera, *Faust*: February 1

World of Wheels: February 6–8

Saint Paul Chamber Orchestra: February 14, 19, 20, 21

Scottish Ramble: February 14–15

Minnesota State High School League Girls' Hockey Tournament: February 25–28

Fourth Friday at the Movies: February 27

Historic Saint Paul Concert with The SPCO: February 28

Minnesota Opera, *The Adventures of Pinocchio*: February 28

See pages 288–310 for more information and more events

➩ Middleweight boxer Mike "the Harp" O'Dowd, also known as "the Saint Paul Cyclone," was the only world's champion to fight at the front during World War I while serving in the U.S. Army.

FEBRUARY

S	M	T	W	T	F	S
1	2	3	4	5	6	7
8	9	10	11	12	13	14
15	16	17	18	19	20	21
22	23	24	25	26	27	28

2 MONDAY

Groundhog Day

3 TUESDAY

4 WEDNESDAY

5 THURSDAY

Photo © Patricia Bour-Schilla

Mississippi River bottom

FEBRUARY

6 FRIDAY

World of Wheels

7 SATURDAY

Saint Paul Farmers' Market

World of Wheels

8 SUNDAY

World of Wheels

One of the first places where Bob Dylan performed in 1960 was the Purple Onion Pizza Parlor in Saint Paul.

SOME CHEERS FOR WINTER

Judith Niemi

My sister phones. "Storm!" she says, disgusted. "They're calling this a storm. No wind, maybe an inch of snow. It's winter, for Pete's sake, we're *supposed* to have snow. Get a grip!" My sister is not one of your hardy outdoors types, but we're Iron Rangers, and even though between us we've spent six decades in Saint Paul, we retain the Ranger's right to scorn urban wimpiness. It's the TV weather people who have set her off. "They are trying to brainwash us into weather wimps."

FEBRUARY

Up North, people take some pride in cold. My cousin who lives in the Embarrass bog country, where it really does get to 40 below pretty often, cheerfully argues about a late July frost they had—was that their earliest or latest killing frost on record?

But how is it that all Minnesota gets tagged as the Abode of Winter, even in these days of climate change and a lot of, frankly, substandard winters?

Here's my theory: meteorologists, nationwide, must include a lot of Minnesotans. (Who else talks so much about weather?) They value our quality of life—and know that overpopulation is the quickest way to wreck it. So, I figure, enthusiastic loyal Minnesotans who love weather, and cross-country skiing, and maybe even ice fishing, take temporary posts in exile, where they deliberately slander our state. "Mosquitoes in summer and 40 below keeps out the riffraff" is their battle cry. They report on the Icebox of the Nation, and every cold day in the Embarrass bog—any fragment of bad weather news. Like the summer a friend's mother called from Maryland, frantic: "Are you OK?" "Sure. Why wouldn't I be?" "But the Tornado!" (She says "tor-nah-do!") We thought hard. Oh, yeah, there was a little one—took the roof off a barn, no cows hurt. But it made the news in Baltimore and Washington.

The problem is this new generation of local TV weather people, who seem to believe the hype about terrible weather. Their standard is tropical beaches: sunny and hot is good. In steamy 95-degree August, they chirp about "gorgeous weather," even if we're in a drought. "Plagued by rain," I heard one say, predicting half an inch. Any cold, and some low-seniority reporter gets sent outside, wrapped in a muffler, to warn us about wind chill. It's probably a ratings thing: our station has the most exciting weather.

Saint Paulites have not all been brainwashed by the winter-haters. Right after a good snow, Como Park, Highland, and Crosby Farm are

Photo © Allen Swain

Winter Carnival Ice Palace, Central Park, 1886

FEBRUARY

covered with ski tracks. A lot of people play hooky or leave work early to catch the snow before the thaw ruins it. People smile: "Finally, a real old Minnesota winter!" Neighbors I never see give each other a hand shoveling out, or just meet in the alley, appreciating the new plow guy we've hired.

Heating bills aside, we could use more consistent cold, not these damn thaws and black ice. The friend who most recently broke her leg on black ice celebrated recovery by a skating party on the anniversary—that is Minnesota style. My niece credits her safety to our winter neighborliness; driving through one of Saint Paul's tonier neighborhoods, she spotted a cardboard sign tacked to a tree. "SLOW DOWN! ICE AHEAD! SLICKER THAN SNOT!"

And the Winter Carnival—any city can celebrate lakes and summer—it takes more spirit to celebrate winter. So what if these days ice sculptures are in danger of premature melt? Famous artists have made careers of ephemeral art. And in a bottom-line, tight-fisted age, building an Ice Palace is a lovely, extravagant gesture. Traveling in the Amazon, I once brought, along with photos of family and home to ease conversations with local people, Saint Paul postcards, including old ice palaces. Nothing could have impressed and delighted people more.

"Turn off the TV," I told my sister. "You'll get high blood pressure." While the weather news was on, I went for a short walk in the "storm." The lightly falling snow was very pretty under the streetlights.

➩ Charles Schulz drew the cartoon *Li'l Folks* for the *Saint Paul Pioneer Press* from 1947 to 1949 before he created the popular comic strip *Peanuts*, which was nationally syndicated in 1950.

FEBRUARY

S	M	T	W	T	F	S
1	2	3	4	5	6	7
8	9	10	11	12	13	14
15	16	17	18	19	20	21
22	23	24	25	26	27	28

9 MONDAY

10 TUESDAY

11 WEDNESDAY

12 THURSDAY

Photo © Patricia Bour-Schilla

Sign on Payne Avenue at Foreign & Domestic Repair Shop

13 FRIDAY

14 SATURDAY

Valentine's Day

Saint Paul Farmers' Market

Saint Paul Chamber Orchestra

Scottish Ramble

15 SUNDAY

Scottish Ramble

Famed aviator Amelia Earhart came from Kansas and attended Saint Paul Central High School in 1913 and 1914.

I [HEART] SWEDE HOLLOW

Michelle Leon

I pulled up in my blue Honda SUV. "New Orleans, Proud To Call It Home" read the bumper sticker. I had just arrived at my new house—the house I bought without ever seeing. In my life, at that moment, that decision made perfect sense. It was a time when things much more unthinkable than buying a house without ever seeing it in person made perfect sense too. An unthinkable world had been my reality for the last year: New Orleans AFTER. I was gone eight years and was just now returning to Minnesota, where I had grown up. I had left all those years ago, a dreamy young bride, all velvet and chenille, and returned, a shell-shocked divorcée, all knowing smirk and wise sage. I scraped off my bumper sticker two days later—that was one of the hardest moments, really. I really had been proud to call New Orleans my home.

I could tell the neighbors had been anticipating my arrival. The house had been vacant for over a year. Later they would come around with brownies and bottles of wine—for real. Welcome to Swede Hollow! And, there she was—my little hot dogger. She is a Victorian dating back to 1887, painted dusty rose, with mossy green and sunshine-yellow trim. The minute I saw her picture at 3 a.m. on realtor.com, I knew she had to be mine. She had a rusty iron gate with little bells hanging off the bottom. Hundreds of lilies of the valley come up in the spring and now I have a mailman—Mr. Mailman, I call him! The mail, it comes everyday. We didn't have that in New Orleans.

Swede Hollow—the very name sounds sweet, like the kind of place where strudels cool on white Victorian windowsills and blue birds land on your finger tips in the morn. I heard tell of the olden days here. The scratchy black-and-white movie that plays reel to reel in my mind tells the tale of shanty shacks with tin roofs and children running round in lederhosen (did Swedes wear those?) crossing wooden bridges over streams. Neighbors talked to neighbors and sang songs together while stars shone brightly over the valley. Front porches doubled as living rooms on hot summer days and in the wintertime smoke billowed out of brick chimneys as old folks huddled under scratchy gray blankets in their johnnies during the long nights.

The truth is that this place was not so ideal. In fact, all the homes were burned down in the 1950s because of inhumane living conditions and pollution in the nearby stream. It was home to poverty-stricken immigrants

Photo © Patricia Bour-Schilla

Swede Hollow porches

who worked hard manual labor until their hands were raw and their bodies exhausted. From this view in the valley, the onetime residents looked up to the opulent Victorian homes on the bluff as a reminder of a faraway dream.

Okay, I'll admit it: in the past, winter and I, we have had our differences. Now it was time to make friends. It really was the only way this all was going work out, the whole coming home thing. My friend Hayley told me that the only way I was ever going to find peace with grumpy ole man winter was to get out and walk with him. Walk. Walk outside in the snow. So we did. We put on vintage Dr. Zhivago hats and coats and we went—two little Laras. It was -5° and we headed down into the hollow. Dried cattails, sumac, and milkweeds pushed brittlely out of soft white snow. The trees were covered with glassy white icicles. It was quiet shivery white quiet. We turned a corner and saw green and gray mallards gliding on an icy pond with silvery steam rising. It was at that moment that I knew everything was going to be all right.

FEBRUARY

S	M	T	W	T	F	S
1	2	3	4	5	6	7
8	9	10	11	12	13	14
15	16	17	18	19	20	21
22	23	24	25	26	27	28

"Blacks have traditionally had to operate in a situation where whites have set themselves up as the custodians of the black experience."
—August Wilson, Saint Paul playwright

16 MONDAY

Presidents' Day

17 TUESDAY

18 WEDNESDAY

19 THURSDAY

Saint Paul Chamber Orchestra

Photo © Patricia Bour-Schilla

That darn cat is on my porch again!

FEBRUARY

20 FRIDAY Saint Paul Chamber Orchestra

21 SATURDAY Saint Paul Farmers' Market

Saint Paul Chamber Orchestra

22 SUNDAY

KSTP television of Saint Paul began broadcasting in 1948, a year earlier than WTCN in Minneapolis.

SKIING ON PIKE ISLAND

Nora Murphy

Pike Island ought to be the perfect place for a novice cross-country skier like me. Bounded by the Mississippi and Minnesota rivers, the island is flat—no hills, no moguls, no sharp twisty turns. This desolate wooded island is also close to home, just a seven-minute car ride from the center of Saint Paul. Only the occasional planes overhead remind you that urban life is just around the corner. The closeness to the city may explain the park's amenities. There's a lodge with heat and a drinking fountain, an after-hours port-a-potty that smells like fallen snow, and parking just a few feet from the trailhead. Yet I am afraid to ski on Pike Island. I am afraid because the island is haunted. Haunted by the unrelenting echoes of women and children who suffered here one long-ago winter.

In the fall after the U.S.–Dakota War of 1862, hundreds of Dakota women and children were force-marched for seven days to Fort Snelling from their reservation in western Minnesota. That winter, over fifteen hundred Dakota were detained on Pike Island below the fort. Under military patrol and with only thin blankets, the prisoners watched this wooded island fill with snow. Dozens never lived to see the snow melt or spring arrive. Those who did survive the long winter endured starvation, rape, and disease. Hardest of all was the heartbreak of not knowing whether their husbands, their fathers, and their sons, shackled in chains in prisoner-of-war camps further south, were still alive. Exile was the reward for survival. When the ice melted on the rivers, the Pike Island survivors were loaded onto boats and moved out of the state, out of their homeland.

Makoce, pronounced mah-koh-chay, means homeland in the Dakota language. The *makoce* of the Dakota is the land surrounding the confluence of the Mississippi and Minnesota rivers. It is the land we call the Twin Cities today. In 1863, over fifteen hundred Dakota women, children, and elders were held in a concentration camp at the heart of their *makoce*. From this frigid base of horror they were exiled.

After the Dakota were gone, non-Natives like my own ancestors took the rest of their land and built the schools where we educate our young.

Photo © Benjamin Franklin Uptor

Dakota woman Wenona, daughter of Chief Red Iron, at Fort Snelling prison compound on Pike Island in 1863

Photo © Benjamin Franklin Upton

Dakota Indians in fenced enclosure at Fort Snelling prison compound on Pike Island

We built the farms and the companies that feed our people. We strengthened a government that serves and protects. We even designated leisure lands like Pike Island, where we can cross-country ski on a winter's afternoon. We've built so much over the *makoce* of Minnesota's first people that it's easy to forget that this is the Dakota homeland. It's easy to forget that after 150 years, we're visitors in another people's ancient holy land.

When I pole ahead in grooved tracks designed for pleasure and thread my way alongside the frozen rivers of beauty, I feel the eyes of the Dakota women and children who endured that long-ago winter. They are watching me. When I watch the deer rummage through the snow for buried roots and when I watch the woods fill up with snow, I hear their cries reverberate like a sharp whistle through the barren river oaks. Part of me wants to turn away from this chilling echo. I can't. Each time I visit the island for a winter ski, their uneasy song sounds louder than the last visit. The women ask me to stop, to listen, and to witness their pain with the tenderness of a mother swaddling a child who may not make it through the winter. When I unstrap the bindings on my boots and reload the skis and poles into the back of my car, I'm not weightless and free. Their raw grief lingers, awaiting release, like river water under the icy surface. The women plead to me, "Remember our story in the snow as if your life depends on it."

It does. For until we remove the bindings on the Dakota people who have returned home and heal the tragedy that lingers in our land and rivers, the past may continue to haunt us all.

➪ Harry Shepherd, the first African American photographer in Minnesota, operated at several different Saint Paul locations from the 1880s to the early 1900s.

FEBRUARY

S	M	T	W	T	F	S
1	2	3	4	5	6	7
8	9	10	11	12	13	14
15	16	17	18	19	20	21
22	23	24	25	26	27	28

23 Monday

24 Tuesday

Mardi Gras/Shrove Tuesday

25 Wednesday

Ash Wednesday

Minnesota State High School League Girls' Hockey Tournament

26 Thursday

Minnesota State High School League Girls' Hockey Tournament

Photo © Patricia Bour-Schilla

One of the few old Saint Paul bakeries left; Tschidas is on Rice Street

FEBRUARY

27 FRIDAY	Minnesota State High School League Girls' Hockey Tournament Fourth Friday at the Movies
28 SATURDAY	Saint Paul Farmers' Market Minnesota State High School League Girls' Hockey Tournament Historic Saint Paul Concert with the SPCO Minnesota Opera, *The Adventures of Pinocchio*
1 SUNDAY	

"Love is a Fallacy."—Max Shulman, Saint Paul humorist

LIFE SEEN THROUGH TWO WINDOWS ON PAYNE AVENUE

Gunilla Bjorkman-Bobb

I am a proud resident of Payne Avenue on Railroad Island in Saint Paul. I moved from New Hope, a quiet, safe, and aged western suburb settled in the 1960s by young families looking for a suburban lawn and a picket fence. I lived there for the first year of my life. It was okay.

Then we moved to Saint Paul into a new brownstone on Payne Avenue. I am definitely no longer bored. I have all the adventure I need right in front of me. I have two windows. They are both tall and handsome. One is on the main floor and overlooks Payne Avenue; the other one is on the back of the second floor, overlooking Swede Hollow Park.

First I'll tell you about life through my main floor window. I take my seat at the window after 8 a.m. in time to see G leave for work. If I am lucky, she will delay going to work and I will have another hour under the covers. The street is busy in the morning; I guess people from all over the county use Payne Avenue to go to work. I don't mind them doing that—it gives me something to look at. The street hasn't been paved since 1933, so you can hear them long before you see them. Trucks tend to drive away from the city for some reason, and they bounce as they hit the potholes. Sometimes things fly off them and land in the street. The fire trucks are most colorful and the tooting is exhilarating. Police cars fly by at incredible speeds; I sometimes wonder how they know that there isn't some old person or a kid crossing the street at that very moment. That could end up very exciting.

I can always tell when it is 9 a.m., because that is when Bobby comes past on his way to the local liquor store. G tells me he lives in the dry house up on Dayton's Bluff and supplies much-needed refreshment for himself and his friends. When I see him go past, I know he means business, and I let him know that doesn't scare me none.

As things calm down on Payne Avenue, I move upstairs to take my seat at my second window, overlooking Swede Hollow Park. This is an urban forest with more than twenty-two different species of trees. I actually saw one of our nerdy neighbors counting them yesterday, bless his heart—he wants more species planted. This is a different world, a world of natural wonders. Here I am on the look out for deer, fox, rabbits, wild turkeys, squirrels, and even muskrats in the pond. I once saw a deer stuck in the muddy bottom of the pond. I told G about it and she called animal control, who came to the rescue. I spot people with dogs, couples, kids,

Photo © Gunilla Bjorkman-Bobb

Me on the right in my front window with my New Hope girlfriend Maggie visiting

and bums. Birds with huge wingspans like eagles and herons loop above. I bark at them all, telling them that I am taking notice.

During the Saint Paul medallion search, the scene under my window was like a movie set depicting the Middle Ages. I saw hundreds of families charging through the park with pitchforks, spades, sticks, and lanterns. They looked like a mob of Viking pillagers. Long into the freezing night, they dug and scraped in the snow, hoping against all hope to find gold. I stayed at the window rooting for them, wishing them success. Unfortunately, the medallion was hidden elsewhere.

In Saint Paul, life is a constant and daily adventure. On walks, I sniff my way past Italian and Mexican stores, dive through the Druery Tunnel into Swede Hollow Park, burst into the sunshine and the glory of twenty-eight acres of bliss. I chase the ducks in the pond and wade in the stream, lapping clean, clear spring water. I leap up the 185 steps to the top of Dayton's Bluff, panting, but oh! so happy, past great Victorian houses and yes, even white picket fences with climbing roses. I take a shortcut past Minnesota's oldest Lutheran church with the cross I can see from my second window and then past the Swede Hollow Café. I love lying in the garden, while people around me sip coffee and offer me delicious crumbs of sweet rolls, muffins, and scones. Downhill past Metro State, I turn the corner for home and have not crossed a single street!

As I make my way past the brownstone neighbors, I can tell who just took a baked chicken out of the oven, who has a soup simmering on the stove or a cake being decorated. I make myself especially cute and use my best begging technique, which is lying down, pretending to be a good dog, and I almost always strike gold.

Be courageous, choose the tasty bone, and move to Payne Avenue, Saint Paul. This is a lucky dog's life.

KAZOUA KONG THAO

Gaoiaong Vang and Tiffany Lee

The first Hmong American to serve on the Saint Paul School Board of Education, Kazoua Kong Thao has made an impact on how we learn today.

Kazoua is the chair of the Saint Paul School Board of Education; she is serving her second term. She is the third Hmong in the country to serve on a board of education. Kazoua makes decisions on what is best for the Saint Paul Public Schools. As chair, she also schedules meetings and agendas and represents the Saint Paul Board of Education when addressing the City Council.

Kazoua came to America at a very young age. Being the oldest of ten, she couldn't rely on anyone; instead, others relied on her. She attended Jackson Elementary in what we call Frogtown and because she didn't have anyone to look up to, she depended on herself. Because schools did not offer interpreters at the time, she was often pulled out of class to interpret for the Hmong families who had trouble understanding English. She started interpreting for the Hmong families when she was in the third grade. Using that experience, she became the leader she is today.

Kazoua has always been passionate about helping young Hmong women find themselves through cultural identity. She had trouble finding her cultural strength, but the words of her father—"It doesn't matter what other people think. As long as you know who you are, then everything will fall into place"—helped give her the strength to step up and do things she thought she couldn't do.

With her being a part of the school board and having a family, she tries her best to balance time for both of them. When she has to run errands for work, she incorporates her family into her job. She makes sure her kids get what is best for them and makes sure she is able to do what is right for herself and her family. Overall, she is able to balance out her job and family.

She encourages young people to challenge themselves, to take a stand and be heard. She also challenges young Hmong kids to take Advanced Placement classes and other college-prep classes to make it far in education. Today we are informed about good classes we can take, so we should take advantage of them. Back when Kazoua was in school, she did well and could have taken those challenging classes, but she was not told about them.

Photo © Lou "The Photo Guy" Michaels

FEBRUARY

Kazoua Kong Thao

As chair of the school board, Kazoua Kong Thao is an inspirational Hmong woman, a Hmong leader, and she actively takes a stand and expresses her feelings and viewpoints.

THE FUNERAL

Gordon Parks

After many snows I was home again.
Time had whittled down to mere hills
the great mountains of my childhood.
Raging rivers I once swam, trickled now
        like gentle streams.

And the wide road curving on to China, or
        Kansas City, or perhaps Calcutta,
had withered to a crooked path of dust,
ending abruptly at the county burying ground.
        Only the giant who was my father
        remained the same.

A hundred strong men strained beneath his coffin
        when they bore him to his grave.

SAINT PAUL PREDICTIONS 2009

David Tilsen

The capital city, the city of hills, comes to grips with itself and finds its soul.

As the Central Corridor line gets finalized, and the plans to disrupt University Avenue and most of downtown for several years are finally sinking in, the city finds itself forced to deal with very difficult realities.

Housing values continue to plummet, but in defiance of market logic, prices do not. People are simply not willing to sell houses, or rent condos or apartments for less than people have paid for them. So they sit empty. As a result, the city simultaneously has a record number of vacancies and record homelessness. This homelessness is of the working poor. The news outlets show interview after interview of people living by the river in abandoned cars, boats, and shipping containers, going off to minimum-wage jobs.

The school district finds that more and more of its students are without addresses. Attendance rates are getting worse.

But then, things begin to change—for the better.

The first change starts with more and more adult children moving back to live with their parents because housing has become simply unaffordable. Then nieces and nephews also start to move in, and sometimes parents move in with their children. Before long, people with extra space welcome the children, parents, or relatives of neighbors and friends.

This has a lot of advantages. People have large mortgages to pay off, as well as additional home equity and credit card loans taken out to pay for the RVs and cabins that are now living places for their loved ones. These extended families are helping to make ends meet. But even more dramatic is the way homelessness has brought families and communities closer together.

A major shift in people's lives is taking place. Houses become homes, not investments. Not builders of equity, but places to live.

The city first responds by issuing citations for code violations—too many unrelated adults in one house.

But then the police report that personal crimes have dropped to an all-time low. The Humphrey Institute concludes that after adjusting for the arrests of people living in abandoned houses and vacant condos, there are almost no residential break-ins, no rapes, no person-on-person violent crime in the entire city. It appears that neighbors are taking care of neighbors, friends watching friends, and the sidewalks, streets, and parks are safer than they have ever been. Saint Paul has found its community again.

There are block parties almost every weekend, all over—from Frogtown to Dayton's Bluff, from Highland Park to Selby-Dale.

The mayor's office, led by the visionary Ann Mulholland, has stopped citing people and started asking them what they need. People say they need help to remodel their homes: more bedrooms and bathrooms are common requests.

The city turns its attention to the many housing units built with public financing that are now sitting empty and facing foreclosure. A citywide summit called by the mayor with bankers, developers, legislators, and community leaders works out a way to move homeless people into vacant units. Homelessness becomes rare, and now even nonviolent crime, theft, and shoplifting are becoming rare. This during a recession puzzles academicians, and Saint Paul becomes a center of attention nationally.

This new recognition in the city of the value of shelter and the needs of its citizens brings national attention to leaders in the community. Saint Paul is spared the civil unrest and police riots that spread through other urban areas.

Mayor Coleman is now being seen as a potential candidate for national office, and people from other cities are looking to Saint Paul for ideas. President Obama asks Ann Mulholland to chair a national task force on "housing for people," and David Thune is being talked about as undersecretary of Housing and Urban Development.

The strong neighborhoods, the strong family culture within the African American, Hispanic, Asian, Jewish, Catholic, and Lutheran communities are all taking credit for the success of the city. Only the banks are unhappy.

A new age is dawning in America, and Saint Paul is leading the way.

Illustration © Andy Singer

Residents unite for housing

March

Photo © Patricia Bour-Schilla

MARCH

Soon all the snowdrifts shall melt
And we'll feel things we formerly felt
About romance and grace
And getting on base
And improving the hand you were dealt.
—Garrison Keillor

Downtown Saint Paul Winter Farmers' Market: Saturdays through March

Minnesota Opera, *The Adventures of Pinocchio*: March 3, 5, 7, 8

Minnesota State High School League Boys' Wrestling Tournament: March 4–7

Minnesota State High School League Boys' Hockey Tournament: March 11–14

Saint Paul Chamber Orchestra: March 13–14

Irish Celebration Dance: March 15

Saint Patrick's Day Parade: March 17

Saint Patrick's Day Irish Ceili Dance: March 17

Fourth Friday at the Movies: March 27

Donnie Smith Invitational Bike Show: March 28–29

See pages 288–310 for more information and more events

➪ "It seems that every war, regardless of its causes, engenders a spirit of hatred that destroys the hope of achieving those things for which the war is fought."
—Sara Colvin, Saint Paul activist

MARCH						
S	M	T	W	T	F	S
1	2	3	4	5	6	7
8	9	10	11	12	13	14
15	16	17	18	19	20	21
22	23	24	25	26	27	28
29	30	31	1	2	3	4

MARCH

2 MONDAY

3 TUESDAY

Minnesota Opera, *The Adventures of Pinocchio*

4 WEDNESDAY

Minnesota State High School League Boys' Wrestling Tournament

5 THURSDAY

Minnesota Opera, *The Adventures of Pinocchio*

Minnesota State High School League Boys' Wrestling Tournament

Photo © Patricia Bour-Schilla

A view of the Saint Paul Cathedral from the Capitol

MARCH

6 FRIDAY

Minnesota State High School League
Boys' Wrestling Tournament

7 SATURDAY

Saint Paul Farmers' Market

Minnesota Opera,
The Adventures of Pinocchio

Minnesota State High School League
Boys' Wrestling Tournament

8 SUNDAY

Minnesota Opera,
The Adventures of Pinocchio

International Women's Day
Daylight Saving Time begins

Wells Fargo Place, 471 feet and thirty-six stories high, is Saint Paul's tallest building.

CONSTANCE CURRIE AND NEIGHBORHOOD HOUSE

Heidi Grosch

Anyone who knows the history of Neighborhood House on Saint Paul's West Side probably knows the name Constance Currie. Born March 18, 1890, in Saskatchewan, Canada, to a family with a long history of social service, she began her career at Unity House in Minneapolis. But it is her many years as director of Neighborhood House (1918–1957) that best mark her legacy.

Founded in 1897 by the women of Mount Zion Temple, Neighborhood House has always been a place of refuge for those seeking it, the Ellis Island of Saint Paul. From the Eastern European immigrants it first served to the over fifty ethnic groups now using the new Paul and Sheila Wellstone Center, Neighborhood House has been a good neighbor to those who live in the surrounding community.

Miss Currie was still young and naïve on that hot, sultry June day in 1918 when she set off to find Neighborhood House. Assuming the work of helping new immigrants was important enough to warrant the most prestigious structure in the area, she confidently marched up to a large building with white pillars. After pounding on the door for a long time, she became frustrated. Why was no one there to greet the new director of Neighborhood House? She was quickly informed that she was at the synagogue and that Neighborhood House was a block and a half away.

From the beginning, even though surrounded by people from other countries with unfamiliar customs and speaking unfamiliar languages, Miss Currie was determined to make her time at Neighborhood House matter. She felt a community must be built on a foundation of personal relationships, so one of her first steps as new director was to get a job with the school department taking a city census. She and her assistant gathered statistical information door-to-door and soon could greet every neighbor by name. Since she lived on the third floor of Neighborhood House, Miss Currie worked incredibly long hours: "I could look out my window at night and feel the pulse beat of the hundred lights of the 'flats'," she later said.

Currie was a tall, imposing woman, with a strong sense of discipline. "Being at Neighborhood House is a privilege," she would say to her

Photo © Neighborhood House

Constance Currie

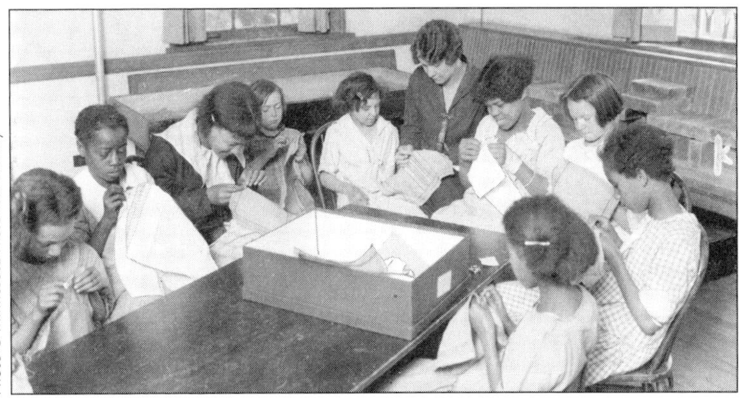

Photo © Minnesota Historical Society

Sewing class at West Side Neighborhood House, probably in the late 1920s or early 1930s

young wayward charges. "If you're not happy then I'm afraid you will have to go home and stay away from everything for 3 days, or 5 days, or 10. And after you've thought about it, I mean really thought about it, we'll have another talk and see if you are really ready to return." One visit with Miss Currie was usually enough to restore order.

She was aggressive in a time when women were not expected to be. Though she kept her personal feelings to herself, Constance Currie spoke up on issues that were important to her. She sat on the board of the National Federation of Settlements and Community Centers as well as on legislative committees, was a consultant to the United States Children's Bureau, and in 1951 served as a delegate to the International Conference of Settlement Houses in London.

Many say that their lives are better thanks to Miss Currie. Many say that under her leadership, Neighborhood House was transformed into the oasis of hope and possibility it is today. People still look to Neighborhood House to find a teacher, an interpreter, a counselor, a confidante in times of trouble, and a community of friends. Services like emergency assistance, programs for children, adults, and seniors, English classes, cultural empowerment groups, transitional services for newly arrived immigrants, and scholarships are still offered. Constance Currie would be proud.

➩ On March 14, 1904, the U.S. Supreme Court ruled that James J. Hill's Northern Securities Company was an illegal combination in restraint of trade and had to be dissolved.

MARCH

S	M	T	W	T	F	S
1	2	3	4	5	6	7
8	9	10	11	12	13	14
15	16	17	18	19	20	21
22	23	24	25	26	27	28
29	30	31	1	2	3	4

MARCH

9 MONDAY

Mawlid al-Nabi

10 TUESDAY

Purim

11 WEDNESDAY

Minnesota State High School League Boys' Hockey Tournament

12 THURSDAY

Minnesota State High School League Boys' Hockey Tournament

Photo © Patricia Bour-Schilla

Photo service sign on Selby Avenue

MARCH

13 FRIDAY

Minnesota State High School League Boys' Hockey Tournament

Saint Paul Chamber Orchestra

14 SATURDAY

Saint Paul Farmers' Market

Minnesota State High School League Boys' Hockey Tournament

Saint Paul Chamber Orchestra

15 SUNDAY

Irish Celebration Dance

During the summer of 1928, Saint Paul's first White Castle opened at 1081 Payne Avenue. It closed in 1944.

LOOKING FOR MY GRANDMOTHER

Mary Jean Port

My grandmother grew up in Saint Paul, poor and Irish. A McDermott, she was the youngest of the six children, and the only girl. Some say that she was spoiled. I have tried over the years to learn more about her, but she is a hard one to pin down.

There is no name on my grandmother's birth record; she is referred to as Marian Irene McDermott on her baptismal certificate. When she was six years old, her parents told the census takers that their daughter's name was Mary I. When she was eleven, they told them it was Irene M. People called her Irene, that much I know, but I'd like to think Mary really was her first name, not her middle name. I'd like us to be, at least in that way, aligned. When I was a child, I was told that I was named after her, this person I'd never met. She died long before I was born.

My grandmother was short, and she had the dark hair and eyes and contrasting ivory skin of certain Irish beauties. Her birthday was March 19, but there are conflicting records of her birth year. Her death certificate and gravestone say she was born in 1898, but her birth and baptismal certificates and marriage license application say she was born in 1899. I take that to be the accurate year. She arrived at the turn of the century, welcomed by a family grieving the loss of eight-year-old Michael, their brother and son, who had died just three months before.

Her father, Thomas B. McDermott, an Irish American, worked as a teamster—that is, he drove a team of horses delivering goods. Her mother, Mary McGrath McDermott, an Irish immigrant, was a housewife. I have two addresses for the McDermotts. They lived at 218 Commercial Street when Irene was six. From the census records, I can pick out the names of children around her age who lived down the block: James Moffitt, Francis and Barbara Freeman, Agnes Madden, and Margaret Soles. I imagine these children were Irene's playmates.

The second address I have is 617½ E. Third Street. In 1909, while living there, Emmet, Irene's brother, just older than she, died of polio.

I know nothing about the courtship between Adolph Port and Irene, only that in 1919, when Adolph came back from fighting in France in World War I, he lived with his parents for a time at 615 E. Third Street, next door to the McDermotts. The following year, he, a divorced Lutheran, married Irene, a Catholic, and in protest her parents and brothers more or less disowned her.

Photo © Mary Jean Port

Marian Irene McDermott, probably around age twelve, dressed for Confirmation

The McDermotts went to St. Mary's Catholic Church on Eighth Street. The parish still exists. The actual church where the McDermotts worshipped is gone, but a new one was built in its place. During a lonely time, back in the mid-1990s, near the end of a long estrangement from my own parents, brothers, and sisters, I went to mass at St. Mary's on Christmas Eve. I especially enjoyed singing the more somber carols that night; my voice sounded better than it ever had. The church's high ceiling allows sound to rise and swell in what I believe are called overtones.

My whole heart was in it. Tears streamed down my face. I sang, for Irene, who died in childbirth when she was just thirty-six, for her husband, Adolph, and the eight children she left behind, for my father, who was only five when his mother died, and for me, too, for what I had never had, and for what I had lost.

At the end of the mass, a woman seated in front of me turned and said sternly, "You have a good voice. Use it." This startled me. I am a writer, and my grandmother had long been my muse. I was piecing together parts of her story while I worked to tell my own. Conjuring Irene McDermott would give me my writer's voice. And somehow this stranger knew.

Write to 3109 W. 50th St. #292, Minneapolis, MN 55410, if you know anything about Irene or her family.

➩ The Saint Paul Curling Club, founded in 1888 and now located at 470 Selby, is the largest such organization dedicated to the sport in the country.

MARCH

S	M	T	W	T	F	S
1	2	3	4	5	6	7
8	9	10	11	12	13	14
15	16	17	18	19	20	21
22	23	24	25	26	27	28
29	30	31	1	2	3	4

16 Monday

17 Tuesday

Saint Patrick's Day Parade

Saint Patrick's Day

Saint Patrick's Day Irish Ceili Dance

18 Wednesday

19 Thursday

Photo © Patricia Bour-Schilla

Spring fishing on the Mississippi River

MARCH

20 FRIDAY

Spring Equinox

21 SATURDAY

Saint Paul Farmers' Market

Spring Flower Show begins

22 SUNDAY

"Law is order in liberty, and without order liberty is social chaos."—Archbishop John Ireland

MABEL SEELEY: THE MISTRESS OF MYSTERY

Steve Trimble

The hall wasn't inviting. It smelled of old gas. It smelled of animals confined to cellars. The ghosts of long-fried dinners, the acridity of long-burned cigarettes haunted the air that was a thicker, foggier dark than the gray day outside; a murk that might have been the grime of the outside walls floated loose and suspended in the hall. Ahead a rectangle of lighter gray showed the door of a room on the right, farther ahead on the right glowered a doorway into pitch-blackness.

—*The Listening House*

"A high priestess in the cult of murder as a fine art" was how Saint Paul literary critic James Gray described her. She was often referred to as "the Mistress of Mystery." But until recently, she was an almost forgotten figure in the city's literary lineup. Her name was Mabel Hodnefield Seeley.

Mabel was born on March 25, 1903, in Herman, Minnesota. Her family came to Saint Paul when her father, a teacher, got a job at the Minnesota Historical Society. Her mother was a natural storyteller, "so I started life with a book in my hand and well-said words in my ears," she once wrote.

Seeley attended Mechanic Arts High School and was encouraged to write by an English teacher. As a result, she contributed some work to the school's literary magazine. Mabel once wrote about her decision to get serious about writing. She was crossing a busy street, was almost hit by a speeding car, and thought, "Here I'm going to die and I haven't written any books." She would eventually pen ten titles, eight of them mysteries, all set in Minnesota.

Mabel won a Saint Paul college scholarship and graduated with honors from the University of Minnesota in 1926. She married fellow student Kenneth Seeley and they moved to Chicago but came back to the Twin Cities for medical treatment when Kenneth was diagnosed with tuberculosis. They later divorced. Mabel became an advertising copywriter for a local department store. After seven years she quit, planning never again to write, but within a year had started *The Listening House* (1938), a mystery set in a seedy Saint Paul rooming house.

To create believable settings, Seeley did field work. While writing *The Crying Sisters* (1939), she ran through fields of tall, dry grass to see how grasshoppers responded when startled. For *The Whispering Cup* (1940),

Mabel Seeley

she spent time at her uncle's grain elevator to experience the wind whistling in the bins and to hear the talk of farmers.

Character development was also important to her. Protagonists were never detectives but ordinary, self-reliant women like librarians or stenographers caught up in unusual circumstances. Seeley empathized with one of her creations so much that she couldn't write for two weeks after killing her off. Mabel even kept a mirror close at hand while writing to see how to describe different facial expressions during various emotions.

Seeley always worked hard to improve her novels. "The only time I'm pleased with myself," she said, "is when I'm exhausted and shaking from having written too much." She was given good reviews by the *New York Times* and the Crime Club of America. *The Chuckling Fingers* (1941) won a Mystery of the Year award. She was an early member of the Mystery Writers of America and served on its first board of directors.

In the late 1940s, Mabel and her son Gregory moved to California. While promoting *The Whistling Shadow* (1954), she met the lawyer Henry Ross. They married two years later, settling down in New Jersey. She never wrote another novel.

Mabel Seeley died on June 9, 1991. At that time, her husband told a *Pioneer Press* columnist that she had quit writing to devote time to the marriage. Mabel never offered an explanation for the end of her active writing career, so it still remains—well, a mystery.

MARCH

S	M	T	W	T	F	S
1	2	3	4	5	6	7
8	9	10	11	12	13	14
15	16	17	18	19	20	21
22	23	24	25	26	27	28
29	30	31	1	2	3	4

➩ Louie Anderson, the stand-up comic and game show host, was born on March 24, 1953, and grew up on Saint Paul's East Side.

23 Monday

24 Tuesday

25 Wednesday

26 Thursday

MARCH

Photo © Tom Conlon

The Science Museum of Minnesota

27 FRIDAY	Fourth Friday at the Movies
28 SATURDAY	Saint Paul Farmers' Market Donnie Smith Invitational Bike Show
29 SUNDAY	Donnie Smith Invitational Bike Show

Phalen Lake on Saint Paul's East Side has a surface area of 220 acres.

POEM FOR THE STATE OF THE CITY

Carol Connolly, Saint Paul Poet Laureate

Any minute now Spring will unlock her door,
windows in every corner of this capital city
will be flung wide open to greet her,
and we will celebrate with a noisy parade.
Some of us will march
out of respect for our Irish ancestors.
Others of us will march
out of sheer foolishness and we are
so good at that. Our faces painted green
will shock the trees to burst into leaf.
Meanwhile, we wait. Driving North
on Dale Street in the dark of early night,
admiring the new in this old neighborhood
where promises that required heavy lifting
have been kept, I don't see the SUV,
as big as a bungalow, following me.
Honking. Honking. Road rage? Blinking lights.
What had I done? The driver was resolute
in his honking blinking blinking following close.
Finally, crowding me to the curb,
he rolled down his window to shout,
"Turn your lights on. It's dangerous
to drive without lights," and so it is.
With lights on bright, we progress
in our livable city, where this sort of initiative
has taken root. We look out for each other.
We do not forget the endless war,
the broken bridges, the broken veterans
who move as quietly, and with the same
hopeful energy, as undocumented workers.
We do not halt progress.
We greet it like Spring,
and do what must be done
to help it sprout and grow.

Photo © Jewish Historical Society of the Upper Midwest

Young adults on the front steps of the Jewish Educational Center in 1940

FROM THE BEGINNING: FORUMS, THEATER, AND MUSIC

Ken Tilsen

I grew up in the Dale-Selby neighborhood of Saint Paul. To be more exact, we lived in the upstairs of a duplex just off the corner of Dayton and St. Albans, one block from Dale and one block from Selby. Then, as now, it was a neighborhood of mostly small single-family homes with a large number of duplexes and a few small apartment buildings. The owners typically lived downstairs in the duplexes.

At that time the Jewish community had mostly, but not entirely, left the West Side and what we called the 14th Street Community, approximately where Regions Hospital now stands, for Dale-Selby. Dale-Selby had a movie house, pool hall, Agronoff's Tailor Shop, Rosen's Barber Shop, a kosher butcher shop, a kosher deli and bakery, Gray's Drug Store, Red Orenstein's Drug Store, and down a couple blocks at Grotto, Boranian's and Anderson's, whose wares defy easy description. Many years later, Red Orenstein told me that he left the candy bars out near the door for the kids to "steal" because they were old and stale and it was better than throwing them out.

On the corner of Dale and Selby, Jack Peck with the help of his younger brother Sid had a newsstand. Nobody subscribed to newspapers in those days. When an extra came out, we would gather our wagons at the newsstand, pick up the papers, and walk down the center of the street hollering and hawking the papers.

If you walked down St. Albans just four blocks past Selby, you were at Webster Grade School. If you walked down Grotto the same four blocks, you were at Marshall Junior High School, later to become Marshall High School, and you would also arrive at the Temple of Aaron, which at that time was the largest Jewish congregation in the city.

Webster and Marshall and the playground between them occupied the entire block between St. Albans and Grotto and between Ashland and Holly. Today Webster and Marshall are linked together by a building addition and serve as Webster Elementary School.

Immediately to the west on Grotto and facing Marshall Junior High was the Temple of Aaron and the Jewish Community Center, separated from each other by a small alley. This geography is important because at age six or seven and for some time thereafter, my whole world lived between these blocks.

We really owned the streets in those days. Jack Christiansen lived across from our house. At age ten or eleven, I remember running a wire from our upstairs porch to an upper window of his house across the street to which we attached some kind of cups to serve as our private telephone.

I entered Webster in the second grade and should have passed on to Marshall Junior High in the seventh. But these were the World War II years. They added seventh and eighth to Webster. Thus, I was a "senior" at Webster for three years. When I entered the tenth grade at Marshall, it had its first graduating class as a high school.

The building housing the Jewish Community Center was built in 1930 and began its life as the Jewish Educational Center, helping teach and integrate immigrants into the community. It served as a cultural and recreational center and as a facility for a Hebrew school. It ran into financial trouble in 1934 and split into three parts. The Hebrew school became basically a tenant, and as the Jewish Activities Association, it became a community chest organization. The present-day Jewish Community Center was organized in 1948.

What I really knew about the center was that we played basketball in the same league as the Neighborhood House, Hallie Q. Brown (now the Martin Luther King Center), Catholic Youth Center, and the Boys Club. They all had better gyms than our center. Originally they had designed a swimming pool for the center and for some reason never built the pool but converted the proposed pool into the gym, so the gym floor was sunken and the out-of-bounds lines were essentially the walls of the pool. It was also the smallest gym I have ever seen. I can always blame the fact that I was never much of a basketball player on the gym and our inadequate coach. But I did learn a little about wrestling and I am, or was,

Photo © Jewish Historical Society of the Upper Midwest

Kids playing ping-pong at the Jewish Educational Center Annex in 1940

a fairly decent ping-pong player. (Only really good players call it table tennis).

Thus it came to pass that I not only attended Hebrew School at the JCC after regular school across the street but also used the center for clubs and basketball and ping-pong and wrestling and generally hanging out.

I had grown to love the place, and during my senior year in high school I met some of the students doing plays with adults and began to see how the center ticked.

So it should come as no surprise that after I returned from a short spell in the Navy, became married, had children, went to the U of M, had more children, began to practice law, and had more children, that I would become active at the JCC.

In the early 1950s I became a member of the Adult Activities Committee. Almost from the days the building first opened, a similar committee had brought in speakers and sponsored a forum. Dr. Abraham Newman spoke in 1940 on "The Emerging Pattern of American Jewry." The same year a speaker talked about Jewish wit, satire, drama, and folklore. In 1949 the Chair of the University of Minnesota Physics Department spoke on "The Social Implications of Atomic Energy."

In 1955 I became chairman of the committee. We brought in Dr. Otto Nathan, who was a close friend of Albert Einstein and executor of his will. His topic was "Communism and Capitalism, Can They Co-exist?"

Not everyone was happy, but the place was packed.

Shortly after Dr. Nathan spoke, we had an open forum on "The World Situation Today" and followed up with "An American Foreign Policy for

1956." It was presented as a round-table discussion by political science professors from Hamline University, Macalester College, and the University of Minnesota. Dr. Mulfred Sibley was the U of M speaker. He should be remembered as a socialist, a pacifist, and indeed the most loved and most reviled Minnesota professor of the era. I remember clearly Dr. Sibley's remarks. At the time, China and the Soviet Union were bitter enemies. The cold war was at its height. Dr. Sibley said simply, "The cold war will pass. In your lifetime China will become the nation whose economy will influence and change the world."

In later years we had Herb Kaplan of NBC speak on foreign policy and Felix Green, a very controversial Far East expert and writer, speak on "What Will Happen in Vietnam?" This was before major U.S. involvement began. He predicted pretty much exactly what happened.

Apparently from its earliest days as the Jewish Education Center, the center also sponsored a theater group known as the Grotto Players. In the middle 1940s, Don Singerman, then known by his stage name "Maxim Man," moved to Saint Paul from Chicago. In Chicago he was part of the Group Theatre, one of the spawning grounds for the great actors of the era. Don, a small, witty, dedicated, and enormously talented man, turned the Grotto Players into what we believe was one of the best nonprofessional theater groups in the community and on a par with the finest groups in the nation.

Among the plays presented in the 1950s were Clifford Odett's *Awake and Sing!* and *Waiting for Lefty*; George Bernard Shaws's *Arms and the Man* and *The Shewing-Up of Blanco Posnet*; E. Y. Harburg and Fred Saidy's *Finian's Rainbow*; Arthur Miller's *Death of a Salesman*; Arthur Laurents's *The Time of the Cuckoo*; and Paul Osburn's *On Borrowed Time*.

I hung around the Grotto Players doing miscellaneous little tasks while my wife, Rachel, along with my friends, including Bob Levey, acted in several plays, including *Death of a Salesman* and *The Shewing-Up of Blanco Posnet*. Rachel also co-directed *The Time of the Cuckoo*.

Although I played no active role in the center symphony, it always had a special place in my heart. It began in 1933 and, like the Grotto Players, was pushed to excellence by a director whose life was devoted to his art. Peter Lisowski was always a little scary for those of us who were not part of the symphony. He had an incredible scowl and a booming voice that defined authority and power.

We did not tread in his territory.

My doctor as a child and our family doctor was Cecil Warren. He was the concert master beginning around 1936. His name was listed in 1943

Photo © Jewish Historical Society of the Upper Midwest

The Grotto Players perform The Golden City *in 1940*

MARCH

with an asterisk and the explanation that he was "in the armed forces." After the war he returned to the symphony as first violinist. His wife, Edna, a friend and wonderful woman, was the featured pianist and piano soloist. The orchestra's musical level was incredible, widely acclaimed, and often compared favorably to some of the best-known professional groups.

The three most significant programs at the center for me were the Forum, the Grotto Players, and the Center Symphony. All began in the center's earliest days and all continued to enlighten and inspire for several generations.

Photo © Patricia Bour-Schilla

AN ODE TO UNIVERSITY AVENUE

Mary Kay Bailey

MARCH

I like to think of University Avenue as the Twin Cities' own El Camino Real. Rather than linking missions, presidios, and pueblos, it connects Hmong and Somali neighbors; African Americans and Saint Paul Irish; the State Capitol and the Turf Club; the U of M and the Love Doctor. It is a street lined with dreams and contrasts; its buildings relay the constancy of urban change.

At first glance, there's not much to love about University Avenue. It's a wide street, with acres of parking lots, scads of empty buildings, unattractive big-box stores, and no street trees. But if you look closer, gems shine along this hardworking roadway. University is the backbone of Frogtown, complete with the best Asian food in the region.

In the Midway, the corridor's past as a haven for auto sales is echoed by scores of empty car lots and showrooms screaming to be converted into new arts venues. The area palpitates with opportunity, just as it must have for prospectors decades before.

University takes you past gritty and functioning industrial areas—a rarity in many cities. Somehow, the warehouses and manufacturing plants manage to fit in while rubbing elbows with lofts and gracefully restored commercial buildings.

As it has in the past, University will again witness sweeping change. According to plans, the Central Corridor Light Rail Transit line will travel along the avenue by 2014. Light rail is likely to bring back more vitality and elegance to our underappreciated artery. It's also likely to bring disruption and heartache—common afflictions of urban change.

For now, I celebrate the avenue as an eclectic, messy, adaptive hodgepodge of old and new, smelly and shiny, tacky and lovely. But I will also celebrate a future of exciting opportunities and the organic change that keeps the city alive.

APRIL

Photo © Patricia Bour-Schilla

It's April! Spring! Le printemps!
Let's sing! And dance! Call up Mom!
Let's look at flowers
For hours and hours—
And real ones—not CD-ROM.

—Garrison Keillor

Downtown Saint Paul Farmers' Market: Saturdays and Sundays through October

Saint Paul Chamber Orchestra: April 4, 24, 25

Minnesota Opera, *The Barber of Seville*: April 11, 14, 16, 18, 19

Historic Saint Paul Concert with The SPCO: April 18

Fourth Friday at the Movies: April 24

Saint Paul Art Crawl: April 24–26

Festival of Nations: April 30

See pages 288–310 for more information and more events

John Dillinger shot his way out of an apartment building at 93 South Lexington with a machine gun on March 31, 1934, eluding police and a federal agent.

APRIL

S	M	T	W	T	F	S
29	30	31	1	2	3	4
5	6	7	8	9	10	11
12	13	14	15	16	17	18
19	20	21	22	23	24	25
26	27	28	29	30	1	2

30 MONDAY

31 TUESDAY

1 WEDNESDAY

April Fools' Day

2 THURSDAY

Photo © Patricia Bour-Schilla

Garden of Poetry on Thomas Avenue

3 FRIDAY

4 SATURDAY

Saint Paul Farmers' Market

Saint Paul Chamber Orchestra

5 SUNDAY

Palm Sunday

Saint Paul Farmers' Market

Newell Park's development began in 1927, and the pavilion, which still stands today, was built in 1929.

APRIL

THE LAST CHILD TO SLEEP IN SAINT PAUL

Sasha Aslanian

It's 8 p.m. at City Hall and the lights in the mayor's office are still on. He sets down the stack of reports he's been reading, glances at the clock in his office, and reaches for his briefcase and keys. It's time to make the rounds. He flips off the lights and walks down the echoing corridors of City Hall to the door. Everyone is long gone.

The mayor turns the ignition in his car, turns up the radio, and swoops down Shepard Road. His usual route is through Highland Park, then Mac-Groveland, Desnoyer Park, Como-Midway, North End, Frogtown, Crocus Hill, Summit University, downtown, the East Side, and finally the West Side. He checks his clipboard.

All the children in the city are listed. Most have even rows of check-marks by their names, a few have some notes scrawled in the margins. The twin boys on Pinehurst have been giving their mom some trouble, but tonight all looks to be quiet. There was a family on Otis Avenue that held the record under Mayor Latimer for being the last kids to sleep in the city, but those children are parents themselves now. Thank goodness they moved away from Saint Paul, the mayor thinks, because their kids would surely be holy terrors too.

APRIL

It's 9:00 p.m. by the time the mayor wraps up in Frogtown. Street by street, he checks that the lights are out in children's bedroom windows and he can't hear parents shouting anymore. The blue light of television glows in most living rooms as parents wind down for another day of work tomorrow. Every so often the mayor has to get out of the car and gently convince a child to go back to bed. The parents always nod gratefully, a little embarrassed they needed his help. The mayor tries not to make a big deal out of it, slipping past the parents, murmuring that little Quinn was a bit riled but he'll settle in now. Crocus Hill is a breeze tonight. Sometimes the au pairs let the kids stay up too late, but all seems to be quiet. The mayor turns down Ramsey Hill, passes Irvine Park, riverfront condos, the farmers' market and chugs up the East Side. Some of the families haven't been here long and it's a struggle to get to know them all. The mayor does his best, checking names off as he drives through Dayton's Bluff and Swede Hollow. The East Side feels sleepy and so does the mayor. He stops at Dunkin' Donuts to refill his morning coffee cup. There's more to go. He travels down Seventh Street, cuts over the river, and finds Cesar Chavez Street on the West Side. He slowly ticks off the

Nighttime in Saint Paul

easy blocks and streets of sleeping children. His own house is calm. He'll kiss his sleeping children when he gets home tonight. Finally, the car climbs up George and he takes a right on Bidwell. There at the corner, the mayor pulls over and sighs. The lights are still on in Liv Marit's room. Her big sister Kaia has probably been asleep for hours, but Liv Marit, age five, is pulling toys out from under her bed, spreading peanut butter on crackers in the dining room, and making little footfalls on the hardwood floors. My husband and I have retreated to the basement, exhausted, to watch a movie. The phone rings.

"Hello?" the mayor says. He sounds tired.

"Hello, Mr. Mayor," I say. "It's been kind of a tough night."

"I know," he says. "Well, she's it again." The last child to sleep in Saint Paul. I try to keep my composure for the mayor and walk upstairs to motion to Liv that the mayor's on the phone. Her eyes get wide, and she abandons her potion of soap and toilet paper in the bathroom sink and dives for her bunk bed.

"Thank you for calling, Mr. Mayor." I say. "I'll talk with her. You don't have to come in tonight. We'll be OK."

"If you're sure," he says, sounding a bit relieved.

I hang up the phone and walk to her room. Through the shades, the headlights of the mayor's car making a U-turn briefly light up the room. I look at Liv's closed eyes and even breathing. She's out. It's 10:20 p.m., the end of a long day for the mayor and a long night for me.

Sasha Asianian made up this bedtime story for her daughter, Liv, but fears it may have created an incentive for her to stay up late to see if the current mayor really calls.

➪ The corpse plant, *Titum arum*, bloomed at the Como Conservatory on April 9, 2008, the second time a corpse plant ever bloomed in Minnesota.

APRIL

S	M	T	W	T	F	S
29	30	31	1	2	3	4
5	6	7	8	9	10	11
12	13	14	15	16	17	18
19	20	21	22	23	24	25
26	27	28	29	30	1	2

6 MONDAY

7 TUESDAY

APRIL

8 WEDNESDAY

9 THURSDAY

Passover begins

Photo © Patricia Bour-Schilla

Lock and Dam no. 1 on the Mississippi River

10 FRIDAY Good Friday	
11 SATURDAY	Saint Paul Farmers' Market Minnesota Opera, *The Barber of Seville*
12 SUNDAY Easter	Saint Paul Farmers' Market

"I have a feeling that when my ship comes in, I'll be at the airport."—Charles M. Schultz, Saint Paul cartoonist

THE DATE

Phyllis Moore

Remember that date? You know—the one when you were a teen and had so much fun you'll never forget it?

At eighteen, a cute blond co-worker, Sue Larson, caught Danny Kress' eye. He asked her for a date.

"Wear running shoes," he told her. He didn't think to also tell her to wear dark clothes. She arrived in a bright yellow jacket, complementing her blond ponytail. She also brought three girlfriends.

Danny took his gang to Como Zoo. After hours. There was not much to see, since most of the animals were locked up. They went for the excitement of doing something dangerous.

As they walked along the chain-link fence to the wolves' den, one lone gray timber wolf distracted the group; they didn't notice the two wolves lying against the fence. The wolves yelped and howled at the little group. The girls screamed, turned to run, stumbled into Danny, and pinned him against the fence.

The girls ran until they reached the outer wall. Danny helped the first girl over, but as she was preparing to descend the other side, a police car came cruising by.

The front end of the car tilted forward as it came to a sudden halt.

"Run," Danny yelled.

Everyone scattered.

Danny ran through the zoo to the back and jumped the fence to freedom. Just when he thought he was in the clear, a security car came around the bend. He dove into the bush. Maybe security hadn't seen him.

The car slowly rolled up to where Danny was hiding and stopped. Through a loudspeaker, the guard said, "Danny Kress, come on out."

Busted. The police had caught the girls and they had given him up.

Once Danny was in the car, the guard asked, "Did you do any damage?"

"No."

"Then I won't press charges. I snuck in the zoo after hours to have a look around when I was a kid." The guard grinned, remembering his mischievous teen years.

Danny left his sporting goods job soon after that and never saw Sue again. He liked her and would have asked her out again, but he was afraid

Photo © Lou "The Photo Guy" Michaels

Wolf at Como Zoo

he'd blown it. Some years later, through a mutual friend, Danny learned Sue still fondly remembered their date. She really liked him and had so much fun she would have gone out with him again. Unfortunately, her parents were not so understanding.

➪ The sweet pea was chosen by students as the official flower of Saint Paul on April 15, 1912, in a vote sponsored by local women's clubs.

APRIL

S	M	T	W	T	F	S
29	30	31	1	2	3	4
5	6	7	8	9	10	11
12	13	14	15	16	17	18
19	20	21	22	23	24	25
26	27	28	29	30	1	2

13 MONDAY

14 TUESDAY Minnesota Opera, *The Barber of Seville*

15 WEDNESDAY

16 THURSDAY Minnesota Opera, *The Barber of Seville*

APRIL

Photo © Patricia Bour-Schilla

Tuffy's view of downtown Saint Paul

APRIL

17 FRIDAY

18 SATURDAY

Saint Paul Farmers' Market

Minnesota Opera, *The Barber of Seville*

Historic Saint Paul Concert with the SPCO

19 SUNDAY

Saint Paul Farmers' Market

Minnesota Opera, *The Barber of Seville*

The number of homeopathic physicians in Saint Paul grew from three in 1857 to thirty-six in 1896.

THE BIRD MAN OF DUNN BROTHERS

Matt Jackson

The first time I met the Bird Man at Dunn Brothers about three years ago, he introduced himself as Mark, but he added that if I wanted to, I could call him Smooth. I wondered why Mark, somewhere in his forties, with a daily scruff, a casual concern for his hairstyle, and an everyday outfit of jeans with a workman's jacket, was called Smooth. I say this with all due respect to Mark.

Dunn Brothers on Grand seems to have an especially loyal and varied lot of regulars, and Mark quickly became one. I watched as he met and began sitting with the other daily regulars. He was accepted into the network of altruistic table sharing. This is one of the benefits of being a regular in the dog-eat-dog atmosphere of the Dunn Brothers afternoon rush. In the spring, Mark made the seasonal switch and sat out front on Grand Avenue. He baked in the sun like a pro.

As Mark sat outside one day, a large sparrow hopped onto the arm of his bench. The sparrow circled him, and landed on his table. Mark threw a small piece of bran muffin toward it, and the bird caught the crumb in midair. By that same afternoon, Mark had Bessie eating out of his hand. When Mark arrived at Dunn Brothers the next day, the others outside told Mark that Bessie had been waiting for him.

As the spring turned toward summer, Mark was buying several bran muffins a day and supporting a population of twenty or so sparrows. He named them all and kept track of Bessie. They greeted Mark when he pulled up each day, fluttering around him with anticipation. He would then stroll through the parking lot, tossing the crumbs like seeds to either side, and practice his whistling. Mark told me he knows many distinct whistles, but admitted he doesn't know what they mean.

Another regular, Radke, from the prudent and conservative front alcove of Dunn Brothers, told Mark he couldn't keep buying muffins for the birds, it was too expensive. He told him to go buy birdseed instead. Mark took his advice and began bringing it with him every day in his truck. Mark confided in me, however, that he was sure the birds liked muffins better.

The next spring, Mark and Clint, the carpenter, hung a bird feeder underneath the VIOLATORS WILL BE TOWED sign outside of Dunn Brothers, but it created huge piles of seed shells and poop where people sat,

Photo © Lou "The Photo Guy" Michaels

Mark "the Bird Man" of Dunn Brothers Coffee Shop

and it needed to be moved. The following year, Mark's friend Chuck got a pole from work, and with the permission of Doug, the owner of Dunn Brothers, and Macalester College, they installed a freestanding bird feeder and a bird bath in the bushes between the two parking lots. This has been the center of Mark's operations ever since. Mark told me he goes through a twenty-pound bag every two days now, and thought there were 500 to 600 birds using his facilities.

With the size of his current flock, Mark isn't sure he can still recognize Bessie. He told me Bessie had a raspy voice, and that sometimes, amidst the chaos, he can hear it, but usually it's just a robin who sits across the street on a wire fooling him. Mark says it doesn't bother him that he lost Bessie. When he loads the food into the bird feeder, the birds engulf him. They rub up against his cheeks as they rush in, and graze his hair with their wings.

Mark seemed to become the Bird Man of Dunn Brothers almost unconsciously. He was not overtly looking for a niche, or pretentiously trying to fit in. He also did not begin calling himself the Bird Man, and after watching him earn that nickname, I'm sure he did not begin calling himself Smooth. I wonder if Mark introduces himself as Bird Man in other areas of his life, and if people wonder where the name comes from. I wonder if he secretly knows how to whistle his name to the birds. I wonder if some of the birds have a nickname for him too.

➯ Red House Records, a Saint Paul distributor of folk and rock music, was resurrected in Bob Feldman's apartment in 1983 when he relaunched Iowa singer-songwriter Greg Brown's label.

APRIL

S	M	T	W	T	F	S
29	30	31	1	2	3	4
5	6	7	8	9	10	11
12	13	14	15	16	17	18
19	20	21	22	23	24	25
26	27	28	29	30	1	2

20 Monday

21 Tuesday

22 Wednesday

Earth Day

23 Thursday

Photo © Lou "The Photo Guy" Michaels

Conny's Creamy Cone at Maryland Avenue and Dale Street

24 FRIDAY

Saint Paul Chamber Orchestra
Saint Paul Art Crawl

25 SATURDAY

Saint Paul Farmers' Market
Saint Paul Chamber Orchestra
Saint Paul Art Crawl

26 SUNDAY

Saint Paul Farmers' Market
Saint Paul Art Crawl

DIRTY WORK

Mike Hazard

He holds out his hands in a beam of sun.
Dirt jammed under finger nails, informed
by ceremonies of dust and mud, he teaches
"Every day above ground is a good one."

Frank Sinatra asked to sing at Vice-President Hubert H. Humphrey's 1978 funeral in Saint Paul, but the officiating minister refused.

MIGHTY MISSISSIPPI MEMORIES

Linda Straley

Memories often take on a life of their own and go where they will. This one leads me down memory lane to helping my grandfather, Floyd W. Anger, mayor of Lilydale from 1959 to 1970, move his essentials to higher ground every year that Lilydale's lowlands flooded where Water Street becomes Lilydale Road. In 1965 he lost his home to the river; one day it was off its foundation, the next day it was down the road, having slammed into a telephone pole, and the day after it was gone— pictures, treasures, and lots of essentials. In one newspaper article, my grandfather was quoted as saying, "They [the residents] say they won't come back—but they do," and so did he and his wife, Evelyn. After the 1965 flood, he built a home at 944 Lilydale Road, down the road and across the street from his lost home. Not only did they go back after every flood, but Grandpa would often pay his friends who helped him by giving them a lot of land. At one time, he owned a considerable amount of land in Lilydale.

I lived down there for a year in the mid-1950s just past the "new" road for the Lilydale Boat Ramp, and on a recent drive (I hadn't been down there for thirty years) with my dad, Floyd's son, I was shocked (because memories freeze things in time) that the only sign of where our house used to be is the pine tree that stood between our house and Grandpa Floyd's. There are no houses down there anymore.

Life in Lilydale was idyllic; the closest I can come to a description is that it was sort of a Huck Finn/Tom Sawyer kind of life—everybody knew everybody. Lilydale was little more than a wide spot in the road, and the road itself was so narrow in a few places that one car would have to pull off the road to let the oncoming car pass. There were no speeders or hot-rodders; Lilydale was a peaceful, family-oriented community, and as a child I never realized the river could be such a threat.

Grandpa drove the school bus for Lilydale. He was always in a good mood and loved to joke, but when he said to do something, you just knew he meant it. I don't think he ever met a person he didn't like, or if he did, he kept it to himself. It was fun going to his house because he loved his ice cream and he always treated us to a huge bowl of it covered in Hershey's chocolate syrup. He played in a band at local taverns, too, and I've often thought that was why he was always tapping his foot; even while he was sitting, he seemed to be tapping a beat. He played drums in the band but he could play any instrument—piano, sax, accordion,

Photo © Linda Straley

Lilydale Boat Ramp

banjo, viola—just anything. He'd pick up or sit at the instrument and just know how to play it.

Grandpa is dead now and all of Lilydale's homes are gone—bought by the government and razed for future park use. I wonder what Grandpa would think of all this—the changes to his "kingdom"—and every year I wonder what the Mighty Mississippi has in store for us.

Photo © Linda Straley

Floyd W. Anger, mayor of Lilydale from 1959 to 1970

Photo © Linda Straley

Lilydale Village Hall boarded up

➪ In 1859, Colonel D. A. Robertson became the sixth mayor of Saint Paul, taking office on May 3, 1859. He was the founder of the *Minnesota Democrat*.

APRIL

S	M	T	W	T	F	S
29	30	31	1	2	3	4
5	6	7	8	9	10	11
12	13	14	15	16	17	18
19	20	21	22	23	24	25
26	27	28	29	30	1	2

27 MONDAY

28 TUESDAY

29 WEDNESDAY

30 THURSDAY

Festival of Nations

Photo © Patricia Bour-Schilla

Sculpture in front of Children's Hospital

1 FRIDAY	Festival of Nations Cinco de Mayo Festival Como Memorial Japanese Garden opens
2 SATURDAY	Saint Paul Farmers' Market Festival of Nations Cinco de Mayo Festival Living Green Expo Historic Saint Paul Concert with The SPCO Summer Flower Show begins
3 SUNDAY	Saint Paul Farmers' Market Festival of Nations Living Green Expo

Four police substations were opened on May 1, 1887, in different neighborhoods of the growing city.

IRISH IN RONDO

Patrick O'Dougherty

I must go down to the place where all the ladders start,
the bone and rag shop of the heart.
—William Butler Yeats

Flashback: I was going through some old family photographs after my Irish Catholic father died of cancer at Mount Sinai Hospital in 1986. I came across a photo of my mother taken of her while at St. Benedict's College at the time she met my father. It was a black-and-white photo in which she was wearing a beautiful bonnet. It reminded me of the song, "I Dream of Jeanie with the Light Brown Hair."

My Story: problems with schizophrenia and a mother conflict. James Joyce thought the "one true thing in life is a mother's love." My social worker/writer mother, Patricia Coyne-O'Shaughnessy, got me involved with Hope Transition Center and Guild Hall after I was the victim of an armed robbery, which gave me post-traumatic stress disorder. I lived at Guild Hall in the mid-1970s and early 1980s. I was under commitment while a resident of Guild Hall.

APRIL

I had problems with unconscious protrusions while a freshman at St. John's University, where I was a history major. Unconscious protrusions are unwanted thoughts and dreams and nightmares that protrude into the consciousness against one's will. I had problems with racing thoughts and fragmented thinking, such as problems with focusing thoughts and thought-tracking problems. I also had mother-conflict problems. My mother has a very strong personality that cuts both ways. My mother lost her first child, so my father named me Patrick after her.

My mother recently sent me some articles about the opening of *The Great Gatsby* at the Guthrie. She recollected she met my father while her relatives were living on 669 Grand Avenue in the old F. Scott Fitzgerald neighborhood of Saint Paul. James O'Dougherty, my father, proposed to her on the landing going down the steps from Summit Avenue to Smith Street by the James J. Hill Mansion.

My mother and I had a long talk about Guild Hall, which was a psychological/psychiatric group home where I lived and worked after a psychiatric commitment. Guild Hall is run by the Guild of Catholic Women. It was originally a home for single, working women who moved to Saint Paul looking for work. While I was there, Guild Hall was directed by Jan and Russ Djvergstan. I was the janitor at first. Later I worked in the kitchen

Photo © Patrick O'Dougherty

James O'Dougherty and Patricia Coyne-O'Shaughnessy

with Mrs. Christiansen and Glen Pittlekow.

Fascinated by labor history, I did history research during the day at the Minnesota Historical Society. I studied Civil War census data and city directories. The city directories of Saint Paul showed fluidity in the turnover rates of occupational categories, and this suggested that the thrust of economic change came through changes in economic occupations and their new landscapes. I privately worked at Industrial Steel, loading barrels onto trucks, at Twin City Hide, sorting the hides, and at the Victory Parking Ramp as a cashier. These jobs made labor history a lived experience for me. Manual labor gave focus to my thoughts and helped stabilize my thought-tracking problems. Medications brought my schizophrenia under control.

My doctor at the time was a young physician named Patrick Stokes. He was a dark Irish Catholic, the son of a police officer from the Washington Park part of Chicago. Dr. Stokes was not very good with the medications, and his personal advice would not be approved today. For example, if you asked him about sex, he told you to find a girlfriend. Father Tegeder got us involved with a book discussion group in the basement of the cathedral's rectory on *Christ Amongst Us: A Modern Presentation of the Catholic Faith* by Anthony J. Wilhelm. Through the pain of therapy and the joys of living together, we learned to see Christ in each other. This is the truth of Guild Hall. Located on Marshall Avenue, Guild Hall became the Marshall of our hearts. The Guild Oblates, Father Mike Tegeder, and later Father Michael Skluzacek, introduced us to the Benedictine Oblate movement. The word *oblate* relates to gift and to charity. Through this spiritual discipline, I became a Benedictine tertiary, a minor status. This discipline

Photo © Patrick O'Dougherty

Patrick O'Dougherty

gave a spiritual and justice focus to my fragmented schizo-affective personality. My own diagnosis is that I have a narcissistic personality with a creative, divergent-thinking cognitive style.

We frequently went on dates to W. A. Frost, Gallivan's, and the Commodore Bar, where F. Scott Fitzgerald used to hang out. We went to the Wabasha Caves and to the Ford Caves when they were still open, where we wrote *I love you* notes in the limestone with candles. The Ford Motor Company used the sand in the caves to make automobile windshields. We danced at the Prom on the Midway, which featured the Dick Kast Combo. After my father's death, Dick Kast married my mother and became my stepfather.

I attended Central High School for computer class instruction in the evenings and learned how to create a computer menu. While attending Central and Guild Hall, I read James Joyce's *Portrait of an Artist as a Young Man*, Richard Wright's *Native Son*, and James Baldwin's *Another Country*. I was heavily influenced by these artists. I went back to graduate school and I won a fellowship to study in Havana, Cuba.

In 2001, I moved back to Saint Paul after a court hearing, and I joined St. Peter Claver Parish, the old traditional Black Catholic Parish in Saint Paul. At a birthday party at Golden Thyme, the staff told me my mother resembled me. The photo I had found helped me deal with repressed issues in my relationships. Are my mother and I like repressed dream sequences formed out of old *Great Gatsby* narratives? In part, the answer is yes. My mother's photo turned my childhood and my dreams into a meditative reflection on growing up in the Fitzgerald Rondo Guild community of Saint Paul. This is growing up Irish in the Rondo/Fitzgerald community of Saint Paul. Get the picture? Blow it up!

A SUNDAY MORNING IN SAINT PAUL

R. Allen Miner

Twenty-three years ago I spent a memorable spring break in Saint Paul with my wife and two daughters. Now I am a grandfather of two, and as a birthday gift my daughter and her husband decided we should revisit the places that made that long ago trip special: the Como Park Zoo and Conservatory, and the Sunday Brunch at the Lexington Restaurant. Now, as then, the Minnesota winter was not cooperative, with temperatures in the low forties and playful snow flurries. But we were a game group: my wife and I, our daughters and their husbands, and our grandchildren, two-year-old Lily and six-month-old Charlie.

Como Park on a Sunday morning is a busy place, with parents pushing strollers and shepherding toddlers and young children along the many pathways seeking out favorite animals. During our visit there was an Earth Day "Party for the Planet" celebration going on at the newly opened Leonard Wilkening Children's Gallery, with special family-friendly activities, like decorating clay pots to be toad homes. Because of the weather, we concentrated on the indoor exhibits like the giraffes ("Who knew they could bend their long necks into an almost complete circle?"), primates, sea lions and penguins, but did find time to seek out the lions, and other "big cats" and were serenaded with impressive roars.

When we decided we'd had enough of the sights and smells of the zoo animals (the hooved stock are particularly memorable when it comes to aroma), we headed for the indoor gardens of the Marjorie McNeely Conservatory. If one ever needs an antidote to the seemingly endless Minnesota winter, it is a visit to the Spring Flower Show in the Sunken Garden. Tulips, lilies, buttercups, hyacinth, blue and pink hydrangea—an explosion of color and fragrance. I loved encouraging two-year-old Lily to not only look but stop and smell her namesake flowers. Before leaving the conservatory, I also took her on a quick trip through the Tropical Encounters rainforest exhibit. How nice to experience in April being too warm and seeing Lily's hair curl up from the humidity.

Having worked up an appetite viewing distinctly un-Minnesotan flora and fauna, we headed off to the Sunday Brunch at the Lexington Restaurant. What a family-friendly place! Unlike most fancy restaurants, where young children are received as if they were hooved stock, the Lexington made every effort to keep young children (and their parents) happy. And

Photo © Patricia Bour-Schilla

The Lexington at Grand and Lexington Avenues

the place was packed, mostly with families—children, parents, grandparents, great-grandparents. Clearly here was another Saint Paul tradition that we had happened upon and would now make our own. The couple next to us, who looked like they may have been teenagers when the restaurant first opened, was working their way through a hot turkey dinner. (I'd heard them order "our usual.") But our group decided to stick with the breakfast specialties like eggs Benedict, corned beef hash, and strawberry waffles. Everything was delicious. Even the bill seemed family-friendly and old-fashioned.

The Lexington boasts of its reputation for "seventy-three very good years," but we hadn't been back since our dinner there twenty-three years ago. I know it won't be another twenty-three before we go back again.

CASS GILBERT AND "POPE" TIFFANY: AN ARCHITECT'S PROGRESS

Charles Locks

In 1878, Cass Gilbert left Saint Paul to attend the two-year architectural program at the Institute of Technology (MIT) in Massachusetts, after which he planned to travel in Europe. Gilbert checked his finances after his first year. He had sufficient funds to complete his coursework or travel, but not both. He chose travel. Upon his return to the States, he caught on with the iconic architectural firm of McKim, Mead & White in New York.

Working in New York was a heady experience for the twenty-one-year-old Gilbert. His rapport was solid with the firm's principals, who served as his mentors and provided him with his first projects when he started his own architectural practice. His best friend was his fellow draftsman, Joseph Wells, a descendant of John Adams. Wells was a brilliant designer who is credited for the Italian Renaissance design of the Villard townhouses on Madison Avenue, formerly Random House headquarters and now part of a Helmsley Hotel.

One of several projects Gilbert worked on in New York was the Louis Comfort Tiffany House at 72nd and Madison, a fifty-seven-room, five-story townhouse. Ten years older than Gilbert, Louis Comfort Tiffany, son of the founder of Tiffany & Company, had begun his career as a painter but switched to glass making. He declared that his lifelong goal was "the pursuit of beauty," a quest in which he was so successful that his name became synonymous with the term. Wells, a first-class skeptic, felt Gilbert's reverence for the artists of the day approached religious fervor. To chide Gilbert, Wells coined the term "Pope" Tiffany, and suggested Gilbert's faith was misplaced.

Gilbert did believe in the symbolic Pope Tiffany as well as the flesh-and-blood Tiffany; his artistic aims mirrored those of Tiffany and the leading artists of the day, and he never gave up the faith. When given the opportunity to design the interior of a motor yacht for James Gordon Bennett, Jr., the publisher of the *New York Herald* and the man who financed Henry Stanley's search for the explorer David Livingstone, Gilbert specified Tiffany windows.

Gilbert didn't abandon his artistic sensibility when he returned to Saint Paul in 1882 to set up his architectural practice, but he found it difficult to find clients prepared to spend money on art glass from Tiffany. In

Photo © Minnesota Historical Society

Cass Gilbert on roof of State Capitol

1885–1986, Gilbert and James Knox Taylor designed the Dayton Avenue Presbyterian Church at 503 Dayton Avenue. Gilbert queried The Tiffany Glass Company about providing windows for the building. A representative of the company replied that even if Tiffany had no other work, the company could not afford to provide windows at the budgeted price, and the church went without.

Gilbert strove to include Tiffany windows in his other churches. Thanks to the generosity of Mrs. Theodore Eaton of New York, Gilbert was able to acquire twenty-one Tiffany windows for St. Clement's Episcopal Church at 901 Portland Avenue (1895–1896), but not without controversy. Mrs. Eaton demanded a larger window behind the altar. Gilbert felt a larger window ruined his design. Mrs. Eaton went behind his back to the glass company. The company denied taking sides in the dispute, but Mrs. Eaton got the larger window. J. P. Morgan attended the dedication and afterward lunched with Gilbert at his Grand Hill home. St. Clement's later donated one small Tiffany window to St. John the Divine Episcopal Church (1898–1899), which Gilbert designed in Moorhead.

Gilbert won the competition to design the University of Minnesota Campus Plan in 1908, while he was president of the American Institute of Architects. His design was never built. Aside from the question of funding, a quarrel arose between Gilbert and his erstwhile friend and classmate at MIT, Clarence Johnston, the Minnesota state architect, who believed all work at the University of Minnesota fell under his purview. It didn't help matters that Pierce Butler, a university regent (later the first U.S. Supreme Court justice from Minnesota) had an ax to grind; he was miffed that Gilbert penalized his family's construction firm (general contractor for the Minnesota State Capitol) on an East Coast project. Gilbert did, however, receive a letter from Tiffany Studios soliciting work on the project.

A decade after winning the design competition for the University of Minnesota, Gilbert received a note from Tiffany's secretary: Gilbert (now world famous) had left his gloves in the great man's automobile—Gilbert had kept the faith and got his interview with the "Pope."

MAY

Photo © Patricia Bour-Schilla

Downtown Saint Paul Farmers' Market: Saturdays and Sundays through October

Festival of Nations: May 1–3

Cinco de Mayo Festival: May 1–2

Living Green Expo: May 2–3

Historic Saint Paul Concert with The SPCO: May 2, 16, 30

Saint Paul Civic Symphony Mother's Day Celebration: May 13

Sur Seine Music Festival: May 14–24

Minnesota Dance Festival: May 16–18

Fourth Friday at the Movies: May 22

Saint Paul Chamber Orchestra: May 22, 23

Flint Hills International Children's Festival: May 26–31

See pages 288–310 for more information and more events

MAY

S	M	T	W	T	F	S
26	27	28	29	30	1	2
3	4	5	6	7	8	9
10	11	12	13	14	15	16
17	18	19	20	21	22	23
24	25	26	27	28	29	30
31	1	2	3	4	5	6

➩ Hamline University hosted the first intercollegiate basketball game in history in 1895, losing to the U of M's School of Agriculture by a score of 9–3.

4 Monday

5 Tuesday

Cinco de Mayo

6 Wednesday

7 Thursday

Photo © Tom Conlon

Saint Paul Central High School Girls' Basketball team wins the State Championship in 2007 and 2008. 2008 team: Back row, L to R: Megan Tate; Samantha Robinson-Ricks; Megan Howard; Kiara Buford; Briana Reeves; Georgie Jones; Maja Cyrus; Natasha Garrett; Theairra Taylor. Kneeling, L to R: Anna Germundson (student manager in stripes); Laura Hansen; Kyana "Bitty" Johnson; Cyonna West; Brittany Dorsey; Maia Wahlberg. Front center: Catavia Jones. Missing: Head Coach Willie Taylor; Asst. Coaches Tom Gunderson, John Robinson; Joey Waters, Chauntyll Allen.

8 FRIDAY

9 SATURDAY Saint Paul Farmers' Market

10 SUNDAY Saint Paul Farmers' Market

Mother's Day

"Have you ever wondered why we exist in Saint Paul?"—Heiruspecs, Saint Paul band, from their song, "Have You Ever Wondered?"

Saint Paul Saints—Change-ups, Curves & Ponytails—1998

As our Saint Paul Saints begin another season this year, here are a couple of stars from a bit ago. Ila Border, the first woman to play in organized baseball, and Darryl Strawberry, down on his luck from stardom from the Yankees. Both players earned the applause and joy of Saints fans in 1998. Here is a poem I wrote for owner Mike Veeck, a star of a person, for the Saints' Yearbook *about these two amazing Saints, with a nod of thanks to John Lennon.*

STRAWBERRY FIELD

Donal Heffernan

1. The Long Winter

The Saint Paul tavern radio could have been talking loss or win
new games of stick hockey, the Chippewa kind
with a different format of scoring,
and we like thawed walleyes this St. Paddy's Day
having melted began flopping and talking once more.
After all, living a ways north of the equator for years,
chatting baseball is a special game in wintertime
and smooth music to our eager ears.

2. The Sporting News

FIRST WOMAN MAY PLAY FOR SAINT PAUL SAINTS—
ILA BORDER IS HER NAME.
We studied the beaten, mahogany box of a radio
as if it were a TV set caught in a lie.

Veeck's done it again, Mike the bartender yelled.
Just like Darryl Strawberry coming to play
and then later hit a home run in the World Series
the season he got on his feet again, some say.

"If spring ever does arrive," the fellow next to me retorted.
Mike hearing this doubter slapped his bar rag down with a smack
furious at the bravado of skepticism,
looking more like Moses being interrupted
by a petty messenger with a weather report
during his big one at Mt. Sinai.
Then Mike revealed what we thought we heard was the plan:
The coming baseball season would star
a woman rather than a man.

Photo © Saint Paul Saints

Darryl Strawberry

Photo © Saint Paul Saints

Ila Border

3. Spring

Along with June's warm winds, Ms. Ila Border
around gardening time
started pitching her way from the sports pages
to the front pages, and on TV
surely a fresh sign of spring
for all fans to see.

She set the style that year, too
For many young baseball daughters:
ponytails and baseball caps:
way ahead of the Saks or Gaps.

4. Summer

Arriving at the Midway for the night
We spotted this special Saint:
a streamlined gal
with wonderfully chestnut brown hair
moving like a deer
then saw her streamlined hands, too
strong
eager to pitch relief in a game that got away
even though she threw some strikes
to Thunder Bay.
But Mike the bartender was right
like Strawberry
she'd leave us, too, one day.

"I believe that in the end the abolition of war, the maintenance of world peace, the adjustment of international questions by pacific means will come through the force of public opinion, which controls nations and peoples."—Frank B. Kellogg, Saint Paul statesman

MAY

S	M	T	W	T	F	S
26	27	28	29	30	1	2
3	4	5	6	7	8	9
10	11	12	13	14	15	16
17	18	19	20	21	22	23
24	25	26	27	28	29	30
31	1	2	3	4	5	6

11 MONDAY

12 TUESDAY

13 WEDNESDAY

Saint Paul Civic Symphony Mother's Day Celebration

14 THURSDAY

Sur Seine Music Festival

Photo © Tom Conlon

Freshman basketball team member Kaylyn Roberts displays her custom-made M&M cookie jacket featuring the numbers of the varsity players and the "ingredients" of the successful team: teamwork, passion, dedication, and confidence (taken before the start of the state championship final vs. Minneapolis South in March 2008 at the Target Center)

15 FRIDAY

Sur Seine Music Festival

16 SATURDAY

Saint Paul Farmers' Market

Historic Saint Paul Concert with the SPCO

Sur Seine Music Festival

Minnesota Dance Festival

17 SUNDAY

Saint Paul Farmers' Market

Sur Seine Music Festival

Minnesota Dance Festival

WHEN I ADMIRE THE SHINING

Mike Hazard

When I admire the shining
strawberries, praise the grower,
shining like a fresh berry,
he tells me they shine the most
the moment they are picked

MAY

Saint Paul–born Dewitt Wallace encapsulated the desire for short factual stories with his creation of *Reader's Digest* in 1922.

IT'S ELECTRIC

Chelsea DeArmond

Gone are the days when I could sneak out of the house to get a few groceries without even brushing my hair. Now I have to look decent because I know people will stare, smile, and wave at me the whole way. Ever since we bought an electric car, I feel like I'm a float in a parade wherever I go.

When we first got it, I felt a little silly driving this contraption that looks like a cross between a golf cart and a mini van. But we have been overwhelmed by the amount of curiosity and enthusiasm people all over Saint Paul have expressed about our little white car. Curious folks gather around it in parking lots and snap photos with their cell phones. At stoplights, people roll down their windows to ask questions. Kids point and laugh.

We've had the car for about a year, and it's given us a whole new perspective on Saint Paul. Since it's classified as a "neighborhood electric vehicle," we can only drive on roads with speed limits of 35 mph or less. So we've found that we can get just about everywhere we would normally go without ever hopping on the freeway. And, since our car is very quiet and has excellent visibility (when the weather is warm we can take the doors off so the sides are open), we see a lot more of places we would normally just whiz by.

Here are a few of our favorite questions people have asked about our car:

Q: What kind of gas mileage does that thing get?

A: It's electric. We just plug it in when we're not using it. It doesn't need gas, oil changes, new spark plugs, antifreeze or radiator fluid, muffler repairs, or catalytic converters (there is no exhaust). It took my husband 20 minutes to do an engine swap.

Q: Is that one of those cars from India?

A: The Discovery Channel must have done a special on cars in India, because we get this question a lot. Actually, our car was manufactured in North Dakota, and we bought it on eBay.

Q: Are those sonar panels? (Yes, he said "sonar," not "solar.")

A: No, those polka-dot decals are just for decoration.

Photo © Chelsea DeArmond

Chelsea's husband, Tyler, driving their electric car

Q: Does that thing run on toilet paper?

A: This question really confused me until I realized that I had put a few large bags of toilet paper rolls in the back seat on my way home from the grocery store.

Q: Do you want to trade?

A: A bus driver shouted this question to me at a stoplight, and the owner of a Hummer I parked next to in a lot was also interested in a trade. I turned them both down.

Q: Can I have a ride?

A: We have been surprised by how often we get this question. One man insisted we take his cab fare after we dropped him off at the store. When we were leaving the Taste of Minnesota, a very tired-looking woman just jumped right in the back seat without even asking. She got off at the lot where her car was parked. So, unless we're in a big hurry, the answer is "sure."

Q: Have you seen the movie Who Killed the Electric Car?

A: Yes, loved it. Based on the huge amount of interest people have shown in our electric car, it makes no sense to me why they aren't being mass-produced. I think an electric car dealership in Saint Paul would do very well.

➩ T. H. Lewis came to Saint Paul in 1878 as the first archaeologist to survey Minnesota's Native American archaeological sites. He later disappeared somewhere in Colorado and was never found.

MAY

S	M	T	W	T	F	S
26	27	28	29	30	1	2
3	4	5	6	7	8	9
10	11	12	13	14	15	16
17	18	19	20	21	22	23
24	25	26	27	28	29	30
31	1	2	3	4	5	6

18 MONDAY

Sur Seine Music Festival

Minnesota Dance Festival

19 TUESDAY

Sur Seine Music Festival

20 WEDNESDAY

Sur Seine Music Festival

21 THURSDAY

Sur Seine Music Festival

Photo © Patricia Bour-Schilla

Bear sculpture on Maryland Avenue near Como Lake

22 FRIDAY	Sur Seine Music Festival Saint Paul Chamber Orchestra Fourth Friday at the Movies
23 SATURDAY	Saint Paul Farmers' Market Sur Seine Music Festival Saint Paul Chamber Orchestra
24 SUNDAY	Saint Paul Farmers' Market Sur Seine Music Festival

MAY

At 7:30 a.m. on June 28, 2008, thousands of people watched as the 570-foot-high concrete Xcel Energy smokestack near the High Bridge imploded.

FROM *THE PAST IS PERFECT: MEMOIR OF A FATHER/SON REUNION*

Alexs Pate

Seeing Willie Mays

At any rate, on this particular night out with my father, the weather was perfect, the food was great, and the baseball game was amazing. It even ended in a most dramatic way. At the bottom of the ninth inning, the score was tied, there were two outs, and the bases were loaded with National Leaguers. Who walked up to the plate? Willie Mays, the "Say Hey" kid.

I turned to my father, my third hot dog trying to escape its soggy bun, my lips smeared with mustard and relish, trying to balance a big cup of Coca-Cola between my knees, and said loud enough for people to hear above the din of the vendors, "He's gonna hit a grand slam. He's gonna do it."

My father looked at me and smiled. In that smile, I know he was trying to say, "Yes, son, I know you have to think about it that way. But the truth is that that kind of thing rarely happens. You have to also be prepared for your hero to strike out this time."

And I know now that striking out is a part of life. Nobody can hit the ball every single time. But he didn't say that to me. He didn't dampen my optimism. He just smiled.

And what does Willie Mays do? He hit a goddamned grand slam homerun. Sure as shootin'. I lost my hot dog and the Coke. Everything went flying.

It was the perfect end to an evening with my father. All the way home, I nursed this feeling that there had been some special connection between us that night, that we had experienced something great together. Willie Mays and Mickey Mantle were on the same field together under the blazing lights.

I thought of that night as I sat with my son, Alexs, puffing away on our cigars and sipping cognac. I suspect that there were many times when my father sat back in his chair and sighed at the power of his love for his children. As his son, I always felt enveloped by him. The experience of serenely sitting with my son was as close as I had come to actually feeling him within me.

I suddenly realized that that was what I sought. I wanted to feel Alexs within me as I now believe all fathers feel their children.

SUNDAY MAY 31, 2009

Tina Dybvik

If I had turned to the others
and asked if they saw her too,
I would know now
it was a Messenger
who lit from the bus at Sixth
and walked downtown
with young men in old pants and loose shirts.

I would know they did not see her
because it was love unseen.
Except by me and the light that shone
on her white haloed hat,
the matching bag and suit,
and opaque stockings,
then disappeared across Robert Street;

a flash of silver shoes among the scuffing.

➩ 1930: Frank B. Kellogg of Saint Paul was awarded the Nobel Peace Prize for his work as U. S. Secretary of State on the 1928 Kellogg-Briand Peace Pact.

MAY

S	M	T	W	T	F	S
26	27	28	29	30	1	2
3	4	5	6	7	8	9
10	11	12	13	14	15	16
17	18	19	20	21	22	23
24	25	26	27	28	29	30
31	1	2	3	4	5	6

25 MONDAY

Memorial Day

26 TUESDAY Flint Hills International Children's Festival

27 WEDNESDAY Flint Hills International Children's Festival

28 THURSDAY Flint Hills International Children's Festival

MAY

Photo © Patricia Bour-Schilla

A party at the Capitol

29 FRIDAY Shavuot	Flint Hills International Children's Festival
30 SATURDAY	Saint Paul Farmers' Market Historic Saint Paul Concert with the SPCO Flint Hills International Children's Festival
31 SUNDAY	Saint Paul Farmers' Market Flint Hills International Children's Festival

MAY

A century ago, Saint Paul sculptor Alonzo Hauser was born in Wisconsin.

GLORIA CONTRERAS EDIN, A NEW HOPE FOR LATINO IMMIGRANTS

Eva Palma-Zuniga

"It's great to help one person at a time, that definitely is needed, but we want to see changes that affect how government conducts itself, how people treat immigrants. We have to look not only at legal issues that immigrants face but the political and public sentiment against them," Contreras Edin states.

Contreras Edin is the executive director of Centro Legal, a nonprofit legal agency that has been providing legal services to the Latino community in Minnesota for over twenty-five years.

Immigration is a current hot-button issue. Of all the cases this agency works with, 80 percent of them have to do with immigration. Taking action in this area, facing a world of people who have little value for Latinos and immigration in general, and getting hate calls is not an easy job, but since the day she took over as executive director of Centro Legal in October 2005, Contreras Edin knew that she belonged there. Her passion for her job is what gives her the strength to keep fighting for Latino immigrants. Where does this passion come from?

"I have this flame of hope that does not go out. I believe I can make the world a better place, I believe it, I believe it, I believe it, and I'm going to keep pushing," she says.

Contreras Edin and the staff at Centro Legal have embarked on a new project that will affect immigration litigation not only in Minnesota but across the country. That is why she filed a lawsuit against the federal government, including the Department of Homeland Security and the Immigration Customs Enforcement Agency, over the residential raids that occurred in Willmar, Minnesota. To do this, she is working in partnership with other law firms in town like Gray Plant Mooty—Centro Legal is not working alone.

Before Contreras Edin ever became a lawyer, she worked with immigrants in rural Minnesota. She was in a coffee shop in a small town, and a local farmer looked at her as she walked in, contorted his face in disgust, and said, "Something smells here now." He got up and walked out and made it known that he wasn't pleased to see her walk into the shop. That day, she decided she would start giving people more information on their rights against racism and discrimination.

Photo © Lou "The Photo Guy" Michaels

Gloria Contreras Edin

Contreras Edin shared a story of how one local judge in the same small town told her, "You can't tell people what their rights are, you are not a lawyer." She responded confidently, saying, "Well, then, I'll become one."

And she did. She applied for a Bush Leadership Fellowship. Her application stated, "If you give me this award, I will go to law school and become a nonprofit lawyer that manages an agency that provides legal services to immigrants." She had no idea that Centro Legal would ever happen. What's really powerful is that she was sworn in as a lawyer along with the son of the same local judge who had told her that she couldn't tell people what their rights were.

Now, Contreras Edin is officially a lawyer, recognized as one of the top up-and-coming lawyers in Minnesota, and she feels a strong sense of resolve to do her job and fulfill her dreams of providing services and changing policy for immigrants in this country.

"I need to change not only the way the law is treating these people, but the way we view each other. . . . I really believe that some day we are going to apologize to the immigrants—Mexican immigrants specially—for the harm that was caused to them."

CAROL BLY—
AFFECTION FOR THE WORLD

Judith Niemi

When Carol Bly died at the end of 2007, obituaries and speakers at her memorial referred to her as a "lion of Minnesota letters" and said "one of the heavy lifters is gone." Carol Bly was not just an important writer—she was a presence, a force to be reckoned with, a voice being scathingly funny about the emperor's missing clothes. In Minnesota, many will remember that voice calling on writers not to be slick, to go deeper, to take on the big ones.

Carol Bly wrote short stories that had weight, complexity, and wit. She was also a prolific writer of essays, a cultural critic, an ethicist, and, in her own terms, "a gadfly." Being that outspoken and opinionated can startle Minnesotans. She was also a teacher of writing at universities, summer programs, the Loft, in her own dining room, and by e-mail. Before I met her in a summer class, I was vaguely aware that some people found her intimidating, even alarming. What I found was a dedicated teacher, very kind, and tremendous fun.

"Every human being deserves the chance to write," she said. "To form a philosophy, and not be thrown off balance by change and chance."

Years later, we worked together on several classes, some in northern Minnesota, in a ratty geodesic dome filled with Early Group Home furniture. She liked the place, chatted up the sled dogs, dug a snow cave—and worked hard. Anything students wrote at night, they'd get back in the morning. She got up at 5 to read them, adding thoughtful, encouraging notes and questions. By 7 everyone was up, even the Night People—no one wanted to miss any of the wild, free talk. There was more robust laughter before breakfast any morning than most women hear in a month.

"Affection for the world" was a quality she admired in writing, and in life. She had it in spades. She built outhouses, studied Icelandic, knit loud socks, took up the violin in her fifties, and planted and tended hundreds of baby oaks for her grandchildren (not conifers—global warming would do them in).

Carol Bly chose writing early, but her public career didn't start until she was almost fifty. From 1955 to 1978, in Madison, Minnesota, where the Bly farm was a center of poetry and politics, she decided to bring up the children—but she kept notebooks. When Carol and Robert Bly divorced, she moved to Sturgeon Lake and Saint Paul and began serious

Carol Bly

writing. Two of her ambitions, a story in *The New Yorker* and a book with Harper & Row, were soon achieved with "Last of the Gold Star Mothers" (1979) and *Letters from the Country* (1981). Her collections of short stories (1985, 1991) were compared to those of Chekhov, Camus, and Flannery O'Connor.

She was often referred to by critics (New Yorkers, often) as a writer of the rural Midwest, but many of her best stories are located in Saint Paul. A gifted violin teacher fends off the dopers and small-time dealers on her lawn. Eleanor Gummel from the farm encounters clueless support groups. Someplace in the south suburbs a fictional chemical plant produces nerve gas, and the genial CEO knows all the demonstrators by name.

The Passionate, Accurate Story: Making Your Heart's Truth into Literature (1990) is her guide for short story writers and a statement of her standards for fiction. Leaving out ethical concerns, she says, is as repressive as leaving out sex would be. Her hope was to help new writers replace reflexive cynicism and "general grunge" with "overall affection and specific wrath."

Fiction, she claimed, is three thousand times harder to write than nonfiction—you need to eat beef when working on plot. She wrote fiction, she said, because people touched her, and nonfiction because the world was too mean, needed fixing up. She wrote a lot of nonfiction. In recent years, Carol Bly took on bad corporations and the Bush administration in a series of pamphlets. A thankless task, but Cynthia Loveland, her friend and publishing partner (Bly and Loveland Press.com), says, "We had so much fun. Carol was the funniest woman I ever met."

Meanwhile, Carol Bly had a novel she had been working at for years; she was reading proofs right up to her death from cancer. Northern Minnesota is the scene this time, and she's got us down with dead accuracy—lots of satire, no cheap shots. It's full of plot and characters, including a foul-mouthed organist and some bears. It's a richly comic, unnerving book about not ignoring evil, taking action, even if imperfect.

A first novel at seventy-seven. *Shelter Half* was published six months after her death. Critics admired its combination of "intelligence and gusto" and some "hilarious moral farce." Oprah Winfrey's magazine made it a summer reading pick. People reading on beaches will get fine entertainment, but perhaps "more truth, and more surprising truth" than they expect.

A young woman's body lay undisturbed for a week in mid-November.
So begins Shelter Half, *a novel about a few people in a northern Minnesota town. Some of them—the town cop, the doctor, and a young couple in love—are smart enough to recognize cruelty that comes at them from huge organizations far outside the town limits. They are not chicken. They don't duck. If their nation and their world look grisly, they still do what they can for love and justice. They look out for one another. Available at your local bookstore or at holycowpress.org for $15.95.*

MAY

This year, Saint Paul Public Schools, with the sponsorship of the Saint Paul Almanac, *held a writing contest for its students. Students shared their experiences of Saint Paul, which included neighborhood stories, coming to America, and personal observations of Saint Paul. The stories remind us of the uniqueness and richness of our city.*

MY LIFE IN SAINT PAUL

Sandra Opokua

Hello. My name is Sandra Opokua. I am fourteen years old and I am writing about my life in Saint Paul.

First of all, I arrived in Saint Paul on May 17, 2007. I arrived with my mother from Ghana in West Africa. I came here to be reunited with my grandmother and my uncle. My grandmother has lived in Saint Paul for ten years and my uncle has lived here for fifteen years.

I arrived in Saint Paul at the beginning of summer. I was impressed by the broad diversity of the population. There are African Americans, Africans, Chinese, Hmong, Japanese, and Somalians. But in my country, Ghana, we were all in one uniform.

Also, when we went out, I was so shocked to see big stores like Wal-Mart, Target, Macy's, JC Penny, Kmart, and Mall of America. And I was wondering, who built these big buildings?

I saw big houses. My uncle took me to Como Zoo and I saw many animals I'd never seen before in my life.

And then one day, I was home and I received a package. When I opened it, it was a jacket. So I asked my uncle why he bought this big cloth when it's hot. He said we were about to enter winter and I needed warm clothes.

The first time I saw snow, I wanted to eat it, because in my country we eat ice. So I went outside and touched it and threw it up into the air.

Saint Paul is the most beautiful city I have ever seen in my life. I would like to thank the people who made it possible for us to stay in Saint Paul. Thanks to all of them. We are grateful.

FROGTOWN: MY NEIGHBORHOOD

Melina Pha

I grew up in Saint Paul in the Frogtown neighborhood. I live with both my parents, one sister, and two brothers. Minnesota is cold, but I still love it.

I love my neighborhood, it's hard to explain. It's not clean, but oh well.

When I walk out my front door, I see children playing two-square, jumping rope, playing tag, and just running around. I see my cousins in their cars, zooming down the street.

In the summertime, there are so many kids that we need two to three ice cream trucks. In the winter, when I come home from school, people are walking their dogs, throwing snowballs, and walking to the hill at the park with their sleds.

Me and my cousin walk to the corner store. I buy Snickers and Sprite, and my cousin buys ice cream, even in the winter.

I grew up there and I want to live there the rest of my life.

MY EXPERIENCE AS AN IMMIGRANT TO SAINT PAUL

Nhia Xiong

My family decided to come to the United States of America because we thought that if we came here we would have a better life than before. A lot of people think that it is easy for refugees to come to America, but it wasn't easy for us. Before coming here, my family had to have blood testing, eat some medicines, do eye testing, and do other things. But at last we got to come here to the United States of America. It was hard for my family because when we came here, we didn't even know how to read, write, or speak English. We didn't even know where to go and we didn't even know how to use the oven and everything in the kitchen. At last, the most important reason for coming to the United States of America is because we wanted to have good opportunities and we wanted to have a good education.

JUNE

Photo © Patricia Bour-Schilla

It's a lovely and languorous June
And winter will come very soon
So be careful, my sweetie
This is not Tahiti
"Sound of Music" or a Disney cartoon.

—Garrison Keillor

Downtown Saint Paul Farmers' Market: Saturdays and Sundays through October

Music in Mears Park: Every Thursday 6–9 p.m.

Saint Paul Chamber Orchestra: June 4–6

Grand Old Day: June 7

Saint Paul Sommerfest: June 13–15

Sommerfest River Cruise: June 13

Emperor's Ball: June 13

Sommerfest Promenade and Picnic: June 15

Twin Cities Jazz Festival: June 18–28

Back to the 50s Car Show: June 19–21

Fourth Friday at the Movies: June 26

See pages 288–310 for more information and more events

➩"We have always followed democratic and legal procedure. . . . The ruling class never does use democratic and constitutional procedure unless it serves its ends."—William Mahoney, Saint Paul labor leader and mayor

JUNE

S	M	T	W	T	F	S
31	1	2	3	4	5	6
7	8	9	10	11	12	13
14	15	16	17	18	19	20
21	22	23	24	25	26	27
28	29	30	1	2	3	4

1 Monday

2 Tuesday

3 Wednesday

4 Thursday

Music in Mears Park

Saint Paul Chamber Orchestra

MMAA Patio Nights

Photo © Patricia Bour-Schilla

Boat slips on Harriet Island

5 FRIDAY	Saint Paul Chamber Orchestra
6 SATURDAY	Saint Paul Farmers' Market Saint Paul Chamber Orchestra
7 SUNDAY	Saint Paul Farmers' Market Grand Old Day

JUNE

The cornerstone for today's Cathedral of Saint Paul was laid on June 2, 1907.

JIMMIE OWENS, MIDWAY BASEBALL AMBASSADOR

Tom Goldstein

There are a number of youth baseball programs in Saint Paul, from city leagues and traveling teams to a handful of Little League organizations. Among these is Midway Baseball, a former Little League affiliate started by the Midway area Dunning Boosters in 1989. Last year, it included more than 275 participants, an all-time high.

What attracts so many kids to the program? One reason is undoubtedly Jim Kelley Field (named for the longtime director of the baseball league), a beautifully manicured stadium built in 1990 with a combination of public and private funds, including support from the former Liberty State Bank, the city's STAR grant program, and the Minnesota Twins. The ballpark-in-miniature features a lush grass infield, enclosed outfield, foul poles, and, since 2003, lights. Although it's just two hundred feet from home plate to the outfield fence, this gem of a ballpark creates the excitement that one might experience at a major league game, minus the bravado and fat paychecks.

Another attraction is the vast number of parents and community members who volunteer as coaches every season, many of whom return year after year even after their own kids have aged out of the program. Unlike the horror stories about parents gone bad at Little League games that occasionally appear on the evening news, Midway has a strong tradition of respect and civility, due in large measure to Jim Kelley, the energetic co-founder of the program, who provides a steadying influence throughout the summer months. But it's also the commitment of the many volunteers who have infused Midway with a generous spirit of giving back to the community, a community whose diversity is well represented among the ranks of adults and players.

Perhaps the best example of this selfless volunteer tradition can be found in the person of Jimmie Owens, a fixture in Midway Baseball who has been a constant on the ball fields for more than twenty-five years. The venerable Owens, now entering his eighty-fifth year, has been volunteering since 1982, when the baseball program was part of Parks and Recreation. He moves with the grace of a man twenty years his junior.

A former customs inspector and postal employee, Owens hooked up with Kelley when the two were coaching at the Jimmie Lee Rec Center. Owens had been a longtime youth football coach but was starting to feel

Photo © Tom Goldstein

Plaque honoring Jimmie Owens

his age when the cold weather rolled around every fall. Although he had only dabbled in baseball as a child, volunteering in the baseball program has been the perfect antidote to retirement.

"It's been a wonderful experience," says Owens. "You show kids that you care about them, that they can trust you, and they open up and start to find themselves. It's a great feeling to know you're helping somebody." Many of those kids go on to become youth umpires in the league or work the concession booth with Owens, where his signature announcement, "Your hot dogs are ready, your hot dogs are ready, your hot dogs are ready" has become a standard ritual during every game.

"Jimmie Owens is the Midway Baseball ambassador," says Kelley of his longtime sidekick. "It's amazing the effect he has on people. There's always a crowd surrounding Jimmie, grown-ups checking to see how he's doing, kids reporting back from high school or college on what they're up to. When Jimmie first started volunteering here, he used to wait on the street corners to make sure kids got rides home. A lot of parents have never forgotten [that kindness]."

"Midway Baseball is like a family," Owens says. "It's a chance for kids to learn baseball, learn something about themselves, and learn respect for one another." It's also a place where kids go on to play ball in high school, earn their college degrees, enter professional careers, and then later return as volunteers and coaches themselves, thus renewing the cycle.

"The wealth of the country, its capital, its credit, must be saved from the predatory poor as well as the predatory rich, but above all from the predatory politician."
—James J. Hill, railroad magnate

JUNE

S	M	T	W	T	F	S
31	1	2	3	4	5	6
7	8	9	10	11	12	13
14	15	16	17	18	19	20
21	22	23	24	25	26	27
28	29	30	1	2	3	4

8 Monday

9 Tuesday

10 Wednesday

11 Thursday

Music in Mears Park

MMAA Patio Nights

Photo © Patricia Bour-Schilla

Panda bear on Wheelock Parkway

12 Friday

13 Saturday

Saint Paul Farmers' Market

Saint Paul Sommerfest

Sommerfest River Cruise

Emperor's Ball

14 Sunday

Flag Day

Saint Paul Farmers' Market

Saint Paul Sommerfest

June

The Augie Garcia Quintet, a West Side rock group, hit the national charts in 1955 with their record *Hi Yo Silver*.

WHO IS FROGTOWN FRED?

Pat Kahnke

Saint Paul is the best city in the world to do what I do.

I plant churches—specifically neighborhood churches (a throwback to the Paleolithic Era—you can read about the neighborhood church at your public library). My wife and I, along with a committed group of friends, have made this our life's work. Our first plant was in Frogtown in 2002, and our dream is to start a new church in each of Saint Paul's seventeen distinct neighborhoods. Our next church, which will be intentionally multicultural, is slated to be launched by our friend Shawn in the Rondo neighborhood in 2009.

Saint Paul is perfect for us because of the importance of neighborhood to this city. To a visitor, the difference between Highland Park and Mac-Groveland, for instance, may be a geographic artifice, but to a resident, it's real and palpable (and a source of inordinate pride, if we're honest).

Planting a neighborhood church in Saint Paul is considered a little bit counter-cultural, for a number of reasons:

1. Let's face it: from a secular point of view, why bother? It would be easier to start a hookah bar—and think how relaxing the work environment would be! I'm keeping that option in my back pocket, right next to the urge to become an over-the-road trucker (which I get about once a week).
2. Evangelicals don't plant churches in the city. We focus on the "booming exurbs," for obvious reasons. I was absent the day they passed out that memo in seminary. . .
3. Who is Frogtown Fred, anyway?

That last point deserves an explanation. In seminary, I was required to read Pastor Rick Warren's book *The Purpose-Driven Church* for *three* different classes. Long before *The Purpose-Driven Life* took the nation by storm, *The Purpose-Driven Church* was the book *du jour* at seminaries across the country.

In that book, we learned to study our community and write a detailed description of our target parishioner. Pastor Warren's neighborhood was the Saddleback Valley in California, so he created the "Saddleback Sam" character to help him get inside the mind of Saddleback's residents. Saddleback Sam turned out to be about what you'd expect. After six years in Frogtown, I still haven't met Frogtown Fred. I see Frogtown

Photo © Patricia Bour-Schilla

Mural on the wall outside J. J. Hill Montessori School on Selby Avenue

Phuoc at the restaurant down the street, Frogtown Fuad selling cigarettes and lottery tickets at the corner store, and Frogtown Fenicia greeting me from her front step when I walk to church. Frogtown Fred? Hmm . . . Maybe *I'm* Frogtown Fred. What a boring place Frogtown would be if everyone was like *me*!

Our tremendous racial, ethnic, and cultural diversity makes Saint Paul the perfect place to do what I do. My friends and I recognize that the "homogeneous unit principle of church growth" (as it's called) has validity, and it would be easy to flow along within the smooth stream of our own monocultures. But we prefer to swim in the choppy waters of multicultural America. Sure, we occasionally get smacked in the face by a wave that we didn't see coming, but the experience is far more exhilarating than simply doing the easy thing. And those waves cleanse our eyes so we can see aspects of the beauty of creation that would be invisible to us if we hadn't taken the plunge.

For a church planter, Saint Paul is a little slice of Heaven.

➩ Elmer L. Andersen was born on June 17, 1909. The former state senator served as governor of Minnesota from 1961 to 1963.

JUNE

S	M	T	W	T	F	S
31	1	2	3	4	5	6
7	8	9	10	11	12	13
14	15	16	17	18	19	20
21	22	23	24	25	26	27
28	29	30	1	2	3	4

15 Monday

Saint Paul Sommerfest

Sommerfest Promenade and Picnic

16 Tuesday

17 Wednesday

18 Thursday

Music in Mears Park

MMAA Patio Nights

Twin Cities Jazz Festival

JUNE

Photo © Patricia Bour-Schilla

View under the Ford Parkway Bridge

19 FRIDAY

Juneteenth

Twin Cities Jazz Festival
Back to the 50s Car Show

20 SATURDAY

Saint Paul Farmers' Market
Twin Cities Jazz Festival
Back to the 50s Car Show

21 SUNDAY

Father's Day

Saint Paul Farmers' Market
Twin Cities Jazz Festival
Back to the 50s Car Show

JUNE

Well-known rapper Eyedea, born Mike Averill, graduated from Saint Paul's Highland Park High School in 2002.

STREETCARS OF SAINT PAUL

Ronee McHendrik

In the early 1940s, we lived on the East Side of Saint Paul near Hazelwood and Seventh streets, where streetcars stopped almost in front of our house. One of my earliest memories is of waiting for the streetcar to bring my grandfather and aunts home from their downtown jobs at the central post office and The Emporium and Schuneman's, two of the large department stores.

In those days Minnesota had no shopping malls, and Dayton's was a Minneapolis store. In Saint Paul, downtown Seventh Street boasted the Golden Rule (another department store), the Orpheum and Paramount theaters, Bridgeman's Ice Cream Parlor, and many other shops along the way from Jackson to St. Peter.

To reach this bustling destination, our family, like most others, used the streetcar nearly all the time. The wicker seats were shellacked to a high gloss and had brass fittings. The bell clanged loudly when the cord was pulled. On the front of the car was a large, heavy mesh semicircle located a couple of feet above the tracks. It was called a cowcatcher. My grandfather told me it was there to catch the cows that jumped over the moon.

As we traveled to downtown Saint Paul, the motorman would call out the names of the intersecting streets, like Johnson Parkway and Arcade. I was mystified when, as we passed the jungly hollow where we played Tarzan, swinging on large vines, he called out "Etna" and "Birmingham." (When we moved back to Saint Paul in the late 1970s, we settled on the east side of Lake Phalen near Arlington Avenue, and lo and behold, there were those missing streets, Etna and Birmingham.)

Sometimes we didn't go all the way downtown. Grandfather might take us to an early evening show at one of the neighborhood theaters, the Radio. It was a few blocks west of Johnson Parkway. We'd walk there and return on the streetcar. The swaying of the car put me to sleep by the time we got home.

The Radio is closed now, and the building houses a floor covering business, but the arched doorways into the theater are still there. Those doors used to be covered with heavy velvet to block the light and noise. I can still feel their softness and weight when I used to push through to find a seat.

Sometimes the Radio raffled off live poultry. One night, my grandfather won. That night we didn't take the streetcar home. With a duck waddling behind, we slowly made our way up Seventh Street, the duck

Photo © Minneapolis Star Journal Tribune

Selby-Lake streetcar in the 1940s advertising war bonds and stamps

tied by a string held in one of Grandpa's hands, and my hand held in the other. It was a long walk home.

It was sad when the streetcars were replaced by buses. There was nothing picturesque about buses. They were smelly; they didn't rock (as in motion); and, worst of all, they didn't have cowcatchers. I guess by then cows had stopped jumping over the moon.

➪ The oldest continuously operating business in the city is Travelers, incorporated in 1853 as Saint Paul Mutual Insurance Association.

JUNE

S	M	T	W	T	F	S
31	1	2	3	4	5	6
7	8	9	10	11	12	13
14	15	16	17	18	19	20
21	22	23	24	25	26	27
28	29	30	1	2	3	4

22 MONDAY

Twin Cities Jazz Festival

23 TUESDAY

Twin Cities Jazz Festival

24 WEDNESDAY

Twin Cities Jazz Festival

25 THURSDAY

Music in Mears Park

Twin Cities Jazz Festival

MMAA Patio Nights

Music and Movies, District del Sol

Photo © Patricia Bour-Schilla

Hmong ABC at 298 University Avenue West

26 FRIDAY

Twin Cities Jazz Festival

27 SATURDAY

Saint Paul Farmers' Market

Twin Cities Jazz Festival

GENESIS

Mike Hazard

How did we get here?
In the market, stirred
by the lavender of Russian sage
the aroma of romantic rosemary
a delicate lingo of cilantro
the ephemeral squash blossoms . . .
How do we stay?

28 SUNDAY

Saint Paul Farmers' Market

Twin Cities Jazz Festival

JUNE

In 1864, James J. Hill met a waitress working at the Merchants Hotel in St. Paul and married her in 1867.

ROSES FOR MARY, FROM PAUL IN SAINT PAUL

Michelle Meyers Berg

This piece is from Blue Collar Diaries, *a show that will be included in the History Theatre's 2009 season. This piece is about my father, who was seriously affected by the heavy combat he experienced in the Korean War, which Truman conveniently downsized into a police action so that he would not need to go before Congress for permission. This war saw nearly as many casualties in three years as Vietnam saw in ten years' time. The failure to identify it for what it really was has been a source of anguish for countless Americans over the years and particularly so for the veterans, whose stories remain largely untold.*

My father used to rust. Especially in the summers. In the heat of the machine shop, his pores would open wide and drink in the micro-fine shavings of metal in the air. Later on, they would re-emerge in an orange stain he would sweat out while sitting in his car or lying on his pillow. Not to worry, though. My dad had a fold-up cushion that he used in the driver's seat of his car and a special pillowcase that he used on his pillow. It's important to take care of what you have.

He had one suit that he said was for hatchings, matchings, and dispatchings. Otherwise, he wore green dickies, white crew socks, black loafers, and a black belt. He had his own chair, just like Archie Bunker, and you couldn't sit in it even if he wasn't home. Ever.

He had a gun in his underwear drawer. For a short period. Once he learned that each of us had quietly slid his drawer open to look at it lying in the folds of his clean tee shirts, he got rid of it. My dad knew a lot about guns. He was an expert marksman and served in the 555th field artillery battalion in the Army in the Korean War. He was in two of the three worst battles documented there.

One day I was sitting on the front porch when he rolled up the driveway. He came into the kitchen holding two dozen roses. I could hear my sister ask him about them through the open window behind me.

"Hey, Dad. Wow! Who're all those roses for?"

No answer.

"Are they for your anniversary?"

"No."

"They're not? Then what are they for? They're not for Mom's birthday, are they?"

Photo © Michelle Meyers Berg

Paul Myers

Photo © Michelle Meyers Berg

Michelle Meyers Berg

"No."

"That's right—her birthday's not until the twenty-fifth. Well then, what are they for?"

"Well . . . when I was over in Korea, I got into a tight spot with Charlie Company. We were overrun. I had to get out of there, and I got separated from my unit. I didn't know where I was. So I prayed to Mary. I said, 'Mary, if you get me out of this one, I'll give you a dozen roses.' And I never had a chance to do that yet. So today, when I got my bonus, I went over and picked some out and I'm gonna bring 'em to her. Down at the cathedral. If your mother calls, tell her I'll be home soon."

Years later I learned that the tight spot that my father was in was a battle called Kum Song Salient. Some 72,000 enemy soldiers, three entire divisions, poured through his company's position, just days before his twenty-first birthday. I'm sure he would have made good on his promise sooner, but money was tight until he got that bonus. It was his first and only bonus.

COUNTER'S SEGUES

Suzanne Nielsen

All are sent into the thicket of life,
Some to hunt and survive, some to be hunted to death . . .
I was a deer compelled to live with the hounds
—Edgar Lee Masters

The year is 1967, the summer before fifth grade, and Emmett and me have a pact. The pact includes club meetings in our fort in Witch's Woods, which only we know about. Emmett lives three blocks away with old people. I can smell them from outside, a blend of mothballs and cabbage. I think they are his dad's parents, runaways from some foreign country because the old lady wears a scarf and whistles gibberish through her toothless grin. Some old people are content being old, I guess, but I don't ask Emmett if this is true with his old people.

Being two boys alone, Emmett and me become blood brothers almost immediately, right outside our fort. I file a twig with the pocketknife I stole from Lou Lepshe's 88-Cent Store on Payne Avenue as sharp as the pin on my mama's hem. I prick first; Emmett winces while a perfect round globe of blood forms on my finger. I am lightheaded just watching it, and my stomach rumbles at the tinny smell. "Did it hurt?" Emmett asks. His face is a similar color to my blood, fake rubies. It might be due to a combination of sunburn, freckles, and fear. I don't know. I don't ask. I pass him the twig. "Go ahead, Emmett, do it quick. It don't hurt as much as a whippin'," I say. Emmett takes hold of the twig and stares at it. He watches a trail of my blood soak into the stick, leaving it looking like dried-out sycamore kindling. He slaps me across the face, and I stare in my knife blade as my cheek shadows the imprint of his hand. "Shyster!" I yelp. My left eye fills with water, soon it's dripping down my branded cheek. "Sorry, Ton," he says. "That hurt me a lot more than it hurt you. Don't know why I do that sometimes," he says. I shrug it off and say, "Just hurry up and bleed, don't think about it. Things don't hurt that much if you're not taken by surprise."

Emmett asks for my knife, wants a clean cut, he says. I don't argue, although I never wanted blood to touch the blade of my knife. Emmett closes his eyes, but at the last minute he watches himself prick his skin with the mirrored blade. Blood draws instantly. Emmett drops the knife, sucks the blood from his finger. I move next to him, squeeze my finger

Photo © Larry Schilla

Waiting for a ride

to draw the blood's attention, telling Em to do the same. We pinch our fingers together, blending our bloodlines. I know right at that moment he will never abandon me.

Emmett whispers under his breath, "Save-diddle-dee-ave-ave-ave-ave-ave-save." I ask him if he's talking Swahili, maybe a new form of Pig Latin, but he says, "Tony Baloney, it's Counterhili, Emmett C. Counterhili. Don't you ever need to count your syllables?" he asks. I figure Emmett can't help that his last name is Counter, so he counts. Plus, I don't want to risk Emmett feeling mental, so I say, "Sure, Emmett, all the time. I count syllables, cracks in the cement, I even count the freckles on your face." Emmett smiles his jagged grin, says he knows how many freckles are on his face, he's counted them. "I can't not count, Tony Baloney," he says.

My name is Tony Anthony. An unfortunate name to have for class attendance. Teachers always start the year off by saying, "Do you go by Tony or Anthony?" I say, "Both." "Choose one or the other," they say, "Tony or Anthony?" I say, "Both." As a result, I spend early fall sitting inside the office with Mr. Grater, the principal, wearing a nametag that reads "wise guy."

When Emmett started calling me Tony Baloney in fourth grade, I perked up. That was the day we became friends. Emmett said that it was a bunch of baloney to send me to the principal's office. "He can't help his redundancy," he lisped to Miss Westerlund, our teacher. Emmett and I spent the morning together in Mr. Grater's office writing an essay on the importance of names. "Does redundancy mean I'm a dunce that likes to dance, Emmett?" I asked. He said, "No, Tony Baloney. Redundancy means your mom had shit for brains when she named you, that's all." We laughed. The idea of my mom's head being full of turds made my day. I started doodling in my notebook, drawing my mom with poop for hair. Then I drew a pile of shrunken skulls next to a pile of doggy-doo. I could smell pee on me and hoped Emmett didn't get a whiff.

I tried to make the smell go away, so I took out my glue. Emmett and I started to coat our palms in white layers. The smell reminded me of Mr. Hall's art room. After one coat of glue became see-through, we put another one on, waving our hands in the air to dry them quicker. We were just about to peel our palms like fresh skin off your shoulders after a bad sunburn when Mr. Grater grabbed my notebook from behind and ripped it into confetti. "Lard butt," Emmett said while making fart sounds under his shirt with his gluey palm and armpit. Then under his breath he said, "Save-diddle-dee-ave-ave-ave-ave-ave-save." "You'll live to regret that talk, Counter," said Grater. "You're working your way back to Totem Town," he added. His big fat cheeks shook like settled Jell-O. I noticed he bit his nails too. He walked to his office and slammed the door and a blizzard of confetti flew through the room. We laughed again. "Emmett," I asked, "what's Totem Town?" Emmett leaned back in his chair and said it's where all the outlaws go for incarceration. Emmett's religious and smart with words. *Incarceration* must be a Catholic word, I thought. The old people he lived with had lots of Jesus crosses in their house. Emmett wore one around his neck, left his skin the color of dirty pond water. He said Totem Town isn't that bad of a place. "As soon as you're twelve," he said, "you can smoke cigarettes."

"What nationality is your name, Em?" I ask. "I mean, Counter." We are resting on the ground outside our trailer fort, sucking on tall grass. "All I know, Tony Baloney, is it's not Bastard," Emmett says. "And my name has four syllables, just like Jesus' name; that's good luck," he adds while sucking his teeth. When Emmett sucks his teeth, he makes the same whistle sound as the old woman he lives with because the space between his two front teeth could fit a molar easy. I think about Jesus' name, Jesus H. Christ, my mom always said. Sure enough, four syllables. "I'm not from a bastard background either, Em," I say. Emmett tucks his hands behind his head, closes his eyes and looks up at the sky, and says, "Don't ever spend any time looking at those long, stringy clouds, they're bad luck." I chalk that one away in my brain. Emmett asks, "Does your ma think you look like your dad?" I write my name in the dirt with the sharpened twig and say, "I don't know if she remembers." "Do you mean," Emmett starts in a Perry Mason-like voice, "she doesn't remember what your dad looks like or she doesn't remember your dad?" "Yes to both," I say. We laugh.

Emmett pulls a cigarette butt out of his pocket. I notice lipstick the color of cotton candy on the filter. It makes me hungry. Emmett pinches off the lip stains, holds the butt between his teeth, and lights it off of a farmer match that he strikes on the patched knee of his blue jeans. He passes it to me after a deep inhale. I watch as three perfect smoke rings come out his mouth. I think of the trestle, of the trains. "Emmett," I say, " let's go ride the trains." I take a puff, and cough up my tonsils. I pass the butt back to Emmett and rub my tongue along the crabgrass. "Knock it off, Ton," says Emmett. "Some dog might have peed there." I look at Emmett and say, "How can you stand to smoke? I'd rather drink dog pee." I wonder if Emmett thinks I do drink dog pee. "It's gotta be about two o'clock by now," I say. "The train comes behind Sacred Heart Church at 2:40. Come on, Em, let's go jump it." Emmett looks over at our abandoned trailer fort we found earlier this summer in the woods. It was just left there by someone, maybe burglars. We don't know. Anyway, we claim ownership of it now. "What about the yard?" Emmett says, smiling. "Who'll water the grass—feed the rose bushes?" I look around and remember hearing Fred MacMurray say something like that on *My Three Sons.* "Why do you always do that, Emmett?" I say. Emmett looks at me, spits on his fingers twice, and rolls the cigarette between them until it's out. "Do what, Ton?" he says. "Why do you always change the subject," I say, "and why do you always spit twice? We're talking about real life here, and you make fun of it. I hate that, Emmett." Emmett stuffs the butt with only one more puff left in his pocket. "Segues, Tony Baloney," he says, "keeps life interesting."

I walk to the trailer, go in and grab my flashlight from under my sleeping bag, along with the bag of money I've been stashing in our secret home. A musty smell follows me outside where I start counting the kale. "Blessmefatherforlhavesinned," says Emmett, "save-diddle-dee-ave-ave-ave-ave-ave-save." "Em," I say, "I've got $27 right here, plus three gold teeth. I've been pinching my mom's purse since last fall. She just got her government check yesterday, so she'll be gone for at least four days. Come on, Em; let's get on that train. Tell the old people you're going out of town with me and my mom to the Badlands for vacation." Emmett looks down at his dirty and gnawed hands. "I'm s'pose to have religion class on Saturday," Emmett says, biting his nail. "But I could always tell them I'm goin' to church in the Badlands," he says. I say that isn't that big of a lie. We're off to some bad land. I can feel it in my bones.

Emmett and me run like deer all the way to Sacred Heart Church. Emmett says he has to use the bathroom in the basement. I wait down by the tracks. I can hear the train in the distance. I start thinking of all the places we can go. New Orleans, maybe. We could go there and get free necklaces. My neighbors did that once. They gave them to my mom last spring just for the heck of it. She put them in my Easter basket, said they were almost as valuable as my grandma's gold teeth. I check my pocket, the envelope with the teeth are safe and secure. And here comes Emmett. "Hurry," I shout. "I can hear the train comin'!" I feel my knees start to shake. I've only watched the Palmer kids hop trains before. Rusty Palmer fell and broke his arm. He had a cast on all summer long and when he got the cast off, his arm looked like it was dead.

"Let's go to New Orleans, Emmett," I say. "We can grab a bunch of necklaces and take them somewheres else, make a bundle." Emmett looks at me, says he lit two candles in the church, one for each of us. "There you go again, Em," I say. "Changin' the subject." Emmett lets out a laugh with a sigh attached. "No segue this time, Tony Baloney," he says. "We need a candle glowin' for each of us, plus one is bad luck." It dawns on me that Emmett doesn't know I've brought along the flashlight. I pull it out of my sock, show it to him, and say, "Em, I'm always thinkin'." I feel smart, almost as smart as Emmett, who uses words like *redundancy, incarceration,* and *segue*—almost as smart as Emmett, who knows all about Totem Town and how to get under Mr. Grater's skin.

There's the train blowing smoke. It's not going to stop for us, but we're not stopping, either. I can feel it. "Watch your limbs," I say to Emmett. "Don't break an arm or a leg." Emmett starts kicking his feet in the dirt like a bull shucking its hooves. "Grab hold of the caboose," Emmett says to me. With that, the train meets up with our spindly legs; Emmett jumps in between the cars. I'm alone, waiting for the caboose. "Where are we going?" I scream. I think I hear Emmett's voice echo off the trestle, "We're goin' to Totem Town, Tony Baloney. We're goin to live with the hounds. Hailmaryfullofgracesave-diddle-dee-ave-ave-ave-ave-ave-save."

He's still a rambler on the go
And shares the curse of every 'bo
Each time he hears the whistle blow
He longs for places far
—Buzz Potter

JUNE

JULY

Photo © Patricia Bour-Schilla

Downtown Saint Paul Farmers' Market: Saturdays and Sundays through October

Music in Mears Park: Every Thursday 6–9 p.m.

MMAA Patio Nights: Every Thursday 7 p.m.

Music and Movies, District del Sol: Every Thursday 7 p.m.

Taste of Minnesota: July 2–5

Hmong International Sports Tournament and Freedom Festival: July 4–5

Nine Nights of Music Series: July 7, 14, 21, 28

Dragon Festival and Dragon Boat Races: July 11–12

Rondo Days: July 17–18

Highland Fest: July 17–19

Rice Street Festival: July 22–25

Fourth Friday at the Movies: July 24

Car Craft Summer Nationals: July 24–26

See pages 288–310 for more information and more events

➪ A century ago, the Saint Paul Automobile Club opened its headquarters in a site on the Saint Croix. It moved to White Bear Lake four years later.

JULY

S	M	T	W	T	F	S
28	29	30	1	2	3	4
5	6	7	8	9	10	11
12	13	14	15	16	17	18
19	20	21	22	23	24	25
26	27	28	29	30	31	1

29 MONDAY

30 TUESDAY

1 WEDNESDAY

2 THURSDAY

Music in Mears Park

Taste of Minnesota

MMAA Patio Nights

Music and Movies, District del Sol

Photo © 2007 T. R. Lacy

Étude I: Path near North Gate of Hidden Falls Park, Mississippi River

3 FRIDAY	Taste of Minnesota
4 SATURDAY Independence Day	Saint Paul Farmers' Market Taste of Minnesota Hmong International Sports Tournament and Freedom Festival
5 SUNDAY	Saint Paul Farmers' Market Taste of Minnesota Hmong International Sports Tournament and Freedom Festival

Yarusso's, 635 Payne Avenue, opened in 1933 and is arguably Saint Paul's oldest family-owned Italian restaurant.

MEARS PARK ADVENTURE

Paul and Linda Bartlett

My wife, Linda, and I moved to Lowertown, along with our friends Ed and Erin Howell, a few seasons ago. We moved from the south burbs, where we had lost all interest in lawn-mowing, raking, and fighting off the neighbors' dandelions. But feeling a little guilty about our new couch-potato lifestyles, we decided some urban frontiersmanship was in order.

Erin suggested we venture across the street to Mears Park and rough it for a while. With chilled chardonnay, brie, and *foie gras* in hand, we dodged the Wild West-like traffic and established base camp under the band shelter. The Howells' Doberman Pinscher, Fu Fu, accompanied us. We rejected Ed's suggestion to cut down trees to build a lean-to, and Fu Fu proved to be of no particular value.

Then our adventure took a turbulent twist. Ed had just put on his waders, strung his fly-fishing rod, and was about to cast into the Mears Park trout stream, when a terrible thunderstorm whipped through.

We were pummeled by grapefruit-sized hail, which endangered life, limb, and Fu Fu. We dashed back to base camp, where Linda managed to snap the following photo of Erin and me holding two of the hail balls. They may not be the largest ever recorded—but they probably are—and all

Photo © Paul and Linda Bartlett

Paul and Erin with two-pound hail balls

Photo © Paul and Linda Bartlett

Ed, with 18-inch trout, caught in Mears Park

these hail balls shared perfect symmetry: each was round and measured exactly 5½ inches in diameter. They weighed in at two pounds each. Maybe no two snowflakes are identical, but these bad boys were.

As the storm passed, we made our way back to River Park Lofts (right across the street), feeling like four of the downtrodden from Cormac McCarthy's *The Road.* Before leaving, Ed hooked a dandy trout.

Well, our Outward Bound days are over; Mears Park is just a bit too Jurassic for these four failed voyageurs. But I challenge anyone from big-brother Minneapolis to share a more harrowing eco-urban adventure than our apocalyptic foray into the Mears Park wilderness area.

➪ Guillermo and Gloria Frias opened the doors of Boca Chica Mexican Restaurant, originally seating only 28 people, on the West Side in 1964.

JULY

S	M	T	W	T	F	S
28	29	30	1	2	3	4
5	6	7	8	9	10	11
12	13	14	15	16	17	18
19	20	21	22	23	24	25
26	27	28	29	30	31	1

6 MONDAY

7 TUESDAY

Nine Nights of Music Series

8 WEDNESDAY

9 THURSDAY

Music in Mears Park

MMAA Patio Nights

Music and Movies, District del Sol

Photo © Tom Conlon

Ordway Center for the Performing Arts

10 FRIDAY

11 SATURDAY

Saint Paul Farmers' Market

Dragon Festival and Dragon Boat Races

A PINT-SIZED CHILD

Mike Hazard

A pint of raspberries rests
in the lap of a pint-sized child.
Lolling in her stroller, she's
living in the lap of luxury.
"Don't eat them," Mom says,
as the little one begins eating,
two-handed, two-fisted,
too much; we laugh until
we grow red as raspberries.

12 SUNDAY

Saint Paul Farmers' Market

Dragon Festival and Dragon Boat Races

The yellow brick Highland Park water tower, built in 1928, is 127 feet high and has 151 interior steps.

A GOOD NEIGHBOR

Anita Dualeh

Concordia University in Saint Paul has opened its doors to some of its newest neighbors by hosting English as a Second Language classes. Since July 2005, Somali Adult Literacy Training (SALT) has met on campus three evenings a week.

The students, united by their goal of learning English, range in age from their late teens all the way up to their sixties. The class for beginners focuses on foundational literacy skills such as learning the sounds of the alphabet and decoding simple words. A second class is for students with some prior learning in English who need focused instruction and practice in reading and writing. A few students attending high school come for help with their homework.

Each day, after an hour of instruction, students, teachers, and tutors enjoy a cup of sweet spicy tea and conversation. This is followed by tutoring time. Volunteer tutors from Saint Paul and surrounding suburbs assist the learners one-on-one or in small groups when there are not enough tutors to go around.

As a former teacher on Tuesday evenings, I found the hours spent at SALT to be some of the most rewarding hours of my week. I saw students making real progress in learning English. It's always a joy to help motivated learners improve their lives through education, but I've also gained some loyal friends, kept my cross-cultural communication skills sharp, and enjoyed some tasty potluck meals.

Photo © Lou "The Photo Guy" Michaels

Many of our lessons provided students with information they could use in everyday life. To supplement the textbook, we used grocery ads, job applications, medicine labels, and other items adults might read in a typical day. When students learned about contacting different businesses, I lugged in copies of the Yellow Pages and asked students to locate phone numbers for a few different places. It was an "ah-ha!" moment for some.

"So if I want to call a taxi, I can use this?" one student asked, checking her understanding.

Another said, "I never knew what this book was for."

Thank you, Concordia, for providing a place to meet. By hosting SALT, you are fostering friendships and learning on many levels for both the students and the volunteers. You truly are a good neighbor.

➭ In July 1859, Thomas Langdon Grace was installed as Bishop of Saint Paul and served until 1884.

JULY						
S	M	T	W	T	F	S
28	29	30	1	2	3	4
5	6	7	8	9	10	11
12	13	14	15	16	17	18
19	20	21	22	23	24	25
26	27	28	29	30	31	1

13 MONDAY

14 TUESDAY

Nine Nights of Music Series

15 WEDNESDAY

16 THURSDAY

Music in Mears Park

MMAA Patio Nights

Music and Movies, District del Sol

Photo © Patricia Bour-Schilla

Marilyn Monroe

17 FRIDAY

Highland Fest
Rondo Days

18 SATURDAY

Saint Paul Farmers' Market
Highland Fest
Rondo Days

19 SUNDAY

Saint Paul Farmers' Market
Highland Fest

The first horse-drawn streetcar began operating on July 15, 1872, with a seating capacity of fourteen.

FRANKIE'S CAVE

Larry Schilla

Frankie's Cave in 1968 was a place where we—as many as fifteen kids—hung out. We would walk the railroad tracks to the caves so we could pick up used flares. Where the trains would cross the streets without warning lights, the railroad used flares to warn cars, and because not all of us had flashlights, we used the flares.

Frankie's Cave was two blocks west of ADM, south of Shepard Road on the Mississippi River. There was an entrance on the north side of Shepard Road you could drive into. Sometimes the entrance was open and sometimes it was blocked by the city. It was easy for us to dig it out because the soil was sandstone.

Part of the cave was the Great Hall. It was massive, with a ceiling thirty to forty feet high and a hundred feet long. There were two ways to get in and out: one real small way and one great archway. One end of the arch was blocked by a brick wall, and we never tried to get through that. Some believe that Schmidt beer was stored in the Great Hall. There were the Three Sisters, which were tunnels around a city block long that ran parallel to each other. They were connected to the main tunnel. There was also a connection to the sewer system, which is a whole other story. The main tunnel connected to the main entrance through the back door, which was on the north side of Shepard Road.

I would pay my little sister 25 cents to not tell Mom we were playing at the caves. We played ditch with no lights, which was very dangerous. I know one day we were playing ditch and I ran into a wall and cut my eyebrow. I put on a bandage. Ma came home from work and looked at it and brought me to the emergency room. Fifteen stitches later, I was told not to go to the caves again. Yeah, like I had permission in the first place.

Photo © Patricia Bour-Schilla

The stories on these pages are written by new learners of the English language: recent refugees or immigrants who left their beloved homelands, usually for reasons beyond their control. They have found a new home here and are studying at the Minnesota Literacy Council or other ESL programs in Saint Paul.

I AM SAD

Lia Yang

A long time ago when we lived in Laos, we had our parents and lived happily as a family. We did not miss anyone because we lived peacefully and there was plenty of food for everyone. We loved one another; we did not live a depressed life. Nowadays, life in America is different and hard. When I think back about life in Laos, I miss my homeland. In America, if you don't work, there is no food on the table and no money to support your family. If you have a lot of children, they all want to do their own things and don't show much support and love like the old days.

Lia Yang

Life before the Vietnam War was peaceful. But when the war broke out, we had to take our family to the jungle and hide there. We did not carry much food with us; when we were out of food, we searched in the jungle and ate whatever we could find. Sometimes we ate grass, cut open tree vines for water, and ate the inside of banana tree trunks for food.

Because life in Laos is very hard, I wanted to let all Hmong children know that your parents risked their lives to save you and brought you to the United States. You should love them and care for them as much as they loved and cared for you when you were young.

PEACE

Abdulaziz Farah

I was born in the countryside of Ethiopia, which is twelve months green. Peaceful people enjoy drinking from its clean and sweet spring water. Colorful flowers grow all over the mountain and fields, and from its organic food there is always health. This is the country I came from.

Because every coming government always puts peace in danger by torturing, beating, taking away properties, and sometimes killing, I left my country. After I came to U.S.A. I could understand how much peace is necessary for development. It is my hope my country will get peace and work for the better of the country together.

➪ Horse-drawn fire engines made their last run in Saint Paul on July 23, 1924.

JULY						
S	M	T	W	T	F	S
28	29	30	1	2	3	4
5	6	7	8	9	10	11
12	13	14	15	16	17	18
19	20	21	22	23	24	25
26	27	28	29	30	31	1

20 MONDAY

21 TUESDAY

Nine Nights of Music Series

22 WEDNESDAY

Rice Street Festival

23 THURSDAY

Music in Mears Park

Rice Street Festival

MMAA Patio Nights

Music and Movies, District del Sol

Photo © Patricia Bour-Schilla

Mural on Selby at Oxford Avenue

24 FRIDAY

Rice Street Festival

Car Craft Summer Nationals

25 SATURDAY

Saint Paul Farmers' Market

Rice Street Festival

Car Craft Summer Nationals

26 SUNDAY

Saint Paul Farmers' Market

Car Craft Summer Nationals

A century ago, Pearson's, the candy company, was founded in Saint Paul. They invented the famous Nut Goodie.

EVERYDAY POEMS FOR CITY SIDEWALK

Diego Vázquez, Jr.

Saint Paul artist-in-residence Marcus Young envisions covering blank surfaces throughout the city with poems. A citywide book on the pavement. This dream took a turn toward reality when he found himself working in a cubicle at City Hall. His neighbors were the staff of the Public Works Department. They are in charge of replacing the pavement. The prospect of turning sidewalks into poetry suddenly became an idea whose time had come.

Collaborating with people in the Public Works Department, Young developed a process to stamp replacement panels used for sidewalk repair with text. The technology for the stamping process is fairly low tech, but finding the proper matching of the stamp process to text so the words will not dissipate rapidly proved difficult. The crew in charge of putting poetry in cement is confident that they will have publications on sidewalks that will stand the test of time, as should all good poetry.

With the technology in place, Marcus recruited Saint Paul's poet laureate, Carol Connolly, to find the poets. Together, they produced an open call to Saint Paul residents, professional or amateur writers of any age, to submit short poems for publication not only in cement but in a companion volume. A website for Everyday Sidewalk Poets will also be developed.

The city poets of Saint Paul responded to the call with enthusiasm. By the deadline on Friday, April 25, 2008, the committee had received more than two thousand submissions. The anonymous review process selected the work of twenty poets to be stamped into the pavement. Congratulations to the poets!

Eleanor Arnason
Naomi Cohn
Esme Evans
Georgia Greeley
*KateLynn Hibbard
Patricia Kirkpatrick
Anne Piper
Terri Ristow
Madeline Schuster
*Diego Vázquez Jr.
*Sasha Aslanian
Caley J. Conney
Sean Fleming
*Margaret Hasse
Zoe Jameson
Eileen O'Toole
Anna Renken
Ryan Ross
Carlee Tressel
Eyang Wu

**These poets' work appears in the* 2009 Saint Paul Almanac *or earlier* Saint Paul Almanacs.

Photo © Marcus Young

Saint Paul artist-in-residence Marcus Young

The first Everyday Sidewalk Poems will appear in the city in the summer of 2008. Special consideration will be made to match poems with their locations. The twenty poets selected will eventually have their poems embedded in five different locations throughout Saint Paul.

The *Saint Paul Almanac* will publish a location finder for the poems in the 2010 edition. To find out where the poems are today, you can go to www.everydaysidewalk.org.

➪ "I dream the writing dream: to live in language forever, to unravel the human story and grant it the power to change human life."—Kao Kalia Yang, Saint Paul writer

JULY

S	M	T	W	T	F	S
28	29	30	1	2	3	4
5	6	7	8	9	10	11
12	13	14	15	16	17	18
19	20	21	22	23	24	25
26	27	28	29	30	31	1

27 MONDAY

28 TUESDAY

Nine Nights of Music Series

29 WEDNESDAY

30 THURSDAY

Music in Mears Park

MMAA Patio Nights

Music and Movies, District del Sol

Photo © Patricia Bour-Schilla

A much-loved program for Saint Paul kids

31 FRIDAY

1 SATURDAY Saint Paul Farmers' Market

2 SUNDAY Saint Paul Farmers' Market

The Charles Symonds House, built in 1850 and now located at 234 Ryan, is thought to be Saint Paul's oldest house.

DOWN ST. ALBANS HILL IN A WOODEN COASTER—PART II

Arthur C. McWatt

One Saturday a month I would accompany Louis and Benny to St. Agnes Catholic Church for their monthly confession. It was a German-speaking parish, and I would wait outside until they were finished. Some of the things they should have confessed to were walking over the forty-foot arches of the Robert Street Bridge and climbing on the backs of the golden horses on the Capitol dome–according to what they told me, at any rate.

Some Sunday afternoons we visited the used car lots behind our houses on University and listened to *Swing and Sway with Sammy Kaye* and *The Smooth Rhythms of Guy Lombardo* on the car radios. We found we could move the cars back and forth by putting them in gear and stepping on their starters. Of course, both maneuvers ran down their batteries and sometimes a watchman would try to catch us, but we always eluded him. One Sunday morning, Bennie and his cousin, Eddie, decided to upgrade vehicular movement. They ran two streetcars together at the car barns on University and Snelling. They were caught and took an involuntary trip to the Boys Farm. Fortunately, while they were doing this, I was serving at the altar at St. Philip's Episcopal Church.

The Rocklitz brothers were the two mad scientists on our block. They were about fifteen and seventeen years old and spent a great deal of time in their basement carrying out chemical experiments. Both of the brothers were very intelligent and loved science. Most of their chemicals came from Chicago via mail order. Their father had died and left their mother a 1932 Packard that sat in the garage because it wouldn't start. Freddie Rocklitz told us that if we could get some gasoline and a battery, he thought he could get it started. Benny and his cousin managed to "find" a new battery and some gasoline behind a motorboat store, and we talked Freddie into a Saturday afternoon alley cruise. Freddie didn't have a license, and the car's license plates were three years old, but he insisted on driving.

After installing the battery and pouring in the gasoline, we all piled in. Freddie started the motor and eased out of the garage. The motor stalled after about a hundred feet, right behind the Saint Paul Police Dispatcher Station behind Engine Company #18. We dropped to the floor while Freddie and Buddie jumped out and opened the hood. After a seemingly

Photo © Arthur McWatt

Arthur McWatt in kindergarten, back row, first child on left

endless wait, they got the engine started again and off we went, bouncing along the alley until we reached Western Avenue.

After some discussion, we decided to take the Charles Avenue alley as the return route. Back home, Freddie's mother was sweeping her back stoop. When she saw us, her mouth dropped open and we sensed that Freddie was in big trouble. We helped him back the car into the garage and quietly disappeared. It was the last we saw of Freddie that summer.

On those long summer evenings, we'd play Duck on the Rock, a version of Cricket and Two o' Cat, in our alley until it got dark and a cacophony of mothers' voices filled the air. I'd be in by 7:30 and we'd be allowed to read for an hour or listen to the radio.

Wedding receptions were big events for all the neighborhood kids because of the possibility of a chivaree. To save money, many receptions were held at the bride's home, and after the ceremony the children would gather outside with cans filled with stones and pots to bang on to make a racket. The shaking and banging would increase until the groom and best man threw coins and candy to the throng outside.

Every summer I retained my racial identity by attending a two-week summer camp sponsored by Hallie Q. Brown Community House on Kent and Aurora. My first camp, when I was eight, was Camp Rock, somewhere on the St. Croix River. We had a wonderful leader, Joe Harpole, and our swimming instructor was Rudy Grimitra, star halfback for the Golden Gophers, national champions that fall. Much of the day was organized, but we often had afternoons to ourselves. Once we found a five-foot bull snake that two instructors could barely hold. On a hike, we

to come

came across a dead man lying beside the trail. A blanket of secrecy was immediately thrown up, and we never heard a word about it.

The next two years I spent at St. John's Landing near Shakopee. It wasn't as nice a camp as Camp Rock, but I had good friends there from St. Philips Church: Larry, Norm, and Gene.

That fall when I was ten and entering fifth grade, I was called to the office by the principal, Mrs. Dunne. She told me she and her staff had decided that both Penny Nichols and I—the two smartest students in school, she said—should skip fifth grade because we were academically ready for sixth. I had mixed feelings. My mother felt I might miss something by skipping a grade, but she went along with the recommendation. I later found, in math, that I had indeed missed something and that my mother had been right.

The 1936 New Year ushered in a year of extremes, with temperatures plunging to 36 degrees below zero that winter, rising to above 100 for ten days straight that summer, and topping off at 114. The ice house on Grotto was soon sold out and my sister and I ranged far and wide with our coaster wagon trying to find ice to keep our food from spoiling in our ice box. I'd try to sleep in pajamas and sheets soaked with perspiration. The Faust Theatre, which was cooled by artesian water, provided a haven for some. Three hundred people in Minnesota died that summer from heat-related causes.

In 1937 the neighborhood baseball team, the Sherburne Aces, disbanded and I began to spend time with Larry, an African American boy who lived on Charles, between Dale and Kent. We both were altar boys at St. Philips. I'd often go home with him after church, as he had a nice pool table and all the newest games. After our games, the pool table would be converted into a dining room table where I ate some of the most delicious dinners of my life.

Larry and I played basketball at the Hallie Q. Brown House the following summer. That fall we joined the Cub Scouts, who were led by a man named Duke Corum, a pleasant, conscientious, caring man. He took us on hikes and campouts and we swam at the YMCA (but only on Wednesdays because the Y was still segregated). The boys all admired Duke Corum. Our den became one of the best in the city, and we always had to turn away boys who wanted to join.

When I was twelve, I joined the Boy Scouts, and again I was blessed with a wonderful leader—Mr. Manning, dedicated, fair, always willing to lend a helping hand, and the kind of man I wanted to be when I grew up. A good judge of character, he also chose good patrol leaders. We learned

Photo © Arthur McWatt

Arthur McWatt in high school

camping skills, and we had overnights and campouts. We learned knot tieing, compass reading, map reading, and how to build a fire without matches.

That summer I got my first two-wheel bike, and it certainly expanded my range of activities. My friends and I took trips to Indian Mounds Park, the Battle Creek ski slide, Harriet Island, and the Como Park Golf Course, where we occasionally caddied.

At school that fall, romance arrived. Ardyce was from Czechoslovakia, and I began walking her home. Her father was concerned about getting his parents out of Europe, and this really sparked my first interest in the study of history. I eagerly awaited the publication of John Gunther's *Inside Europe*.

After Ardyce there was Ruthie. Our romance had lasted only a month when a Golden Glove aspirant named Cyrus lay in wait for me one night and warned me to stay away from her. I knew Cyrus from the Boy Scouts, from which he'd been expelled. We walked toward St. Albans hill discussing the matter. When I told him she had a right to decide, he threw a left hook on my blind side and the lights went out. When I came to, I told him it was a cheap shot and went home. I decided that in the interest of good health, I should look elsewhere for companionship.

In 1939, when I was thirteen, we spent a lot of time at the movies. That was the year for some of Hollywood's greatest films. One of my favorites was *Tarzan*. I was thrilled by Johnny Weissmuller's daring feats and my curiosity was aroused by Maureen O'Sullivan's costume, which I suspected had certain inadequacies. After a third viewing of the film, I felt my suspicions had been confirmed. I left the theater feeling that it was a matter I should immediately bring to the attention of my fellow patrol leaders.

In front of the theater [when I left] was a police car with two officers leaning against it. They asked me my name. I soon discovered that my mother had been worried about my prolonged absence and had asked the police to conduct a neighborhood search. I rode home that night in a squad car.

At the end of the summer, I thought of the nine As I'd received in June and how little they would mean when I entered Mechanic Arts High School. I would no longer be big man on the playground but a lowly freshman in a huge school. I realized my formative years were almost over, but as I looked back on them, I felt they had truly been happy years.

Part I of "Down St. Albans Hill in a Wooden Coaster" appeared in the 2008 Saint Paul Almanac.

DISCOVERING FLAVOR, FUNKY MUSIC, AND FINE ART ALONG PAYNE AVENUE

Chelsea DeArmond

It's been about ten years since we moved to the historic Railroad Island neighborhood at the gateway to Payne Avenue. Before we moved here, I expected that the transition from my small hometown to my new home just across the tracks from downtown Saint Paul would be a struggle. Most of my assumptions about urban life were based on popular TV shows that focused on crime, drugs, and dropouts. But life here has been full of unexpected discoveries that don't show up on TV—like the simple pleasures of front porches, block parties, and parks. Here are just a few of the ways this place and its people have made me glad to call this neighborhood home.

As its name suggests, Railroad Island has always been full of motion. Waves of immigrants arrived by train and settled in Swede Hollow, an area named after one of the earliest groups to arrive. New families continued to fill in the neighborhood between Payne Avenue on the edge of the Hollow and the railroad tracks on the edge of downtown. After the Swedes came the Irish and Italians, and more recently Mexican and Hmong families have settled here.

The homes and businesses along Payne Avenue reflect the neighborhood's flavorful mix. Morelli's Alimentari vero Italiano has unbelievably low prices on great deli meat and wine, and the best spumoni and frozen pizza I've ever tasted. The oldest family-owned Italian restaurant in Saint Paul, Yarusso Brothers, is right next door to Morelli's. These historic Italian establishments have a new Hispanic neighbor, La Palma Supermercado y Carniceria, which features authentic Mexican groceries, deli, and fast food.

When we moved to this neighborhood, I had no idea we were just blocks from one of the best live blues and R&B clubs in the Midwest—the Minnesota Music Café. MMC features live music seven nights a week and serves food until 1 a.m. And I certainly never would have guessed that the brick warehouse next to MMC would be transformed into an art gallery with thousands of original Scandinavian and European paintings! The owner of the new Water and Oil Art Gallery, Jim Davidson, is a third-generation Swede whose East Side roots run deep. He plans to add a premier event center to the existing gallery.

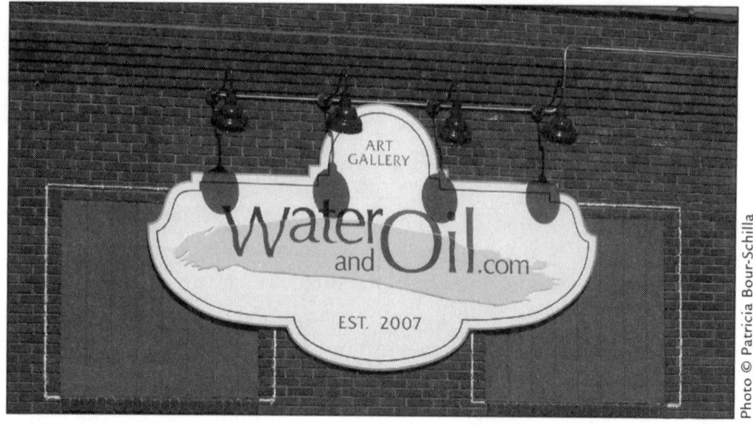

Photo © Patricia Bour-Schilla

Water and Oil Art Gallery on Railroad Island

I've also been surprised to discover remnants of a more rural past so close to the heart of the city. There's an old chicken coop in my neighbor's back yard, and some of the garages in this neighborhood used to be stables. Today, Hmong families and other neighbors have brought back beautiful gardens full of vegetables and flowers. For those of us who haven't learned the art and science of gardening, the downtown Saint Paul Farmers' Market is within walking distance.

The network of surrounding parks, including Swede Hollow, Bruce Vento Nature Sanctuary, and Mounds Park, has contributed to an unexpected wave of new neighbors—white-tail deer, fox, and wild turkeys. Last winter, a possum made its home under my back porch! Thanks to a few neighbors' heroic efforts to get the resident ally cat population off the streets and into caring homes, birds of all kinds are making their way back to the old maple, oak, ash, and cottonwood trees along our streets.

Living here has taught me to cherish the past but also to welcome change and variety. I like the contrast between the old Italian restaurants and the new Hispanic grocery store, the funky music at MMC and the fine art at Water and Oil Gallery, and the bird songs mixed in with city sights and sounds. When we moved to Railroad Island, I guess we were at the point in our lives where we were supposed to find a starter home. But I have a feeling we're here to stay.

Photo © Patricia Bour-Schilla

In two weeks (Good Lord!), Labor Day!
One more summer—drifted away.
BE BOLD! Don't be cautious!
Have fun 'til you're nauseous
And feel sort of guilty—okay?
—Garrison Keillor

Downtown Saint Paul Farmers' Market: Saturdays and Sundays through October

Music in Mears Park: Every Thursday 6–9 p.m.

MMAA Patio Nights: Every Thursday 7p.m.

Nine Nights of Music Series: August 4, 11, 18, 25

Music and Movies, District del Sol: Every Thursday 7p.m.

Irish Fair: August 7–9

Japanese Lantern Lighting Festival: August 16

Circus Juventas: Dates to be announced

Minnesota State Fair: August 27–September 7

Fourth Friday at the Movies: August 28

See pages 288–310 for more information and more events

"Life is essentially a cheat and its conditions are those of defeat; the redeeming things are not happiness and pleasure but the deeper satisfactions that come out of struggle."—F. Scott Fitzgerald, Saint Paul writer

AUGUST

S	M	T	W	T	F	S
26	27	28	29	30	31	1
2	3	4	5	6	7	8
9	10	11	12	13	14	15
16	17	18	19	20	21	22
23	24	25	26	27	28	29
30	31	1	2	3	4	5

AUGUST

3 MONDAY

4 TUESDAY

Nine Night's of Music Series

5 WEDNESDAY

6 THURSDAY

Music in Mears Park

MMAA Patio Nights

Music and Movies, District del Sol

Photo © Minnesota Historical Society

Children swimming at the public baths on Harriet Island, 1912

AUGUST

7 FRIDAY	Irish Fair

8 SATURDAY	Saint Paul Farmers' Market Irish Fair

9 SUNDAY	Saint Paul Farmers' Market Irish Fair

The Bush Foundation was incorporated in 1953 with an endowment from long-time 3M executive Archibald G. Bush.

Photo © Minnesota Streetcar Museum

Grand Avenue streetcar at Prior Avenue

MEMORIES OF GRAND AVENUE

Andrea Taylor Langworthy

For the first four and a half years of my life, my family lived in the upper half of a stucco duplex on Grand Avenue one house east of Prior. My aunt and uncle lived downstairs with my cousins. Kitty-corner across Grand from Thomas Liquors was a corner grocery store with a long wall of windows that faced our side of the street. The streetcar ran down Grand Avenue between the store and our house. We often rode it downtown with our mother to shop at Schuneman's or the Golden Rule.

My year-younger sister must have loved those shopping trips because she used to slide down the front hall steps lickety-split and toddle out to the street, where she would plop herself down on the streetcar tracks before my mother even realized she was gone. It wasn't that Mom wasn't paying attention, but my speedy sibling got going so fast that the grocer had scooped up and was carrying her along the sidewalk at the same time my mother was about to run out the front door in hot pursuit of her tiny toddler.

We moved across the Mississippi to Minneapolis when my brother was born. The two-bedroom duplex had gotten too tight for the five of us. Plus, Dad would go to law school, so we could afford to buy a whole house—with a back yard so my sister could scurry outside and sit on the bricks of a patio instead of a busy street. I wonder if Mom wished the grocer could come with us to keep an eye on her wandering child.

Years later, when we were older, Dad drove us to Saint Paul to visit his sister at the duplex. He gave my younger sister and me money so we could walk across the street with our cousins to buy treats at the corner grocery store. "What will it be, girls?" the grocer asked. Once we'd pointed to our choices, he scooped up penny candy from the case—just as he had scooped up my little sister years before.

BEAUMONT STREET

Mary Legato Brownell

When the Italians came, gardens held their
Secret worlds, and the grace of what was grown
To save became something no one could turn
Away by choice. In each of these lives were
Cracks fissured by pale, slipped roots in summer
Until their bright blood leapt, would awaken,
Not for remembered olives and lemon,
For small seeds and stems, but for dark pepper,
Zucchini, fresh basil, for the low-pitched
Thunder of thick vines rising carefully.
For weeks at a time the thin sky lowered.
The soughing of the white wind steadily
Rustled the ways they loved. From this I learned
To hold the strong hands of my family.

AUGUST

S	M	T	W	T	F	S
26	27	28	29	30	31	1
2	3	4	5	6	7	8
9	10	11	12	13	14	15
16	17	18	19	20	21	22
23	24	25	26	27	28	29
30	31	1	2	3	4	5

➪ *Asian Business & Community News* became the first Asian-American publication in Minnesota in 1982. It was renamed *Asian American Press* in 1990.

AUGUST

10 MONDAY

11 TUESDAY

Nine Nights of Music Series

12 WEDNESDAY

13 THURSDAY

Music in Mears Park

MMAA Patio Nights

Photo © Patricia Bour-Schilla

Western Sculpture Park at Marion Avenue and Ravoux Street

14 FRIDAY

15 SATURDAY Saint Paul Farmers' Market

FREE SAMPLES

Mike Hazard

Among a giggling gaggle of girls one gal,
in front of the table loaded with chocolates,
laughs out loud, "Let's try them all."

16 SUNDAY Saint Paul Farmers' Market

Japanese Lantern Lighting Festival

William Crooks was the first locomotive to operate in the state. It started running between Saint Paul and Saint Anthony in 1862.

ACCORDION HEAVEN

Jan Zita Grover

On a quiet stretch of lower Randolph in the West Seventh neighborhood stands a small, fortress-like business building. From its long, skinny dimensions, I imagine it was once a neighborhood tavern. But for the past twenty-five years, it has been Mahler Music Center, an independent accordion shop, instruction studio, and repair depot, and more recently home too to Accordion Heaven.com, a web store, all of these run by Ken Mahler.

The store, as you'd imagine, is filled with accordions, many of them retired, many of them in need of repair, most of them flashy in the mid-twentieth-century way of accordions. Mahler works on them when he can, which is to say when he isn't teaching would-be accordionists, tending to his website, and keeping up with the voluminous queries generated by his website and status as the only retail accordion shop in the five-state area.

A West Seventh boy ("St. Stanislaus") grown to affable middle age, Mahler stumbled into his unlikely calling early in life: "I wanted to learn an instrument when I was a kid, and finally my parents bought me a guitar. First I taught myself to play from the Mel Bay books, so then my parents tried to find me a guitar teacher. But they couldn't, so they sent me to Turlindi's instead. Turlindi's accordion store was where Five Points Hardware is now, across the street from Cossetta's.

"I took lessons, and then I started cleaning and washing Turlindi's windows. By the time I was in high school, I was teaching classes. One day I was outside washing Turlindi's windows, and I thought, *This is what I want; I want to have a store like this.*"

Mahler got his wish after Ed Turlindi died in 1981; after the estate closed in 1983, Mahler started his own business on lower Randolph. He had only three accordions as stock. He had learned to repair squeezeboxes from Ed Turlindi, and repairs soon became the major part of his business. The accordion's popularity, so great in the 1930s–1960s—"There used to be an accordionist on every block in Saint Paul"—was waning by the time Mahler opened his store; the schoolchild accordion bands many people now over sixty can remember had disappeared by then. "The kids just stopped. I don't know why, but they just stopped being interested by the 1970s." Until the dawn of the commercial Internet, Mahler's business was devoted mostly to repair; he also played in Mancini's house band until his recent retirement as accordionist.

Photo © Larry Schilla

The king of the accordion: Ken Mahler playing his signature Planet Squeezebox

These days, Mahler's sales are mostly to those long-ago child accordionists, now in or nearing retirement. "The majority of the Internet buyers live in New York, Florida, California, Nevada, Arizona"—retirement states, except for New York. "These people are buying good accordions; they know what they want. They're the bulwark of the industry. And as students, they are faithful to keeping up lessons." Accordion Heaven serves these dispersed buyers online, while Mahler Music Center caters to regional buyers, most of whom still drive to the store to choose their be-rhinestoned, chromed, multicolored beauties, often trading in instruments that have become too big, too heavy, or too in need of repair to play.

An accordion of Mahler's own manufacture is his middle-of-the-line, seventy-two-bass *Planet Squeezebox*. Mahler sought permission from the producers of Planet Squeezebox, a delightful two-CD compendium of world accordion music, to use the name, and received it. Then he embarked on what became an eight-trip quest to northern Italy to find the right parts suppliers and assemblers to produce his line of accordions.

And now they here sit in Saint Paul, Planet Squeezebox accordions, red-blue-white-black, patiently awaiting their new (old) owners.

"I want to help the accordion," Mahlers says somewhat plaintively. "I want to be a place where people can find answers."

➪ Fifty years ago, the Amherst H. Wilder House, a priceless piece of Saint Paul's architectural heritage on Summit Avenue, was torn down.

AUGUST

S	M	T	W	T	F	S
26	27	28	29	30	31	1
2	3	4	5	6	7	8
9	10	11	12	13	14	15
16	17	18	19	20	21	22
23	24	25	26	27	28	29
30	31	1	2	3	4	5

17 MONDAY

18 TUESDAY

Nine Nights of Music Series

19 WEDNESDAY

20 THURSDAY

Music in Mears Park

MMAA Patio Nights

Photo © Tom Conlon

Looking westward on Fourth Street

21 FRIDAY

22 SATURDAY St. Paul Farmers' Market

Ramadan begins

23 SUNDAY St. Paul Farmers' Market

A century ago, St. Louis King of France Church, supported by French-speaking residents of Saint Paul, was built at 506 Cedar.

HOME DELIVERY

Judith Niemi

The Egg Man came on Thursdays, and for several years I arranged to be home then. It wasn't a convenience, I couldn't order online in advance—in fact, I never knew exactly what he'd bring.

This started when I read Patricia Highsmith's *Beastly Murder*: in one story, hundreds of chickens, crazed by life in tiny cages, escape—abetted by a human accomplice—and peck to death the greedy farmer. I love eggs, and the cholesterol thing doesn't bother me, but the story did. My qualms were aesthetic and maybe ethical, but I called it a health issue: "Eating eggs from psychotic hens cannot be good for me."

It wasn't so easy, not that long ago, to find eggs from free-range chickens, even at some farmers' markets, so I was happy to meet the people I'll call Larry and Allie. Their farm wasn't officially organic, just an authentic old-style place with a lot of different crops, and where chickens ran around and had real lives, and produced delicious eggs. When the market closed in fall, I said, "Now what am I going to do?" and they said, "Oh, we deliver." It started, I think, when they were coming to Saint Paul's West Side anyway, visiting aging relatives, and then it got to be a habit. Their customer list grew casually, as we told friends about them.

It was Allie I'd first chatted with, because she reminded me so much of my farmer aunt—warm, sensible, and wheezing from the chicken coop. For a while they both drove the route, until health and community work started to keep Allie home. Larry was the gregarious one, anyway; he loved the route.

There was no point being in a hurry on Thursdays. The old van would arrive, and Larry'd walk, a bit stiffly, up the stairs. We'd stand on the porch, talking drought and frost, township politics and national politics. Finally he'd take my order. It was a point of pride never to write it down. He just ticked things off on his fingers, disappeared into his van, and came back with eggs, and chickens, fresh and frozen, whole and cut up. Also apple cider, squash, Yukon Golds, onions. No steaks—"forgot 'em this week"—but a nice roast. He always added up the total in his head.

He was always adding new foods but often forgot to mention them. It started when a neighbor grazed a few Black Angus on the back pasture, and they cut a deal with the local butcher. One year they raised ducks. "Never again!" he swore, after the whole family spent days pulling pinfeathers. He tapped other sources for cheese curds, pepperjack, butter,

Wisconsin cranberries. Sometimes a neighbor would visit Florida, and then there were grapefruit.

One year the farm had two peacocks. Larry walked into the barnyard and there they stood. "Guess they escaped from one of those hobby farms," he said happily. "I always sort of wanted peacocks." He fixed them an apartment in the barn, and read up on peacock care, but they weren't of hardy northern stock.

Larry delivered across the river, too, Crocus Hill and Mac-Groveland. (West Side prices, not Crocus Hill.) It was a very personal service. "Hey, do you think your sister's home yet?" he'd ask. "Missed her last time." "No, she's working late today–give me eggs and a roaster for her."

Gradually, though, visits became less frequent and then ended. You knew this was too good to last in this era, as gas got pricier and the hobby farms and McMansions spread. A developer bought the farm, named it something like Arcadia Hills, and bulldozed the hills. Allie and Larry took the greenhouse with them, and now grow flowers.

I really miss those chickens–the ones that ran around doing whatever chickens do to make life meaningful, and, at the point when I met them, tasted delicious. Dinner guests would ask, hopefully, "Is that one of Larry's chickens?" These days you can find organic, omega-3, vegetarian-fed brown eggs all over–"cage-free" is still what I look for first. You can find really good chickens, too, at higher prices than Larry's. But none of them come with weather predictions or news of wandering, free-range peacocks.

➪ A century ago, McGill-Warner, a printing company, constructed a new building at 225 East Ninth Street. It was recently turned into the Ninth Street Lofts.

AUGUST

S	M	T	W	T	F	S
26	27	28	29	30	31	1
2	3	4	5	6	7	8
9	10	11	12	13	14	15
16	17	18	19	20	21	22
23	24	25	26	27	28	29
30	31	1	2	3	4	5

24 Monday

25 Tuesday

Nine Nights of Music Series

26 Wednesday

27 Thursday

Music in Mears Park

Minnesota State Fair

MMAA Patio Nights

Étude II: Path near North Gate of Hidden Falls Park, Mississippi River

AUGUST

28 FRIDAY — Minnesota State Fair

29 SATURDAY — Saint Paul Farmers' Market
Minnesota State Fair

30 SUNDAY — Saint Paul Farmers' Market
Minnesota State Fair

In 1859, the Saint Paul Bridge Company constructed its toll bridge across the Mississippi, spurring development on the West Side.

DOCTOR GREASE MONKEY

Drew Tilsen

I do not remember where I heard this, but I find it amusing: "Doctors have it way too easy—they only have one make and two models."

Your Saint Paul automobile technician, on the other hand, has to work on a wide variety of makes and models: pickups, minivans, sedans, coupes, SUVs, SUWs, and so on. Your more ambitious auto techs will take on dump trucks, tractors, RVs, snow blowers, and boats. Your auto tech has to work on inline three-, four-, five-, and six-cylinder engines. V6, V8, V10, and V12. Flat four and six engines, diesel, gas, electric, and CNG. Not to mention all of the different valve and computer configurations. If it were as easy as human—male or female—you could probably train a monkey to be a mechanic.

Would you go see a doctor with no education? What if you walked in your doctor's office and saw no certificates or achievements hung proudly on the wall? What if the doctor was wearing a tee shirt and jeans, weighed you on a bathroom scale, and looked in your ear with a giant mag light? Would you still let the doctor treat you? Spend money on drugs you may not need or that are potentially harmful?

I think you should have to have a license to practice auto repair in Saint Paul. At least our vehicles should pass a safety inspection. With the potholes and rusty cars in Saint Paul, extra care has to be taken. Does your mechanic know what pressure your tires should be? Is everything as tight as it should be so when you swerve and brake, you can control the vehicle in an emergency? When you are done with your oil change, are you confident everything is okay at 80 mph?

In a lot of countries where people drive as fast as we do, your vehicle does have to pass a safety inspection. I would be willing to bet that over half of the cars and trucks out there would not pass a safety inspection in other countries. Does your mechanic inform you of potential safety issues, as your doctor does when you have high blood pressure?

Since we do not have emissions testing in Saint Paul anymore, who is responsible for keeping our vehicles running clean? You are! When your check engine light comes on, it is telling you that you are a polluter! Do not continue to drive around. Do not pass go. You need to get it fixed. It is part of your personal responsibility to take care of our environment.

Some health problems are directly related to smog. Your doctors would appreciate you keeping your car in good health so they don't have to treat unnecessary diseases and broken bones when you crash.

Illustration © Andy Singer

Drew's Gutless Cutless

Are you and your mechanic doing all that is necessary to keep our air as clean as possible and the roads safe? Is your mechanic disposing and recycling the waste from your car properly? I can't be the only one on the road looking over at the car next to me and seeing a little orange glowing light on the dash, signifying a major polluter. I bet these cars would not pass a safety inspection either. Do you feel safe driving next to them when they lose their steering? Or do you drive behind them and breathe their smog? What should be done about this? I believe police should give tickets if they see the polluter light.

If we got the word out in Saint Paul, we the people could set a nationwide standard for auto service and have no need for the government interfering with our everyday drives to work. Is it time to see your qualified automobile repair professional and ask about your pollution and safety? Please be responsible.

MISSISSIPPI MARINER

Diego Vázquez, Jr.

I was leaving the Bean Factory on Saratoga and Randolph in Saint Paul, when the small white car with a kayak on the roof bounced up to the curb. The driver of the car got out and reached for the roof to check for the tightness of the straps holding the kayak. We passed each other when he lumbered inside to order coffee, and I asked him if he could surf with that thing.

"Ha—I tell you what, I don't need to get wet using this thing. But there are characters in this world who actually ride the surf on kayaks. I think my time has passed for that. Hell, I'm just trying to make it down river without having to take a nap." His laughter was loud with pure joy. He carried the serious politeness of a good teacher. He reminded me of the best professor I ever knew: there was a gentle hospitality in their histories, this kayaker being so welcoming of a stranger like me, and responding to my humor.

I don't know what turned us both around, but we sat down at a table and drank away hours with coffee and stories. Toward the end of our first meeting, John said that I could be the missing link, because he was in need of someone crazy enough to assist in his journey on a ten-mile stretch of the Mississippi. He had a solo kayak, and he needed to be dropped off to launch and then to be picked up at journey's end. I agreed to be the kayak helper even before John could finish. John estimated about three hours on the river, which would allow me enough time to find the pickup spot. On the day when I dropped off John at the landing in Lilydale, he was just a month past his seventieth birthday.

Almost a year to the day after our first meeting at the Bean Factory, we both sat inside the coffee shop again, recollecting John's fabulous journey through downtown Saint Paul on the river with a kayak.

On the morning of the launch, the boat landing was empty and the sun was warm. The river stretched quietly. For John, rowing with the current was a relief. The beginning mile or so was as calm as an afternoon nap, and he had yet to face into the wind.

The first bridge, officially known as Omaha Road Bridge Number 15, is an old railroad bridge that opens and closes periodically but remains mostly unnoticed by passersby. The earlier version of the bridge was one of the original fifteen bridges built over the Mississippi.

Downstream from Lilydale and to the left (starboard) is the old NSP plant. To the right is the Mendota Road stone arch bridge, another aged structure. Then comes the Smith Avenue High Bridge. The newer version is less than twenty years old. Up comes Harriet Island, home to many a

Photo © Lou "The Photo Guy" Michaels

Mississippi kayaker John Murphy

winter carnival snow castle. Wabasha Street Bridge, Raspberry Island, the Saint Paul Union Pacific's vertical-lift rail bridge, Robert Street Bridge, the Lafayette Bridge. Then come the cliffs where the Indian Mounds oversee the passage of time. Pig's Eye no. 1 and Pig's Eye no. 2, Holman Field, and Saint Paul's downtown airfield, built for the 3M execs. The kayak came ashore shortly past the Wakota Bridge.

At the start of the ten-mile journey, I held onto the kayak after we had placed it in the river, while John drove his car back up to the parking lot. His most recent stroke had resulted in a more noticeable hobble, and he walked back to the river in slow motion, pointing out a barge hauling Mankato limestone. We decided that it was coming from Shakopee. Big rocks floating on the river and looking so pretty turned our thoughts to all the things that need water and the connection that every living thing on this planet has with water. Everything that lives, everything, needs water for survival. I am not surprised that John needs to float and row on it alone, using his favorite form of transportation for this epic journey. He knew that this would be the last time that he could do it on his own.

This time John saw his hometown in a way he never had before. Seventy years, and looking now at the downtown where he had made a living for many of those years with the Saint Paul Companies, and seeing it from the vantage point of being on the river in his kayak. The Landmark was a federal building. He knew it well because his father, who had worked as a federal prosecutor, had an office in the Landmark. When the feds handed the building over to the city, it almost became a parking lot. A friend of John's served on the local committee that decided the fate of the newly acquired building. The friend originally favored razing the old structure to free up space for parking cars. Happy to have been wrong, he is now proud that the building survived. So is the city.

On our day of recollection, sitting in a corner of the Bean Factory, we captured an audience who listened to the retelling of the kayak mission. Sorting through all of the nuances of the river trip, I told John that I was such a weak swimmer that I am always afraid of being on the water. My favorite activity on a river is being on the bank. Still, John talked about the episode as if we both had been on the river. "When *we* did the river trip, I hadn't had the really bad stroke yet. I had some strokes that weakened me, but I had not yet had that really debilitating shot. I wouldn't do it again now because I don't have the stamina. I just don't feel strong enough that if I capsized, even with a lifejacket and knowing that I am a good swimmer, I just don't have the stamina anymore. I couldn't."

A few years ago, an organization sponsored river runs for nonmotorized vessels. John had planned on entering one of the ten-mile events, but by the time he decided to do it, the group had gone broke. The Mississippi Mariner solo ten-mile special for people seventy and over was John's reaction.

He practiced for weeks, using short stretches of the rivers that are accessible from a Fort Snelling boat landing. The most noteworthy of the small runs was circumnavigating Pike Island on his seventieth birthday. On that day, John paddled the kayak on both rivers and the channel that connects the Mississippi and the Minnesota.

"I e-mailed a buddy of mine and told him about my circumnavigation. He wrote me back offering congratulations and confusion. He said, 'John, for the life of me, why would a guy seventy years old want to get circumcised? And why would he want to get circumcised on Pike Island?'"

One of John's friends, this one an important board member of a major corporation, had driven off the High Bridge and survived. "Can you believe that? I can't recall all the particulars, but he actually drove off the bridge. The old one, before this new one was built. He must have driven off somewhere on the sides close to the banks, because the guy lived to tell about it. Don't know of anyone else who has survived a fall off of that bridge."

Another piece of history from John about the river explained why the great mansions that were built up on Summit Avenue deliberately faced away from the river: their owners disdained the people who worked the river. All river traffic ended in Saint Paul. St. Anthony falls is the only falls on the Mississippi, the only natural falls on the entire Mississippi, and there were no locks and dams to move vessels any farther north. The riverfront of Saint Paul bore the traffic of all commerce from the Red River oxcarts to the road and trails that would take over for the river.

John realizes there is a star in your eye when it is your turn to meet the river. He was seventy years old, and he knew that with his debilitating health, he needed to make the journey when he did. The kayak journey, the Mississippi adventure of ten miles solo through the heart of Saint Paul, was one of his finest achievements. A river runs eternally through his soul in a universal engagement with water.

Almost in a whisper, which is rare for his grand voice, John recollects, "I was so happy when I saw my daughter and my grandson waiting for me at the landing underneath the Wakota Bridge. You surprised the hell out of me. I never knew that you would think of bringing them along to pick me up. I tell you, that made the effort all worthwhile, to see them waving at me. Ha, I could barely move my arms anymore, but I knew they had given me back just enough inspiration to finish the voyage."

The most enchanting view of the journey can be seen up on the cliffs where the downtown Saint Paul Holman Air Field's beacon stands and where the ancients positioned their souls to rest on mounds that are eternally pointed toward the infinity of natural light. I am proud to know a particular soul that rests on the endless movement of this magnificent river, who on one particular day in September rowed on the ride of a lifetime.

Photo © Patricia Bour-Schilla

Working at the Saint Paul Farmers' Market

OVERHEARD IN THE MARKET

Mike Hazard

Once upon a time, it was all organic. Now, not.
Wow, I've never seen that before.
Holy buckets, look at those radishes.
Climate is what you expect and weather is what you get.
We're up to our eyes in groceries here.
Soda pop is liquid corn.
Paradise was a garden.
On a farm, everything is dangerous.
I love to watch stuff grow.
Plant your corn by the light of the moon.
A farmer farms soils and a writer farms brain cells.
If it was easy, you'd see it on every table.
I've known these Brussels sprouts since they were seeds.
Enjoy every blade of grass. Don't miss the miracle.

SEPTEMBER

Photo © Patricia Bour-Schilla

Downtown Saint Paul Farmers' Market: Saturdays and Sundays through October

Minnesota State Fair: Through September 7

Payne-Arcade International Harvest Festival: September 10–13

Selby Avenue JazzFest: September 12

Annual Twin Cities Black Film Festival: September 18–20

Fourth Friday at the Movies: September 25

See pages 288–310 for more information and more events

➪ "Larry Ho" was the nickname of Lawrence Hodgson, a Saint Paul mayor (1918–1922 and 1926–1930) who was also a journalist and published poet.

SEPTEMBER

S	M	T	W	T	F	S
30	31	1	2	3	4	5
6	7	8	9	10	11	12
13	14	15	16	17	18	19
20	21	22	23	24	25	26
27	28	29	30	1	2	3

31 MONDAY Minnesota State Fair

1 TUESDAY Minnesota State Fair

2 WEDNESDAY Minnesota State Fair

3 THURSDAY Minnesota State Fair

Photo © Patricia Bour-Schilla

Foreign & Domestic Repair Shop

4 FRIDAY	Minnesota State Fair
5 SATURDAY	Saint Paul Farmers' Market Minnesota State Fair
6 SUNDAY	Saint Paul Farmers' Market Minnesota State Fair

In 1859, Cass Gilbert was born. He designed the State Capitol and many of Saint Paul's elegant homes.

Photo © Patricia Bour-Schilla

Saul Lu

KAW THU LEI

Saul Lu

Saul is one of many ethnic Karen (pronounced kah-ren*) refugees forced out of their homeland in Myanmar, formerly known as Burma. After spending years in Thailand refugee camps, many recently immigrated to Saint Paul. Saul is learning English at MORE Multicultural School.*

My name is Saul Lu. My country's name is Burma. Burma has many peoples, and they speak many languages because we have many ethnic groups. Our Karen people lived in the highlands, and we called the place Kaw Thu Lei. It has good forests, high mountains, many animals, clean streams, beautiful waterfalls, and many fish in our rivers. Especially I miss my farm on the side of the river. I planted coconut trees, butternut trees, lemons, and mangoes. Every year I sold the vegetables and fruits and got money for my family.

Then in 2006 I came to the United States. I have five children, three boys and two girls. My wife and I work at the same place. The first time I came to Saint Paul, I saw many different things like the buildings and snow and deer that lived with the people in town. In the winter we walked on the lake because the water changed to ice. I never saw that in my country. But I miss beautiful Kaw Thu Lei.

FIRST DAY OF KINDERGARTEN

Margaret Hasse

The bus steps are high, but William clambers up gamely.
Doors shut. He peers out a print-marked window.
From the street corner, I wave, wistful as a soldier's bride
as his bus pulls away and turns a corner.

At noon the yellow bus returns him
to the same place where I'm standing again.
He thinks I stood there all day, waiting in his absence.
When he finds out I left to play tennis,

his forehead crumples like paper in a wastebasket.
Now he knows I can move on my own without him.
Tears drawn from the well of desertion form in his eyes.
I'm his first love and his greatest disappointment.

➩ The McDonough Homes, named after a mayor, opened in September 1951 as Saint Paul's first subsidized rental housing community.

SEPTEMBER

S	M	T	W	T	F	S
30	31	1	2	3	4	5
6	7	8	9	10	11	12
13	14	15	16	17	18	19
20	21	22	23	24	25	26
27	28	29	30	1	2	3

7 MONDAY Minnesota State Fair

Labor Day

8 TUESDAY

9 WEDNESDAY

10 THURSDAY Payne-Arcade International Harvest Festival

Photo © Saint Paul Dispatch & Pioneer Press

Advertising sign "Growing with St. Paul" on roof of Commerce Building as seen from the roof of the Hotel Lowry, 1962

SEPTEMBER

11 FRIDAY

Payne-Arcade International Harvest Festival

12 SATURDAY

Saint Paul Farmers' Market

Payne-Arcade International Harvest Festival

Selby Avenue JazzFest

13 SUNDAY

Saint Paul Farmers' Market

Payne-Arcade International Harvest Festival

City Academy became the first charter school in the United States when it opened on September 7, 1992.

TRYING TO LEAVE SAINT PAUL

Jim Moore

1

Little streets of Saint Paul

that lead nowhere. One of them
ends where quiet drunks sit
in the old September grass
on top of a hill.
Street cars used to run here,
through a tunnel cut into the hill.
The sun rides so low
in the cloud-filled western sky,
it makes the empty bottles glow.

2

How far away

it is possible to go from Saint Paul
in a single night of raucous dreams:
I wake up before dawn,
joyful, moon shining
through broken slats
of an old bamboo curtain.

3

A boy and his father

cross the street. The first depends
on the second. The second
fumbles for a map.

4

Yesterday we almost did it,

took off from Saint Paul,
        driving south thirty hours
to Florida, almost gave in
        to sunlight, warmth, the sea.
The biopsy report had come back negative,
        making me greedy for more:
coconuts, fresh shrimp, crickets
        past midnight under a full moon.
I did so want
        to begin driving and not stop
until I knew for sure
        I would live forever.

(reprinted from *Pleiades*)

SEPTEMBER

S	M	T	W	T	F	S
30	31	1	2	3	4	5
6	7	8	9	10	11	12
13	14	15	16	17	18	19
20	21	22	23	24	25	26
27	28	29	30	1	2	3

➪ "Those streets in Saint Paul must have been designed by drunken Irishmen."—Jesse Ventura, former wrestler and Minnesota governor

SEPTEMBER

14 Monday

15 Tuesday

16 Wednesday

17 Thursday

Photo © Patricia Bour-Schilla

Costello's Bar on Selby Avenue

18 FRIDAY	Annual Twin Cities Black Film Festival
19 SATURDAY Rosh Hashanah	Saint Paul Farmers' Market Annual Twin Cities Black Film Festival
20 SUNDAY	Saint Paul Farmers' Market Annual Twin Cities Black Film Festival

In 1859, Fort Road between Fort Snelling and downtown Saint Paul was completed.

MEMORIES OF ST. LOUIS SCHOOL

Kathryn Lindaas

We moved from Riverside, Rhode Island, a suburb of Providence, in 1961. My father, an airline sales manager, was transferred. He took us—me, Mom, Christine, and Susan—to Howard Johnson's to break the news.

"We are moving," he said. "Can you guess where?"

We guessed: "California? Colorado? Hawaii?"

It was none of the above, but rather to a place with no oceans, no mountains, no year-round balmy weather.

Dad tried to sell Minnesota to us. "Minnesota is very clean. In summer there's no humidity. It's dry heat. Though it's cold in winter, it's dry, not damp; more tolerable." Regardless—it was a done deal. Prior to this time, our folks had spared telling us about possible transfers. We knew this was for real or we wouldn't be hearing about it.

So we packed up our 1957 Ford station wagon and headed west, taking a scenic trip, up northwestern New England, through Niagara Falls, around the Great Lakes, and then to Minnesota.

Despite many trips schlepping around looking at potential homes, my folks hadn't found the right house or even the part of the Twin Cities in which we would settle. So in that early summer with the "dry heat," Capp Towers Motor Hotel on the corner of Fifth and Cedar became our temporary home in Saint Paul. We had two adjoining rooms with a balcony. I was impressed by the red shiny-like-patent-leather bricks that were the interior walls of the motel's Firehouse Restaurant. We ate most breakfasts, lunches, and dinners there.

As fall approached with still no home sweet home, my sister Chris and I needed to start school. I was entering eighth grade and she, fifth. A block north and a couple more east was St. Louis Catholic Church and School. It was run by the Sisters of St. Joseph of Carondelet. We registered.

The classrooms each housed two grades. I was in the seventh-eighth room and Chris in the fifth-sixth room. The sisters were missionary nuns, and Saint Paul's inner city was their mission. They were truly dedicated to their vocations, the school, and its students. One day, I forgot to bring my lunch. Mom was out with a real estate agent, and it was the 1960s—no cell phones! So Sister Christine gave me enough loose change to go to Woolworth's and buy a grilled cheese sandwich. The nuns also asked my mother if we had any clothes we didn't wear anymore. My mother did, and in the playground we would see kids wearing our outgrown hats and mittens.

Photo © Eugene Debs Baker

St. Louis Catholic School,
Tenth and Cedar streets

Tired of eating restaurant food (yes, really!), we moved to the Lowry Hotel on Wabasha. This time, we had an efficiency suite with a kitchen so we could have home-cooked meals. Every day, Chris and I would take the elevator to the lobby and pass a doorman on our way to school. We walked several blocks past markets and stores. One was a candy shop. Smells of caramel corn wafted through the air. Chris told me recently that we also passed an "exotic dancing club" on our way to school. I don't remember that, but I do remember being greeted by friendly Saint Paulites all along the way.

I called the Sisters of St. Joseph recently. I couldn't remember the names of our teachers, and I hoped they could help me. The director of communications said she would have the archivist call me back. She did, and I had a delightful conversation with Sister John Stephen, soon to be eighty years old. She had been Christine's teacher. Sister reminded me that the school closed in 1962 and that I was in the last eighth-grade graduating class. Most of the sisters have passed away. But the church is still there and has an active congregation.

I now live in a suburb of Minneapolis and love both Twin Cities. But I loved Saint Paul first.

➪ A century ago, F. Scott Fitzgerald's first appearance in print was in a literary magazine published by his school, Saint Paul Academy.

SEPTEMBER

S	M	T	W	T	F	S
30	31	1	2	3	4	5
6	7	8	9	10	11	12
13	14	15	16	17	18	19
20	21	22	23	24	25	26
27	28	29	30	1	2	3

SEPTEMBER

21 MONDAY

Eid al-Fitr

22 TUESDAY

23 WEDNESDAY

24 THURSDAY

Photo © Patricia Bour-Schilla

Westside of the Blair Arcade Building on Selby Avenue

SEPTEMBER

25 FRIDAY	Fourth Friday at the Movies
26 SATURDAY	Saint Paul Farmers' Market
27 SUNDAY	Saint Paul Farmers' Market

Nobel Prize-winning author Saul Bellow once lived in the St. Anthony Park neighborhood.

AN OASIS

Mahmoud El-Kati

Dedication to the Golden Thyme Coffee Café

This could be the place where free *social space* is afforded for us the people,
you and me,
who would meet other people, that is,
people unlike ourselves, and yet, we learn something fresh about
ourselves from
this chance encounter.

This *should* be the place, this space,
where we all, in an instant,
might discover the truth, the way, to transcend the murky waters of colors,
creeds, and enslavement to myth.

It *can* be here, this place, this space,
where social boundaries are crossed, where high meets low, flesh to flesh,
wherein
that complexity that is called *human*
might begin the process of living broader, truer, fuller lives,
where we begin to learn how to learn, and indeed, learn how to live together
without having to live alike.

This *would* be the place, this space,
our crossroad to begin that tomorrow that is so much talked about,
and wished for, by so many, where finally through this narrow prism of
infinite possibility,
we will discover the spirit and the will to make the great leap forward
toward
building a sturdy, indestructible bridge to diverse human connections.

Yes! *This ought to* be the place, this space of our times,
in which we walk that talk into a wellspring of democracy, engaging our
fellows, sharing and liberating our minds from conventions that separate,
isolate, and alienate.
A communal outburst is awaiting!

Golden Thyme Coffee Café on Selby

It is here, this place, this sacred space, that could be, should be,
may be, will be, shaped by an energizing ambience that shall inspire quite fun,
Soft, warm, and beautiful kinships, and a quiet, untheatrical love,
wherein our essence will be *NOT* be, just being, but becoming ____ all the time.

AGONY AND ECSTASY ON THE TWIN CITIES MARATHON

Brad Richason

Shortly after crossing the ten-mile marker in the 2007 Twin Cities Marathon, I was gripped by an unanticipated fear: *I might not finish*. Until that point, even during the toughest days of training, I had never even considered the notion of not crossing the finish line. But at that instant, with well over half the distance remaining, my head was throbbing, my feet were soaked, and I could feel the ominous hint of a leg cramp. Try as I might, I could not deny my rapidly deteriorating condition.

SEPTEMBER

I squinted at the exuberant crowd lining the street. At every moment, another runner's name was shouted, encouraging hands were extended, and benevolent strangers provided a variety of snacks. For all their support, though, I began to resent the incessant cheers. The last thing I wanted was an audience to my imminent collapse. Runners I had passed earlier were now passing me. My fight gone, I watched each pass with resigned acceptance and mounting amazement. Were these people really so masochistic? What was I doing amongst such lunatics? I pondered the question, thinking back to when the idea of running the Twin Cities Marathon still seemed sensible.

Even though I had long been a recreational runner, I had never considered tackling a marathon until a friend of mine, someone with zero experience, had successfully completed the Twin Cities course. Awed by his accomplishment, I resolved not only to run next year's marathon, but to cover the distance in perfect form, striding strong for the entire 26.2 miles.

Because my training started during winter, my earliest runs were confined to treadmills at a local gym. Though treadmill running was numbingly repetitive, the machines forced me to recognize speed limitations when an overambitious pace made my legs feel ready to snap off at the knee. I also learned that cotton can breed blisters large enough to swallow an entire foot and that the wrong shoe can cripple a runner for weeks. Painful lessons each, but they could not dissuade me from my goal. At a specialized runner's store, I bought dual-layered socks to wick away sweat and new shoes that fit the contours of my feet. I was ready to forge forward with renewed ambition, when Missy, my wife, startled me with her plans to run the marathon herself.

Photo © Lou "The Photo Guy" Michaels

SEPTEMBER

2007 Twin Cities Marathon

Aside from some shared recreational jogs, Missy had never been a dedicated runner. Spurred on by my lofty pronouncements, however, the marathon had taken hold of her imagination. Her announcement coincided with the dawn of spring and, living in Saint Paul near the Mississippi Parkway, I was well aware of the picturesque miles of pathways that lined the river. So regardless of our unbalanced paces, I was glad to have my wife join me.

I soon came to realize how seriously she took the training. Her face beet red, her breathing ragged, she never quit. Inspired by her determination, I stayed at her side, encouraging her on to the next mile. Mindful of my need to maintain a pace, Missy would insist that I speed off for the last few miles. In this way we trained together, waking to run at 4:30 a.m., when the sun rose in summer over the Mississippi.

Weekends were for longer distances, starting as low as eight miles and topping out at twenty-three. Together we charted routes, learning the location and qualities of every bathroom in a ten-mile radius. We ran from Saint Paul to Minneapolis and back again, first crossing the Mississippi at Ford Parkway and crossing back at Marshall, then Franklin, and finally Washington. Never had I felt so strong or confident.

One month before the marathon, however, a series of business trips impeded my training. Maybe I would have tried harder to stick to my training schedule had I not felt like I was in the home stretch. In those waning days of training, my mind was already reveling in the glory of sprinting across the finish line.

By the morning of the marathon, Missy and I were tense with excitement. We hopped on the Hiawatha light-rail train to transport us to the starting point at the Metrodome. The train was packed with marathoners, each sharing our sense of anticipation. We were tightly coiled with anxious nerves, ready for the penultimate test to our months of preparation.

At the Metrodome, runners spent the waning time stretching out muscles, joking out tension, and lining up at restrooms to relieve bladders. As minutes ticked down, a corral of runners formed behind the starting line. All in all, over seven thousand runners had amassed to cover the 26.2-mile course starting in downtown Minneapolis and ending at the Capitol building in Saint Paul.

After a moment of silence for the victims of the 35W bridge collapse, the marathon began. Tightly packed waves of runners moved forward, some jockeying for space, others content at a conservative pace. Missy and I focused on the spectators, the cheering men, women, and children that covered every inch of sidewalk. Distracted by the characters in the crowd, my wife and I passed the first five miles with ease.

But things were about to change. We had agreed that after five miles, if Missy was still feeling strong, I could move ahead at my faster pace. After numerous reassurances, I wished her luck and ran forward. I managed another four miles before sudden exhaustion surged through me. Only then did I recognize the dangerously high heat and humidity. All along the path, fallen runners were on their backs being given assistance by EMPs. Ignoring my own waning condition, I clapped hands with kids, nibbled on sugary snacks, and rehydrated at every refreshment station.

Despite my best efforts, though, my pace was self-defeating. If I didn't readjust, I'd never make it all the way.

Slowing my speed, I accepted that my original goal would be sacrificed. When an ill-fated attempt to run under a water hose left my shoes and socks soaked, all I could do was trudge on in wet feet. Miserable with discomfort, I took a walking break, hoping to revive my senses. I continued to alternate between a run and a walk for the next several miles. Time was no longer a concern. I just wanted to finish. But with every stop I walked a little longer, ran a little less. Still, I kept managing to spur myself on, trapped in a cruel exhibition of prolonged suffering. Better to keep moving, I resolved, until I had either crossed the finish line on my feet or was carried away on a stretcher.

Shortly after lurching through mile twenty, I developed a cramp in my right leg. Covering over six more miles in this condition felt impossible. Overheated and exhausted, I considered a suicidal sprint for the finish line. I was sure to collapse along the way, but at least I would go out in an extraordinary meltdown. On the verge of this despair, I noticed an extraordinary thing: Missy ran up beside me.

Her face gleamed with exertion and determination. Seeing her expression, I felt renewed resilience. We pressed on together, feeling stronger with each numbing step. Cresting Cathedral Hill, we could see all the way down to the finish line. Disregarding the pain, I ran the remaining distance in unison with my wife. I hardly remember our names being announced as we crossed the finish line, so elated was I with achieving this impossible victory.

After collecting our finisher's medals, we staggered to a grassy area and collapsed. Relief swept through me. Covering the 26.2 miles proved far harder than I had imagined, but we had both succeeded. Better still, we had done it together. Now that the ordeal was over, I couldn't have been more satisfied, except for the nagging thought that I had finished over an hour past my original goal.

Eventually I accepted that there was only one proper way to achieve closure. Maybe I am a bit of a masochist after all, but I'll be running the next Twin Cities Marathon, this time with a score to settle.

EXCELLENCE PERCEIVES ITSELF

William S. McDowell II

William is taking classes at the Minnesota Literacy Council's learning center in the Rondo Community Library, working toward obtaining his GED certificate.

If I had the opportunity to teach something I know well, it would be writing rap lyrics. These lyrics would be based on a life in the fast lane and a life in poverty. The fast life got me nine years in a state correctional facility for crimes that I committed. During my long stay in this horrible place called jail, I learned a lot about life. I learned there is much more to life than just living a fast one. As time continued to pass, I found myself writing a lot of letters and poems. The poems that were written became rap lyrics. So, as I continued on with writing these lyrics, it became my hobby and something that I enjoyed doing.

I then started to say these lyrics to other people in jail, and they loved it. I spoke about my life in the fast lane and how living in poverty had promised me one to three years in jail for selling drugs and carrying guns in the street. I spoke about how we could change when we are set free. I would teach someone something that would change the world if they could just take focus. I would tell them how to meditate with love and faith, that's all it takes. I know because I did it, I changed by writing lyrics with a good spirit inside of me saying I could do it.

OCTOBER

Photo © Patricia Bour-Schilla

A philosopher walking down Selby
Asked where might a Hilton hotel be?
What is time? What is space?
Where's the nose on my face?
And where is the light b-u-l-b?
—Garrison Keillor

Downtown Saint Paul Farmers' Market: Saturdays and Sundays through October

India Day: October 4

Twin Cities Marathon: October 4

Saint Paul Art Crawl: October 9–11

Zoo Boo: October 17, 18, 23, 24, 25

Fourth Friday at the Movies: October 23

Dia de los Muertos Family Fiesta: October 25

Great Pumpkin Festival: October 25

See pages 288–310 for more information and more events

➪ "Why should I pine for halls of science and literature, when such glorious privileges were mine—when to my weak hand was accorded the work of rearing the fabric of educational interests in the unorganized territory?"—Harriet Bishop, pioneer Saint Paul teacher

OCTOBER

S	M	T	W	T	F	S
27	28	29	30	1	2	3
4	5	6	7	8	9	10
11	12	13	14	15	16	17
18	19	20	21	22	23	24
25	26	27	28	29	30	31

28 Monday

Yom Kippur

29 Tuesday

30 Wednesday

1 Thursday

OCTOBER

Photo © Tom Conlon

A view of Saint Paul from the First National Bank Building

2 FRIDAY	
3 SATURDAY	Saint Paul Farmers' Market
4 SUNDAY	Saint Paul Farmers' Market India Day Twin Cities Marathon

OCTOBER

In 1859, Saint Paul began to enjoy the game of baseball and within a decade, a State Association of Base Ball Players had been formed.

ON THE MOUSTACHE

Abram Sauer

A man with hair on his face's upper lip has a moustache. A moustache is not facial hair's natural form; neighboring regions must be maintained without fail, or the moustache will cease to be. Add hair to this same upper-lipped arrangement, and now it's a goatee, a beard, or something else.

The first moustache on record appeared on a Scythian horseman around 300 BCE. Assuming he had *the* most advanced tools of his day, this Pazyryk rider enjoyed scraping a single, dull, possibly copper blade across his wind-swept cheek. Things have only mildly improved. Even with the Gillette-Schick cartel's recent move to five-bladed razors, shaving technology has moved forward at a molasses pace with one blade improvement every 450 or so years.

But if you get the right blade, you don't need the other four. To experience the proper care a gentleman's moustache should receive, you should turn to Saint Paul's own Moustache Jim, master barber at Heimie's Haberdashery on Saint Peter Street.

Visible through a large street window, Moustache Jim's shave station is nestled in a sizeable room at the back of the haberdashery. To get there, you pass through the very impressive bespoke spectacle that is Heimie's. This sartorial wormhole transports patrons into a mind-set where, by the time they arrive to shake hands with Jim, the thought of a complete stranger putting a very sharp, unguarded razor to his neck seems logical.

Jim piles hot towel after hot towel on my face. My softening cheeks are rubbed with pre-shave oil and then put under an even steamier wrap. Reclining on the padded vintage leather chair, I try to remember if the wall-mounted animal's head above me is a boar or some other unfortunate beastie.

The moustache-wearing male and society's general consensus about him are paradoxical. Moustaches themselves are by far the most difficult of the basic facial hair arrangements to maintain, requiring a large amount of conscious primping. So while the modern moustache is believed to be favored by men who care not much for fashion or personal appearance, the truth is that the moustached man is, at least in terms of his facial hair arrangements, a vain, vain creature indeed. A moustache says, "Why, yes, I did shave. But very intentionally—and with great care and calculation, I did not shave this bit here."

Photo © Abram Sauer

Moustache Jim

It is with great care and calculation that Jim's blade drifts across my jawline. Though no doctor, I do believe that is where the jugular is. Yet I am confident. Moustache Jim is a Saint Paul native and has been putting men under a knife or shears for almost a decade now. His favorite moustache is Bill the Butcher's, which Jim's own resembles in both style and flamboyance. His *Gangs of New York* bloodthirstiness seems thankfully, especially at this moment, absent.

Jim sits me up to appreciate his work. And what work it is. It's not enough to say that my face feels shaved; it feels proper. And here's one more thing that I suppose a potential client should know: Moustache Jim happens to be a singing master barber. Surely Saint Paul's only. And he is quite not bad.

Once the mark of the true gentleman, the moustache has become a joke in the minds of those who usually consider themselves open-minded. No U. S. president has worn a moustache in three generations. No current senate member wears one, and if opinion polls continue to dominate politics, which they will, there won't be any soon. The moustache now finds itself maligned, alive only on the fringe.

A 2007 poll found that more than half of American women would refuse to kiss a man with a moustache. And for me, therein lies probably the single most persuasive argument for the moustache: appearance martyrdom. In a culture where physical attractiveness is increasingly important in all levels of one's personal and professional life, a moustache can be seen as an open protest against a warped value system.

➩ The Saint Paul Garden Club was founded in 1927 by thirty-two women who planted 1,700 tulips in Rice Park as their first project.

OCTOBER

S	M	T	W	T	F	S
27	28	29	30	1	2	3
4	5	6	7	8	9	10
11	12	13	14	15	16	17
18	19	20	21	22	23	24
25	26	27	28	29	30	31

5 Monday

6 Tuesday

7 Wednesday

8 Thursday

Photo © Patricia Bour-Schilla

Mural on Midtown Business Center Building at Dale and University

9 FRIDAY	Saint Paul Art Crawl
10 SATURDAY	Saint Paul Farmers' Market Saint Paul Art Crawl Fall Flower Show begins
11 SUNDAY	Saint Paul Farmers' Market Saint Paul Art Crawl

Elsie Shaw taught children, trained teachers, conducted choirs, and was Saint Paul's music supervisor from 1898 to 1933.

BEST FRIEND

Margaret Anzevino

As I knew it then, in September of 1938, Beaumont Street, on Railroad Island, was only three blocks long. We lived in the middle of the block between Bedford to the east and Burr to the west. And although it was only another block and a half from our house to Lincoln School, on Burr and Collins, my mother was not going to let me walk alone for my first day of kindergarten—that was how important it was to her that I be properly dropped off. With her bib apron over her cotton dress, she held my hand and we set out for the five-minute walk.

Just as we reached the door of the school, another little girl accompanied by her mother climbed the school steps. The other mother was much more modern-looking than mine, mostly because her hair was short and permanent waved, while my mother wore braids wound around her head. Our mothers knew each other—everyone knew a little something about everyone else in the neighborhood—so they tucked our little girls' hands together and told us to go into the building. The other little girl, Bobbi, had light brown hair cut into a Dutch bob, which I much admired; my hair was in long pigtails closed at the ends with ugly rubber bands.

We walked into the classroom and immediately spotted the big dollhouse with a doll sitting beside it. We headed straight for the doll, both of us grabbing her head and feet, and began to pull the poor thing from side to side. The teacher, Miss Will, came over immediately, grabbing my arm and Bobbi's until the wobbled doll dropped on the floor between us. Miss Will picked it up and took her away, leaving both of us utterly dismayed, thereby forging an irreparable bond of lasting friendship with the quick anger we held against Miss Will. Thus began the Beaumont Street friendship between us that lasted more than fifty-five years, until the day she died.

When we were to enter third grade, Bobbi's family moved one house away from us on Beaumont. What could be greater? Morning, noon, and night, summer, spring, fall, and winter, we could do everything together. We played cops and robbers; we gave shows that other children could come to watch, paying a safety pin as ticket price; we played ball in the street; we made bonfires of leaves in the fall and roasted potatoes in the ashes.

By the time we were twelve and allowed limited freedom from our street, we would beg for 12 cents to attend the Sunday matinee at the

Photo © Patricia Bour-Schilla

Beaumont and Burr streets

Capitol Theatre on Payne Avenue. There was not a big thing about ratings then, and almost any movie was okay. When we were lucky, or our parents had pennies to spare, we were given a nickel extra for a big bag of popcorn.

But the actual movie wasn't the big event—it was the walk home. With complete abandon and total unselfconsciousness, we acted all of our favorite scenes from the movie we had just seen. Sometimes I became Jeanette McDonald singing the "Indian Love Call," Rhett and Scarlett's daughter falling off a horse, or Esther Williams gliding through the perfect waves in her smooth bathing cap. It usually took us over an hour to complete the fifteen-minute walk. Much time was used up arguing about which scene we should do next or who was going to get the best part. Bobbi was better at acting, but I was better at remembering the scenes. We loved our small lives, and to this day I am still remembering my lines.

➯ In 1859, Saint Paul reported that the Métis brought more than 500 fur-laden carts from the Red River area and spent $100,000 in the city.

OCTOBER

S	M	T	W	T	F	S
27	28	29	30	1	2	3
4	5	6	7	8	9	10
11	12	13	14	15	16	17
18	19	20	21	22	23	24
25	26	27	28	29	30	31

12 Monday

Indigenous People's Day

13 Tuesday

14 Wednesday

15 Thursday

Photo © Patricia Bour-Schilla

Fishing the Mississippi River in October at Hidden Falls

16 FRIDAY	
17 SATURDAY	Saint Paul Farmers' Market Zoo Boo
18 SUNDAY	Saint Paul Farmers' Market Zoo Boo

OCTOBER

President Dwight Eisenhower made a speech in Rice Park on October 16, 1956.

COMPAS (COMMUNITY PROGRAMS IN THE ARTS)

Daniel Gabriel

One by one, they read their pieces—the tall, slender girl in the billowing robes and headscarf, the bouncing, gap-toothed second grader with the sly humor, the swaggering teen in the hoody ripping off rhymes about the streets—and then they flee the stage, stunned at the rising applause that envelops Landmark Center's columned cortile. Every December this scene is played out again with different actors, as COMPAS's annual Anthology of Student Writing brings young writers from across the state into downtown Saint Paul.

On a steaming July day, a dozen young musicians splay across Ecolab Plaza, belting out proto-jazz that slides into hip-hop, followed by a slow ballad tinged with mournful violin. The COMPAS ArtsWork apprentices are hard at work, demonstrating chops and possibilities that will lead them forward into future jobs, or passions, or any manner of new discoveries.

In over one hundred schools across the state, COMPAS artists are at work each year, producing arts projects that connect kids with unnoticed talents, with broader horizons, with penetrating questions and deeper understandings of both ancient and contemporary cultures. Poets, dancers, sculptors, muralists, photographers—here is where the connection happens and where tomorrow's catalysts are conjured. Graffiti art murals redefine a school's image. Landfill robots transform garbage into art. Reed pens are dipped in ink and slid across Egyptian-style papyrus to create fresh hieroglyphics of the heart.

In hospital rooms where patients struggle to regain muscle memory, mental balance, or a clear sense of why their life is ending, there are COMPAS artists teaching them how to use a mural, or a dance, or a slice of graphic memoir to come to terms with the curves life has thrown at them. Here the arts are a lifeline, a re-imagining . . . a ladder, perhaps, to heaven.

The COMPAS offices have been on the third floor of Landmark Center since the building first re-opened in the 1970s. But the work of COMPAS is all around: check out the mural on the side of the old Schmidt Brewery. Watch the mosaic project developing in McDonough Rec Center. Peek in the window of a dozen different Saint Paul schools. For that matter, next time you attend a local theater performance, visit a gallery, or watch a

Photo © COMPAS

COMPAS artist Leo Lara works with Saint Paul Public School students

dance troupe transport you to another time and place . . . check out their funding sources. There's a good chance COMPAS had a hand in making it happen.

And you wonder why I like to work here? COMPAS has a roster of over sixty artists doing residencies through Writers & Artists in the Schools, as well as another fifty individuals and groups from around the world who work in the Global Arts & Culture program. Toss in an arts-crazed staff, and you have a roiling stew of creativity and connections to many of the hottest happenings in town.

Artists see the world from perspectives beyond the usual horizons. And once they've dug within themselves to give expression to work of their own, so does everybody else.

➯ A century ago, Griggs, Cooper & Company and Dickerman donated and dedicated Dickerman Park, located at University and Fairview avenues.

OCTOBER

S	M	T	W	T	F	S
27	28	29	30	1	2	3
4	5	6	7	8	9	10
11	12	13	14	15	16	17
18	19	20	21	22	23	24
25	26	27	28	29	30	31

19 Monday

20 Tuesday

21 Wednesday

22 Thursday

Photo © Patricia Bour-Schilla

Jax Building in Lowertown: popular building for artists' studios

23 FRIDAY	Zoo Boo Fourth Friday at the Movies
24 SATURDAY	Saint Paul Farmers' Market Zoo Boo
25 SUNDAY	Saint Paul Farmers' Market Zoo Boo Dia de los Muertos Family Fiesta Great Pumpkin Festival

1974: Women's Advocates, the first battered women's shelter in the country, opened in Saint Paul. Now there are hundreds nationwide.

BRAND NAMES

Phebe Hanson

"When to the sessions of sweet, silent thought,
I summon up remembrance of things past . . ."
—Shakespeare, *Sonnet XXX*

I am driving down Grand Avenue, hoping
for a red light, so I can put on my lipstick,
Revlon's "Mauve Mystique," whose smell
summons up my first date with you.

March 1, 1948. I wore Revlon's "Fire and Ice,"
borrowed from my sophisticated friend Irene,
because my father disapproved of any makeup
("Be happy with the natural color God gave you").

I wore a borrowed dress, too, a "Jonathon Logan,"
black crepe sheath, long and sinuous and clingy,
and borrowed perfume, "Tigress" by Fabergé,
rich, musky scent promising delights of the flesh.

Only my bra belonged to me, pale blue nylon
"Permalift," bought at Dayton's with money I'd
earned as a summer girl in White Bear Lake, and
matching blue panties trimmed with delicate lace.

As I sat beside you in the Edyth Bush Theater
watching *Street Scene*, Elmer Rice's 1930s play,
the "Tigress" wafted up to us its message of passion,
while the "Permalift" kept my breasts firm and safe.

"Put brand names into poems," Jim White once
said to his class, and his poems are still alive even
though he's been dead now for twenty years, his
body crumbled almost to dust, as has my love for you.

What's left is the remembrance of all our years together
and the poems I write to keep the memories alive.

ALLITERATIVE ANALYSIS & ASSESSMENT OF (MPR) ANNOUNCERS

T. R. Lacy

Lost in the thicket of
Extraneous verbiage is some
Vital verification, from some
Announcers, concerning the
Classical composers, their
Compositions, conductors, *etc.*

That's often missing! Not needed are the
Clichés, the contrived and the convoluted
Recollections from the
Anchor's sunken childhood.

What's needed, along with fewer
Painfully persistent pledge pitches, is an
Antidote to the asinine allusions and
Atrophied anecdotes. Amen.

➩ Anne Bilansky of Saint Paul, who was convicted of murdering her husband, was hung in March 1860, the only woman ever executed in Minnesota.

OCTOBER

S	M	T	W	T	F	S
27	28	29	30	1	2	3
4	5	6	7	8	9	10
11	12	13	14	15	16	17
18	19	20	21	22	23	24
25	26	27	28	29	30	31

26 MONDAY

27 TUESDAY

28 WEDNESDAY

29 THURSDAY

Photo © Tom Conlon

Brooks Building (originally Merchants National Bank, 1892) and Galtier Plaza on Jackson Street

30 FRIDAY

31 SATURDAY — Saint Paul Farmers' Market

Halloween

1 SUNDAY — Saint Paul Farmers' Market

The final run for streetcars in Saint Paul was on October 31, 1953.

FOURTH FRIDAY AT THE MOVIES

Dwight Hobbes

Mahmoud El-Kati, Twin Cities historian and scholar, revered in African American communities as a griot, *offers a splendid film series, Fourth Friday at the Movies, with Saint Paul's Golden Thyme Coffee Café, of long-obscured contributions to national and international cinema by Black producers, directors, screenwriters, actors, and technicians.*

Mahmoud El-Kati spoke at length with Dwight Hobbes about Fourth Friday at the Movies.

DWIGHT HOBBES [DH]: Whose brainstorm was it to have Fourth Friday at the Movies?

MAHMOUD EL-KATI: It's germinated a while. At Golden Thyme, that's my favorite spot, and they happen to be proprietors as well as friends. So, this was not like I walked in one day with this idea and said, "Let's have this film series." It grew from a conversation between Mychael Wright and myself, just trying to do good things for the community in the same vein that Golden Thyme sponsors the Jazz Festival, that kind of stuff. Right along those lines. It's not my idea as such, okay? It's collaboration. It evolved out of conversation.

DH: So, the two of you got to kickin' it back and forth and somebody made a move to do something about it.

EL-KATI: Somethin' like that . . . We agreed it's a good idea . . . in doing these films, first of all, to [sustain] a little bit of community around Black films. To build a sense of what was going on prior to the 1960s, prior to "Blaxploitation."

DH: Now, wait a minute. How you just gon' come with that? There were exceptions. Not everything in those days was about being "superbad." You have *Across 110th Street*, a fine detective movie. And *Superfly*, despite the goofy title, was about an individual outwitting the system, including corrupt police and politicians.

EL-KATI: I won't argue that. Still, we decided to begin at the beginning. When Edison was makin' movies, you had Black folks in them. When the movie industry was in New Jersey, that's where it started, before certain forces moved filmmaking to Hollywood, California. By the 1920s, filmmaking became the institution as we know it. African Americans were in films almost since day one. As part of the ambiance, background, and all that.

Photo © Tobechi Tobechukwu

Golden Thyme Coffee Café

DH: Butlers, maids, slaves, and such.

EL-KATI: Yeah, okay.

DH: Well, they wasn't playin' presidents.

EL-KATI: Up pops the collection of Black filmmakers. It's a remarkable story, because what parallels Black filmmaking is the fact that there were Black movie theaters owned by Black people. At one point, during the 1920s and 1930s, there were roughly a hundred spaces or movie houses that were Black owned. A classic such theater still stands in Macon, Georgia. The theater was named the Douglas Theater, which has been refurbished, and still stands in its original location. My mom saw Bessie Smith on stage as a teenager at one of these theaters in Savannah, Georgia—the Pekan Theater—that was owned by a Black woman. I myself as a high school student in Miami, Florida, often attended the Lyric Theatre, which was built from the ground up and owned by a Black man. It still stands today on Second Avenue in Miami. It has been renovated and is now an African American historic site.

DH: So, it was theaters where they showed movies and had performers.

EL-KATI: Yeah.

DH: How's Fourth Friday being received?

EL-KATI: Good. Growing response—we've had a lot of people in that little space . . . In addition to showing the movies, there's the educational piece underneath this. We want to educate ourselves on our role in the history of filmmaking. For instance, Spencer Williams, whom you and I have seen on television as Andy in *Amos 'n' Andy*, was a brilliant director of many Black films, and occasionally acted in them. He was a pioneer in Black filmmaking. What the world didn't know was that Williams had a huge name in the Black community before *Amos 'n' Andy*. One of the unintended benefits of the oppressive system of segregation has to do with showcasing Black celebrity within this segregated environment. Back then, there were these bigger-than-life names that the outside world did not know, such as producer/director/screenwriter Oscar Micheaux. Mr. Micheaux produced, directed, and acted in Black films for more than thirty years. He made more than three dozen films over that span of time. Black filmmaking lasted in some form from 1915 to the end of the 1950s. What has educational value here for viewers of Fourth Friday at the Movies is that a whole range of human emotions and experiences are revealed in these films. Unlike today, they were not stereotyped and confined to the urban ghetto. Among the genres of these films were love stories, stories of religious and rural life, street and intellectual life, murder mysteries, and even sports—all of what you don't see today that Black people do in their full complexities. For instance, love triangles, cowboy stories. We showed a cowboy movie last year starring Herb Jeffries. The larger society knew Herb Jeffries as a silver-voiced supperclub singer. I'm now trying to find a particular film starring Ralph Cooper titled *Murder on Lennox Avenue*. Ralph Cooper was perhaps the most popular star in these films made for the most part for and by Black people.

DH: Just how long has Fourth Fridays been going on?

EL-KATI: About two years.

DH: Are white folk allowed to attend?

EL-KATI: Of course. Why would you even bring something like that up?

DH: Well, it's about Black people connecting to their culture and history. Aside from it being illegal to discriminate, why have them there?

EL-KATI: "Understanding is the best thing in the world," said Ray Charles. So they can understand. Part of the showing of these films has to do with understanding, has to do with those minds that are curious. It's for everybody who wishes to reach understanding. People who come, whoever they may be, are sure to get a rich experience. It will certainly blow their minds to see the kind of movies that Black people made historically. Those who have come seem to appreciate it.

DH: The socializing time before and after the screenings, what has that amounted to?

EL-KATI: People talk. They connect. I can't say in any scientific way, but from conversations I've overheard people say they're getting something out of the experience. That it's been beneficial. They say so themselves, that they enjoy it, that they've learned things, and I think that is wonderful.

DH: Can't argue with that.

EL-KATI: No, you can't. It's been and continues to be a positive experience. For everyone involved.

Fourth Friday at the Movies

Fourth Friday of each month
6:30 p.m. Social hour
7 p.m. Film showing
Golden Thyme Coffee Café
921 Selby Avenue
651.645.1340

CHOOSING SAINT PAUL

James McKenzie

Moving to Saint Paul during my sixty-fifth year represents the first time I have had the joy of selecting the community I live in, rather than following the dictates of circumstance. Famously a nation of immigrants, we are also nomads. Born and raised in western Pennsylvania's Monongahela Valley steel towns, I've also lived around the American South and Hawaii (the army), Indiana, and North Dakota, before getting to choose Saint Paul.

It was not a difficult choice, one made easier by my wife's landing a good, challenging, job at a Saint Paul nonprofit with a national mission. I was ready to leave academe and had but two criteria for relocation: that we be no farther from a daughter and grandchildren in North Dakota than the Twin Cities, and that we live no more than a half-mile walk from good coffee and a daily *New York Times.* I wanted to come home to "city," I realize now, not yet quite understanding how good that would be.

I felt my first rush of familiarity when we stayed at what is now the downtown Crowne Plaza Hotel for Patti's job interview. Looking out over Kellogg Boulevard and beyond, I liked the curving line of hills, the railroad tracks and lines of traffic hugging the river, the sprawl of industrial buildings and warehouses in the distance, and most of all, the signs of a working river: barges and a fleet of excursion boats, multiple bridges of different designs, especially the dark, heavy steel mechanisms of the railroad lift bridge just west of the concrete arches of the Robert Street span. I had once lived on Pittsburgh's Bluff Street, high above the Monongahela, and gazed down upon a similar spread of landscape. I felt a frisson of recognition, staring down at the cliff on the downtown side of the Wabasha Bridge, the bare rocks of Dayton's Bluff in the distance.

But I have chosen Saint Paul, not Pittsburgh. The sky is bigger here; sunnier, and more often blue. Cass Gilbert's white dome and that gold quadriga glistening above the downtown, surrounded by all those other government buildings, reminds me I'm in the state capital, the city where Minnesota's collective will, with all the necessary pushing and tugging, the compromising and negotiation, is officially enacted. The curved hatches on the Mississippi barges of Lowertown remind me that we also inhabit a grain capital—all that wheat, barley, and oats from Minnesota, Dakota, and Wisconsin farms.

Photo © Patricia Bour-Schilla

St. Paul Corner Drug: still just a nickel for a cup of coffee

My neighborhood retirement criteria turned out to deliver far more than coffee and the *Times* and may offer a litmus test for others contemplating relocations in this new century of changing consciousness about our environment. It is possible to live almost entirely on foot in Mac-Groveland. I've never counted all the bus routes, dry cleaners, good pizza shops, churches, and restaurants—Afghan, Mediterranean, Italian, Thai, Puerto Rican, Vietnamese, the fifty-one-year-old Saint Clair Broiler, for a start—much less how many good coffee shops and *Times* venues my feet can carry me to. Here are a few walkable destinations: Saint Paul's two remaining movie theatres (Grandview and Highland), two library branches, two guitar stores, three hardware stores, a locksmith, two dance studios, a shoe repair shop, several liquor stores (one selling only wine), a small animal clinic, two medical clinics, an antiques mall, Mississippi Market, the Saint Paul Corner Drug Store with its nickel-a-cup coffee counter since 1922. Dozens and dozens more, all on my extended campus.

Before moving to Saint Paul, I dug up a Norway maple seedling from the alley behind our North Dakota home. It's an offspring of another seedling I'd brought from my Monongahela Valley home, planted by my grandfather in 1914, the year my mother was born. I'd climbed in four of them in front of our western Pennsylvania home as a child and wanted

Photo © Larry Schilla

The railroad lift bridge crosses the Mississippi River with the Robert Street Bridge just behind it

some continuity with those Norway maples on the upper Great Plains. I know the Norway maple is not indigenous, though there are now many in Saint Paul. Nor can it provide the sense of belonging that Mdewakanton Sioux descendants of Chief Wabasha must feel still in the Mississippi and Minnesota valleys. But that transplanted maple provides another anchor, makes me feel less nomadic. I promise I'll not let it spread. And we have planted a prairie garden opposite that Norway.

NOVEMBER

Photo © Patricia Bour-Schilla

Downtown Saint Paul Winter Farmers' Market: Saturdays through March

St. Martin's Day: November 8

Minnesota State High School League Girls' Volleyball Tournament: November 12–14

Fourth Friday at the Movies: November 27

Minnesota Hmong New Year: November 27–29

See pages 288–310 for more information and more events

➪ Paul Molitor, baseball player from Saint Paul, had 3,319 hits in his career, which puts him in eighth place in the record books.

NOVEMBER

S	M	T	W	T	F	S
1	2	3	4	5	6	7
8	9	10	11	12	13	14
15	16	17	18	19	20	21
22	23	24	25	26	27	28
29	30	1	2	3	4	5

2 MONDAY

3 TUESDAY

4 WEDNESDAY

5 THURSDAY

Photo © Patricia Bour-Schilla

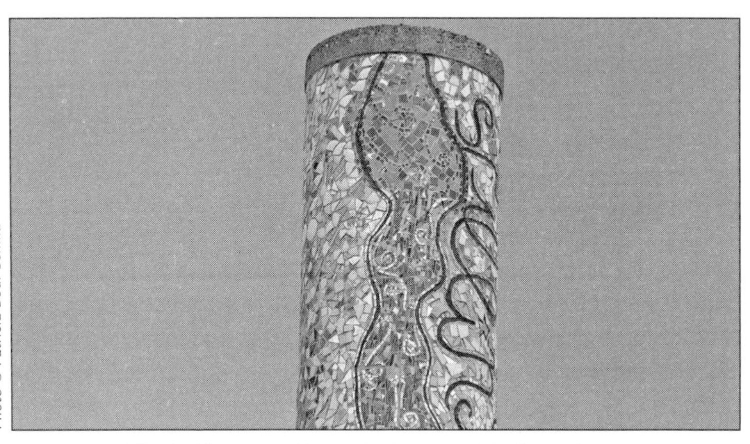

Mosaic chimney on University Avenue at Farrington Street

6 FRIDAY

7 SATURDAY — Saint Paul Farmers' Market

8 SUNDAY — St. Martin's Day

NOVEMBER

"We cannot park the Green Bus"—Rev. Darryl Spence, Saint Paul African American activist and God Squad member

SERLIN'S CAFÉ

Bob Knutson

Serlin's Café is misnamed. It should be called Comfort Café. When my friends and I are tired of eating alfalfa sprouts and arugula and weak green tea and want comfort for lunch, we go to Serlin's Café. The comfort comes not because of the booths, which are wooden, stiff-backed cells lining the sides of this small eatery, the same as they did in 1946, when the café was opened by Irving Serlin after he finished cooking for the U. S. Navy. The comfort comes from the apple pies and meat and mashed potatoes and gravy and lemon meringue pies, with two inches of tanned meringue on top, and cabbage rolls and rhubarb pies and eggs and bacon and toast with jelly and banana cream pies and blueberry pies.

D'ya get the idea they specialize in pies? Not only that—they are the best pies in the world, and that comes from an expert pie-eater who has eaten them all over the world, including my mom's. For Thanksgiving they bake over 150 pumpkin, apple, and mince pies by special requests that must be made about a week before. They begin the crust dough the night before they're baked, using a special pie-roller that was really made for making pasta. And then they somehow or other put water in with the lard-filled crust so that the crust comes out flaky, tanned, crispy, crunchy, light, impossible not to finish.

They are closed on Sundays, but on other days they open at six in the morning for breakfast, and when you order "a couple of eggs, over easy," you get three with a slice of bacon. And for lunches, if you can take it, there are the ordinary entrées, like pork sandwiches and pot roast and turkey and chicken.

This is making me so hungry I can't go on. Excuse me while I dial Serlin's at 651.776.9003, located at 1124 Payne Avenue. If I'm lucky, I can park on the street, right in front.

Photo © Lou "The Photo Guy" Michaels

EIGHT-LAYER JELL-O SALAD

Phyllis Abbott

8 pkgs. Jell-O. Two each of lime, lemon, orange, strawberry, or other red.
4 each 3 oz. pkg. cream cheese

Start with 1 pkg. lime Jell-O. Dissolve in ¾ cup boiling water. Pour into 9 inch x 13 inch pan; set until solid. Next layer: 1 pkg. Lime Jell-O dissolved in 1¾ cup boiling water; add 1 pkg. cream cheese (softened) and whip in blender or mixer. Pour and let stand overnight. Repeat with each color. May take 4 days. Makes a large salad. Keeps well and is very pretty.

Knox Presbyterian Church Cookbook (1985)

➭ Fifty years ago, Buddy Holly, Richie Valens, and the Big Bopper appeared at Saint Paul's Prom Center on January 28 at a special teen hop.

NOVEMBER

S	M	T	W	T	F	S
1	2	3	4	5	6	7
8	9	10	11	12	13	14
15	16	17	18	19	20	21
22	23	24	25	26	27	28
29	30	1	2	3	4	5

9 MONDAY

10 TUESDAY

11 WEDNESDAY

Veterans Day

12 THURSDAY

Minnesota State High School League
Girls' Volleyball Tournament

NOVEMBER

Photo © Patricia Bour-Schilla

Scrap-metal pile on Mississippi River at Childs and Shepard roads

13 Friday	Minnesota State High School League Girls' Volleyball Tournament
14 Saturday	Saint Paul Farmers' Market Minnesota State High School League Girls' Volleyball Tournament
15 Sunday	

"Winter is not a season, it's an occupation."
—Sinclair Lewis

WALKING SAINT PAUL

Kristine Price

Immodestly, sometimes I admit I have good legs but give the credit to growing up in Saint Paul, to place as much as genetics. Every metal grate I poked a stick in; every incongruous staircase jutting out of Summit Hill I climbed; every long walk running my hand along old stone walls, made them.

When Dad moved out, my exploring began. Someone said he had a room at the University Club. After school at St. Luke's, I'd walk up and down Summit Avenue, hoping to find him, the grand street unfolding before me like a great spool of thread I could unravel as far as I dared. My second hope was to spot the governor, but I never saw him either. Eventually I gave up on both, but my wanderlust remained.

In Catechism, I dreamed of digging through notions in Bober Drug and smelling the heady scents in Bungalow Bakery. Doing piano drills, I'd form a plan to stroll past Molitor's house once I ducked past the convent, hoping to catch a glimpse of Paul. Finally, there'd be the wide lawn to cross at Our Lady of Peace, the broad staircase to climb at the Greek Orthodox Church, and the spooky Christian Brothers house to run past before turning for home, where life was willy-nilly, and the mice won the fight for the food.

On nice days, I'd make it as far as the cathedral, where they said JFK had sat in a pew. I spent a lot of time looking for his name on the little gold plates on the pews. Other days, I went downtown to the library, trying to decide between the Selby and the Grand bus. In summer, my sister and I would take the bus down to the squash-colored health center at Wabasha and Tenth, where you could get a monstrously big silver filling and lose it on the caramel corn at Candyland, all in the same afternoon. We'd gape at *Tyrannosaurus rex* in the old museum, run through the library, and ride the glass-windowed elevator to the top of the Hilton until they kicked us out. Undaunted, we would take the bus to the Midway and Montgomery Ward.

Mom told me stories about the old days, so when it was too cold to walk, there was folklore to fuel my imagination. I pictured the F. Scott Fitzgeralds having parties in their row house on Summit, and gangsters hiding out on West Seventh. At night, I worried about Ma Barker rolling into town, and shuddered at the thought of Dillinger lurking behind curtained windows, tommy gun in hand. Like other kids, I went on field trips to the Capitol, but unlike many, I was lucky enough to discover the

Photo © Patricia Bour-Schilla

John F. Kennedy plaque at the Cathedral of Saint Paul

existence of a half-hidden candy store in Rondo, where I could cash in pop bottles and buy penny candy.

I dreamed about the Thompson murder and the Iverson kidnapping, fixtures of my youth, and in my dreams, I gave them different endings. Someone would answer a door in Highland Park in time, and someone else would never have answered the knock on hers at all. Grinning black-faced Vulcans appeared in winter dreams, planting greasy black marks on my cheek. Ghosts of railroad tycoons, presidents, and gangsters peppered my history.

We live in the country now, amidst rolling land and the reassuring sight of farms. But my memories of Saint Paul, with all of its nooks and crannies, walls and stairs, Indian mounds, caves, and bluffs roil through my blood the most. I content myself with Sunday drives in Saint Paul, my legs less willing than before to take me on those golden walks. I wonder if, in the hearts of uprooted Saint Paulites, there lies a hidden plan to return. Like me, do they dream of going back, because no place else ever quite measured up?

NOVEMBER

S	M	T	W	T	F	S
1	2	3	4	5	6	7
8	9	10	11	12	13	14
15	16	17	18	19	20	21
22	23	24	25	26	27	28
29	30	1	2	3	4	5

➩ Fifty years ago, the Science Museum became one of only four museums in the world to have a complete Triceratops skeleton.

16 Monday

17 Tuesday

18 Wednesday

19 Thursday

Photo © Patricia Bour-Schilla

Jewish cemetery in Phalen neighborhood

20 FRIDAY

21 SATURDAY

Saint Paul Farmers' Market

22 SUNDAY

"It's a treat to beat your feet on the Mississippi mud." —James Cavanaugh, songwriter, paying tribute to Saint Paul's beauty.

This year, Saint Paul Public Schools, with the sponsorship of the Saint Paul Almanac, *held a writing contest for its students. Students shared their experiences of Saint Paul, which included neighborhood stories, coming to America, and personal observations of Saint Paul. The stories remind us of the uniqueness and richness of our city.*

SCARED TO DEATH IN SAINT PAUL

Su mya Naing
8th grade
Cleveland Junior High
Teacher Liz McCambridge

When my family first moved to America a few years ago, I remember going to the bathroom with my sister. When we first arrived at our apartment, my sister and I went directly to the bathroom because when we were in the taxicab there wasn't any bathroom at all. When we were in the bathroom we didn't even know where the toilet was or what the toilet looked like. My sister wanted to pee so much that she started peeing in the bathtub, and of course I did that too. Then we washed the pee with water from the sink because we were afraid that the bathroom might explode if we used the faucet that was above the bathtub. When we were about to get out of the bathroom, the door was locked. We pounded at the door as hard as we could. I guess nobody heard us because our apartment was full of Karen people. In the bathroom my sister almost cried just because we couldn't unlock the door. After awhile someone used a spoon to unlock the door and she laughed when she saw us crying and I don't even know why she laughed at us while we were scared to death in the bathroom.

MEMORIES IN SAINT PAUL

See Thao
8th Grade
Cleveland Junior High
Teacher Liz McCambridge

These are some places and memories in Saint Paul that I remember the most. The people in my story are important to me because they are special in many ways. There are a lot of places in Saint Paul to visit and have fun.

The first place is Mounds Park. It is a great place to go sightseeing, especially at night. You see lights and funny "Got Milk?" billboards, highways, speeding cars, and much more. It's best when your friends are there and you're drinking pop, eating junk food, and telling dumb knock-knock jokes. It never happens because my friends have curfews so I do it with my sisters. We go often, usually summertime because it feels good to be outside and feeling the breeze.

Phalen Lake is also a fun place to hang out. My cousins and I usually go walking and exercising around Phalen Lake. We celebrate birthdays there because it has a lot of open space to have cake fights, play volleyball, soccer, and Frisbee. You can do many things at Phalen Lake in the spring and summer.

Como Zoo is so cool. I love the rides and monkeys too. It's a neat place to go with little kids. I go with my nieces and nephews because they run around and laugh at dumb things. It makes me feel like a kid again because it's fun riding the rides with them. Kids brighten up a boring day sometimes.

The most memorable place is RiverCentre. The Hmong New Year is celebrated there every year. It's a crowded place with a lot of colorful clothing and the best of all, FOOD! I love the food because it's so good, to me. My family goes there to see the Hmong pageants. It's a wonderful place to spend time.

These are the most memorable places I've gone to. These places are wonderful and I think they are worth visiting and spending time. It's even better if you're with someone.

➯ A century ago, work began on the Church of St. Agnes. It took three years to complete the baroque-style structure at 548 LaFond.

NOVEMBER

S	M	T	W	T	F	S
1	2	3	4	5	6	7
8	9	10	11	12	13	14
15	16	17	18	19	20	21
22	23	24	25	26	27	28
29	30	1	2	3	4	5

23 Monday

24 Tuesday

25 Wednesday

26 Thursday

Thanksgiving Day

Photo © Patricia Bour-Schilla

View of First National Bank from Shepard Road

27 FRIDAY

Minnesota Hmong New Year

Fourth Friday at the Movies

28 SATURDAY

Saint Paul Farmers' Market

Eid al-Adha

Minnesota Hmong New Year

29 SUNDAY

Minnesota Hmong New Year

"The subject matter is so much more important than the photographer." —Gordon Parks, Saint Paul photographer

FROM *THE FLORIST'S DAUGHTER*

Patricia Hampl

St. Paul had poetry running in the gutters. Its neighborhoods—Irvine Park, Crocus Hill, Mac Groveland, Ramsey Hill, West Seventh—were marked by the illogic of the city's fierce begetting as a French and Indian fur-trading river town originally named by a half-blind whiskey runner: Pig's Eye. Leo the Lion loved that—*we started as a bar*.

Numbered streets crossed each other fecklessly, as if city planners had used a scribble rather than a grid as a template. This was nothing like the tidy squaring of numbered avenues and alphabetical street names that Scandinavian Minneapolis laid like a crosshatched veil over the flat features of its city.

The St. Paul streetlights dissipated their glow rather than truly shed it on the crusted snowbanks. This was strangely beguiling—that light could be conscripted into the service of obscurity, a St. Paul trick. In November, the October blaze of elms and maples was finished, and the bleached, beseeching gray bones of the leafless trees were ranked the length of Summit Avenue, going from church to church, past the old mansions. A faint tea-dance violin floated over it all. *Yes*, one of the nuns at my convent school said, *I danced with Scott at the cotillion . . .*

The damp powder of speakeasy passions and forsaken gangster parties rose from the drenched lilacs in May, and in winter we walked to school through the monastic snow. One of the Irish great-aunts had lived in an apartment on Lexington near Summit for a while. When she moved out, Dillinger moved in. And, my mother delighted in saying, when Dillinger moved out, he moved out shooting. We were proud of our gangster past. Crooks and killers, hoodlums and bank robbers were airbrushed by time, made into lost movie stars from old St. Paul where the cops let them lie low as long as they behaved themselves here.

What a romantic city it was, full of believers, wrapped in pride and insecurity, those protons of provincial complacency. We pulled the blanket of winter around us, we clicked shut the wooden blinds of summer against the killing heat. But our drama was all just weather, the swatted mosquitoes of summer, the dripping ice dams of winter. Our lives were little, our weather big.

A provincial capital of a middling sort as I read with unhappy recognition in Gogol during my Russian period in high school. St. Paul was somehow Russian—I sensed that—minus the aristocrats. Or maybe we had those too. We had Summit Avenue, we had Scott Fitzgerald to draw the blood of class consciousness.

St. Paul was so baroquely Catholic that even Lutherans described themselves as being "non-Catholic." St. Paul Jews, when giving their address, might say, if you didn't recognize the street name, "You know, Sacred Heart," indicating a parish boundary. No one thought this odd.

In some cities, the rare lyric ones, alley shadows and the golden clots cast from octagonal streetlights convey light and shade like communiqués to be decoded, their meanings illusive but provocative. Such fragile civic mysteries hold a promise of things to come—though in St. Paul there was always the sense that everything was happening elsewhere. Or that everything had *already* happened. We were living in an aftermath.

But an aftermath of what? Maybe the great robber-baron age that branded Scott Fitzgerald, the brash age that had cast upon the bluffs of the city the beefy Victorian mansions of Summit Avenue. This was our primary proof of (former) greatness—the brooding piles of Summit Avenue from the age of James J. Hill. "The Empire Builder," my father said, always adding this phrase like a royal title that must be accorded the railroad titan, our Carnegie, our Rockefeller.

But his admiration was tinged with regretful disapproval. As a young man in the thirties, he had been union shop steward at the greenhouse. He believed in the common good. He could never quite understand greed or ambition, not even raw entrepreneurial instinct. He preferred to think such things didn't exist or existed only as imprecise abstractions, not pulsing within the human heart. Not in St. Paul. Not in his town, which was his world. Like all big-time qualities, they resided . . . elsewhere. Not here in the blameless middle.

The Florist's Daughter, *(Houghton Mifflin Harcourt Publishing, $13.95), available at your local bookstore.*

GENERATION AFTER GENERATION

Tou SaiKo Lee

Generation after generation
we've been warned by the elders.
Lost in what is, who we are,
You see, the ignorant youth denies the truth
of their identity,
how free can you be?
the thrusting trees collapse around you,
impacts shatter your pathways,
earthquakes of racism destroy the worth of what's left
on what you stand on,
balancing on these here vibrations,
generation after generation.

Some of our people stay on, some fall off.
I barely held on to the ledge
with ignorance repeatedly stepping on my fingers.
Temptations for self-destruction and
corruption erupt tremendous tremors that
break us away from our bloodline.
Crumbling from existence,
casualties cause cracks in our culture,
like deep wounds that won't stop bleeding.

A healing process that's oppressed and
keeps us from succeeding,
leaving visible scars in abstract shapes
that shape us into what we are.
We shouldn't be forced into knowing our culture,
We should be encouraged,
but first of all we have to
recognize, realize, and identify.

Once I realized what I was it was like an
explosion of emotions.
The blood of my ancestors bursts through my veins,
tidal waves of sublime blood flushing out the

deep-rooted pollution that is my ignorance,
was my ignorance.

I can't express how much pride that I have inside,
Warriors united side by side.
We collide with creativity,
the artistic purity of details intricately interwoven
colors and designs that define unique identity
into our traditional clothing.

Divine dimensions of eternal stories gripping the
piecing thorns throughout our times,
letting it drip down our fingers and splatter to
artistic puddles of
endless emotions on a cloth we
call: *paj ntaub*.

The poetic motion rising and collapsing
cruising steady and overlapping,
flowing like waves of an ocean filled with rice wine.
Drunk off the vision,
thirsting for our attention to an effervescent extension
of the beautiful hypnotizing, traditional dances.

What I call old school spoken word,
in terms of relating to our own culture,
the poetic chants that echo the deepest of devotion,
desperation, despair, depression, death and love.

The melodic symbolic words
vibrate through us internally,
Verbally crushing our emotional senses
bursting to multiple tears,
felt from our own life years.
We call it: *kwv txiaj*.

the food and celebrations,
never had a country of our own,
no place to call home,
we come together for New Year's and
soccer tournaments to create our own nation,

the passion we have for our families,
how we unite at times of devastation,

Respect your bloodline.
It's sacred, you see the sacrifices that were made so
we could have a chance to make it,
so we could even exist,
the perseverance of our people through history
has to be a mystery.
Been through slicing blades from invasions,
been through fatal storms lightning striking our newborns,
been through
the pain that's ingrained in our brains,
been through hot steel penetrating our souls,
walked miles and miles on bare feet,
cold suffering flesh scorched by the sun,
diminished life force,
all we have are our sons . . . our daughters,
our family pride.
For those who don't know it's a dying culture that
we're facing generation after generation.

I'll admit that my second tongue has been eclipsing my
first since birth or since first grade,
And I've been slowly struggling to replenish it.
Look closely into your own mental reflections
and maybe you'll find cracks
of lost pride and identity,
but this broken mirror can extend beyond seven years,
these cracks could eliminate our culture forever.

The spiritual essence of our people
is what gives me life.
The spiritual essence of our people
is what makes us free.
The spiritual essence of our people
is the reason we have survived.
Clashing cultures divide us

The fate of our culture depends on our future.
Educating our youth to embrace and

acknowledge their roots.
Support the cause,
the struggle,
the shining life force.
Our culture is immortal.
Sacred souls of ancestors preserved in salvation
generation after generation.

CHALLENGES IN SAINT PAUL

Najla M.

Living in the United States is a big challenge to me and to other newcomers. Basically, there are different living conditions: culture, weather, thoughts, and, of course, a new language.

The most difficult of these conditions that I faced was the weather in Saint Paul, especially in the wintertime. I came from a hot climate. I don't like this harsh weather because I freeze every day at the bus stop when I go to school or when I have any errands. Also, I see some people fall down on the street because the ground is slippery. So far, I've fallen once and it was embarrassing.

On the other hand, there is one good thing about winter in Saint Paul. When the sun shines on the white shiny snow, the scene reflects one of peace and purity.

Another challenge is learning the English language. As anyone knows who moves here from another country, speaking English is very important. First of all, it helps me communicate with others. Also, English is needed to survive and just make my life easier in this new culture. I know that everything is different and it is not easy to adapt in this new situation, but I will try my best—as I write before in *Saint Paul Almanac 2008*, there's nothing impossible in my life.

The third challenge is to find a job. This job has to fit my skills and put me in a good position. Finally, I am positive that I will adapt to my new environment, overcome all the obstacles, and prosper in Saint Paul.

December

Photo © Minnesota Historical Society

Here on the hill of the crocus
Winter is coming to choke us,
But we shall keep warm
In the teeth of the storm
With coffee, good books, and fast polkas.

—Garrison Keillor

Downtown Saint Paul Winter Farmers' Market: Saturdays through March

Holiday Bazaar: December 3–5

Bouquets Wine Tasting: December 3

SKANDIA: Scandinavian Festival: December 13

Kwanzaa Celebration: December 26

See pages 288–310 for more information and more events

➪ Fifty years ago, Saint Paul's Jeanne Arth teamed with Darlene Hard to win the 1959 Wimbledon doubles championship in tennis.

DECEMBER

S	M	T	W	T	F	S
29	30	1	2	3	4	5
6	7	8	9	10	11	12
13	14	15	16	17	18	19
20	21	22	23	24	25	26
27	28	29	30	31	1	2

30 MONDAY

1 TUESDAY

2 WEDNESDAY

3 THURSDAY

Holiday Bazaar

Bouquets Wine Tasting

DECEMBER

Photo © Patricia Bour-Schilla

The Quadriga on the Capitol

4 FRIDAY Holiday Bazaar

5 SATURDAY Saint Paul Farmers' Market

Holiday Bazaar

6 SUNDAY

DECEMBER

"If you are sure you understand everything that is going on, you are hopelessly confused."—Walter Mondale

NO FINER PLACE FOR SURE

Barbara Haselbeck

In 1964, when Petula Clark's hit song "Downtown" rode the airways, it reflected my sense of what downtown Saint Paul was all about—a place of excitement, distraction, and possibility. My downtown days could be divided into three eras: early childhood, middle childhood, and teen years.

Downtown—no finer place, for sure
Downtown—everything's waiting for you

Downtown was, first of all, the grand department stores: Dayton-Shuneman's (later the revered Dayton's), the Emporium, and the Golden Rule. My grandmother—slender and glamorous with her long red nails and cigarettes—and I would take the bus from her modest Rice Street neighborhood north of town. We roamed the gilded stores, sedately appointed with their marble pillars, brass fixtures, and fine wooden counters. Gliding up the escalator looking at the vast space, people, and counters below or taking a stomach-dropping ride on the fast elevators was as thrilling to me as a ride at a fair. At lunch we sat on red leather swivel stools at Woolworth's lunch counter, eating the day's special or enjoying their 15-cent slices of pizza. I would go home with some gimcrack or a bottle of fingernail polish to seal the memory.

At the age of five, Grandma took me to see Santa at the Golden Rule. A convincing-looking Santa with me sitting on his knee looks out from the sepia commemorative photo. This keepsake was complemented by a $33^1/_3$ vinyl recording of the entire visit. When asked the central question, I said I wanted a Tiny Tears doll and a two-wheeler for Christmas. Every child chose a song to sing: mine was "Away in the Manger."

Don't hang around and let your problems surround you
There are movie shows—downtown

From the age of ten onward, my girlfriends and I would hop on the 12-A bus and twenty minutes later we'd be buying 50-cent tickets at one of four movie theaters. The Paramount and the Orpheum faced each other on old Seventh Street, now Seventh Place between Wabasha and St. Peter; the State and the World (now the Fitzgerald) theaters sat two blocks away, north on Wabasha. Flashing, shapely marquees announced the latest films. My life did not get any more exotic in those days. Where else could you see *Journey to the Center of the Earth* in color with James Mason, Arlene Dahl, and a young Pat Boone? After the movie, we might get a 25-cent hot fudge sundae at Bridgeman's.

Photo © Barbara Haselbeck

Barbara Haselbeck with Santa

On Sundays after Mass, I would read the film ratings, posted in the entryway to the building. The Legion of Decency established the A, A-II, A-III, B (equivalent to today's R-rating), and C ratings. Imagining a movie perverse enough to rate a C was beyond my ken.

So go downtown, things'll be great when you're
Downtown—don't wait a minute more
Downtown—everything's waiting for you.

My last year in high school, 1965–1966, I dressed up and interviewed for a place on Dayton's Teenboard and was selected to represent my school. Each Saint Paul high school, private or public, was represented by a senior girl. Dayton's was beginning to target its marketing to youth, recognizing the approaching tidal wave of baby boomers who were coming of age with their own money. We helped promote Dayton's image as agents of the Youthquake, the marketing concept used in their ads. We modeled Dayton's junior clothing, dancing to pop music, sold their clothes on Saturdays, and published a monthly newsletter featuring styles and tips.

My teenboard experience, the store's savvy and taste, and its local philanthropy made me one of the many loyal customers who still lament the departure of a department store that served as a major artery of the community.

Downtown Saint Paul has changed in many ways since I was in high school and has other features that I value, such as the Farmers' Market and Landmark Center. But as malls have become the new downtowns, it's a pleasure to recall how old downtown Saint Paul broadened my world even as I felt it belonged to me.

➩ On December 7, 1955, Nagasaki, Japan, became Saint Paul's Sister City, the first such partnership between an American and an Asian city.

DECEMBER

S	M	T	W	T	F	S
29	30	1	2	3	4	5
6	7	8	9	10	11	12
13	14	15	16	17	18	19
20	21	22	23	24	25	26
27	28	29	30	31	1	2

7 MONDAY

8 TUESDAY

9 WEDNESDAY

10 THURSDAY

DECEMBER

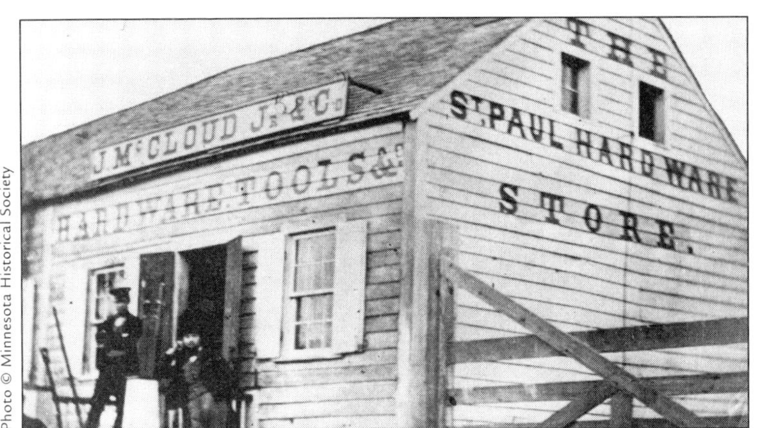

Photo © Minnesota Historical Society

First hardware store in Saint Paul, 1853, situated on Bench Street near Jackson Street

11 FRIDAY

12 SATURDAY
Hanukkah begins

Saint Paul Farmers' Market

13 SUNDAY

SKANDIA: Scandinavian Festival

DECEMBER

Saint Paul-born Edward Lowe created Kitty Litter, using clay instead of sand for the world's domestic cat boxes.

Photo © Patricia Bour-Schilla

José Moreno

The stories on these pages are written by new learners of the English language: recent refugees or immigrants who left their beloved homelands, usually for reasons beyond their control. They have found a new home here and are studying at the Minnesota Literacy Council or other ESL programs in Saint Paul. Their stories are reprinted with permission from the Minnesota Literacy Council's Journeys: An Anthology of Adult Student Writings (2008). *We hope you enjoy reading them and learn a little about the old and new lives of these newest members of our Saint Paul community.*

HOW I DISCOVERED MINNESOTA

José Moreno

José studies English at MORE Multicultural School in Saint Paul.

My name is José Moreno. I was born in Mexico. I came to the U.S.A. in 1983. It was March when I started work in California. I was living there seven years but in 1990 I had few opportunities in my life. In November I went to Seattle, Washington. I was looking for a job, but it was the same thing like California. People on the street with sad faces told me the answer.

Christmas came and I celebrated in the evening. I was talking with an old man and I asked questions and he gave me advice. He told me Minnesota is the best state in the United States I didn't wait. I went to the bus station and bought my ticket to Minneapolis.

New Year's Eve I got here. The good thing was I found two people in the bus station. We were talking about a New Year's party and one of them asked me if I had anything to do and I said no. He invited me to a small party. We were about ten people. The next day we got up late. We had a nice celebration for January 1, 1991.

The owner of the apartment invited me to live in his place. I was so glad I found Minnesota.

Photo © Minnesota Literacy Council

Snow Htoo

I LOVE MY VILLAGE

Snow Htoo

Snow is one of many ethnic Karen (pronounced kah-ren*) refugees forced out of their homeland in Myanmar, formerly known as Burma. She immigrated to Saint Paul, where she is studying English at the Minnesota Literacy Council's learning center on the East Side.*

My name is Snow Htoo. I was born in Burma. I had one brother and one sister. I lived in Burma in my village. My parents worked in the farm. My house was near the field. In my village I didn't go to school. My village is named Eh Oh Klow. I liked it very much because we had many things: animals, trees, hay, and rivers. The river had fish, frogs, crabs, and shrimp. Every day my family caught fish in the river and went to the field.

After my father died, my mother moved to the Karen refugee camp in Thailand because Burmese soldiers came and burned my village and field. I lived in a refugee camp in Thailand. I liked my house because I went to school and studied. In the refugee camp, some people went to school. Some people couldn't go to school because they worked outside the camp and took their families. I worked at home and visited people and children in camp.

I have been in the U.S.A. for eight months, but I never dreamed I would come to the United States. In my first month, the time is changed. Not the same in Thailand and Burma. U.S.A. country is very full of education. I have a difficult time, for I can't speak English but I try to learn more English in this country.

In future I hope I can speak English and have a job because my children go to school and I help my family. I hope my children grow and have education for great ability and strength.

➩ A century ago, the Saint Paul Colored Gophers won the Championship of Black Baseball. One of its stars was Bobby Marshall.

DECEMBER

S	M	T	W	T	F	S
29	30	1	2	3	4	5
6	7	8	9	10	11	12
13	14	15	16	17	18	19
20	21	22	23	24	25	26
27	28	29	30	31	1	2

14 MONDAY

15 TUESDAY

16 WEDNESDAY

17 THURSDAY

DECEMBER

Photo © Tom Conlon

Interior of Nativity Catholic Church in the Mac-Groveland neighborhood

18 FRIDAY

Muharram

19 SATURDAY

Saint Paul Farmers' Market

20 SUNDAY

DECEMBER

Saint Paul's oldest surviving theater space is the Fitzgerald, built in 1910 as the Shubert Theater.

IN RESPONSE TO THE EVANGELIST DOOR-KNOCKING WHO ASKED: *WHAT SAVES YOU?*

Margaret Hasse

Dusk doesn't, dawn does.
Morning splendor,
over and over and over again.
Newspapers don't, with their harpy
human interest stories.
But ah, coffee with milk in a plain white mug . . .

And graves in little cemeteries
in the country, on a hill, with a view.
It's good to think of spirits
having an eye for nature.

Sleep and dreams, the ones remembered,
even dreams about being chased because
that suspicion, that anxiety is given its
own body to run away.

Many books and almost every poem.

What saves often
comes right out of the blue:
a sudden glimpse from a bus
in crowded New York City—
a Lakota woman walking in a jingle dress.

Memory saves, especially random memory
that claims its own borders, its own orders,
makes its own metaphor.

A finger in an atlas seeking a town
on the west coast of Mexico
points to the face of a boy
selling candy on a bus a quarter-century ago

who couldn't talk, who moaned.
Going to work and coming back saves me.
On the Lake Street Bridge spanning the Mississippi,
a man's doing work for us all

waving his hand and his placard:
Support our troops— bring them home.
Honk in solidarity.

Dinner at home last night:
exhausted with meetings and money-making,
I sank into a chair at a table
where all the food was prepared
by my husband and lit by a candle:
salmon with basil and garlic,
deep green beans and a glass of wine.
Dave saying: *I'll rub your feet*
after dinner if you will just lie down
and put them in my lap.

The sight of my two sons saves me
even when they show me their backs.
Today that darkest month,
here in Saint Paul,
it's really cold, down
in the temperature teens.
My real-life teen heads off
to Central High School
at 7 a.m. this morning,
coatless, gloveless, hatless,
his thick dreadlocks
all powdered with snow.

➩ A century ago, the Grandstand at the State Fairgrounds, designed by famed architect Clarence H. Johnston, was constructed.

DECEMBER

S	M	T	W	T	F	S
29	30	1	2	3	4	5
6	7	8	9	10	11	12
13	14	15	16	17	18	19
20	21	22	23	24	25	26
27	28	29	30	31	1	2

21 MONDAY

22 TUESDAY

23 WEDNESDAY

24 THURSDAY

Photo © Patricia Bour-Schilla

The railroad that J. J. Hill built; a caboose at Jackson Street Roundhouse

25 Friday

Christmas Day

26 Saturday

Kwanzaa Begins

Saint Paul Farmers' Market
Kwanzaa Celebration

27 Sunday

DECEMBER

Roger Awsumb began appearing on local television as Casey Jones in May 1954. The show ran until 1973.

TODAY IT WAS BEAUTIFUL OUTSIDE

Michael Teffera

It was Christmas, and this was the first time that I couldn't celebrate it in Ethiopia because I had stayed in Minnesota. My brother, David, was at work. I stayed home alone and opened the window. The weather was beautiful—a forty-degree night. I wanted to go outside.

I picked up my bicycle from downstairs and went out. I rode for an hour from our home at Front Avenue and Rice Street, to downtown Saint Paul. I was so tired. I looked around and I found a seat near a bus station.

I parked my bicycle and sat down for a while. In the meantime, I saw a lady parking her car beside the sidewalk. She had a brand-new Lexus. She came toward me. She appeared to be in her fifties. I thought that she wanted to ask me for directions. But when she reached where I was, she opened her purse and she said, "Merry Christmas." I used to give money to others for Christmas, and now she gave me money.

I took the money and I thanked her very much. I started counting. It was hard to believe. It was $40. I was very surprised. Wow!

An idea came through my mind—I knew a Mexican grill. I went there and I ate a burrito and drank Coca Cola. I stayed there for half an hour. I paid $10 for my meal. Now I had $30 in my pocket, and I decided to buy a bus ticket the next day.

Then I left the restaurant. It was dark, almost seven o'clock. I rode back to my house. While I was riding, I heard a police car's siren behind me. The policeman stopped in front of me. He came toward me. He was angry and asked me for my identification card. He told me it was illegal to ride a bike without a light at night. He gave me a $30 ticket.

Finally, I arrived at my home, enjoying the Christmas day without gaining or losing a cent.

Photo © Patricia Bour-Schilla

GOOBERS

Mary Schauer

Grease jelly roll pan.

Boil:
1 cup light Karo syrup
1 cup light brown sugar
2 Tbsp. butter

Then add:
1½ tsp. salt
1½ cup peanut butter

Mix until smooth, then add 6 cups Special K cereal and mix. Pat in jelly roll pan. Melt 12 oz. pkg. chocolate chips and spread on when warm. Can add crushed nuts on top if you like.

St. Bernard Altar Rosary Society Cookbook

➯ "As we move to assist others, remember it is not what we give them, but how we helped strengthen their own power and ability to positively serve others and self."—Kwame McDonald, Saint Paul African American activist

DECEMBER

S	M	T	W	T	F	S
29	30	1	2	3	4	5
6	7	8	9	10	11	12
13	14	15	16	17	18	19
20	21	22	23	24	25	26
27	28	29	30	31	1	2

28 Monday

29 Tuesday

30 Wednesday

31 Thursday

New Year's Eve

DECEMBER

Photo © Patricia Bour-Schilla

Walleye mural on the Grand Tavern on Grand Avenue

1 FRIDAY

New Year's Day

2 SATURDAY

Saint Paul Farmers' Market

3 SUNDAY

DECEMBER

A century ago, Ellerbe Architects was founded in Saint Paul by Franklin Ellerbe.

FROM *THE LATEHOMECOMER: A HMONG FAMILY MEMOIR*

Kao Kalia Yang

My parents tried their best at English, but their best was not catching up with Dawb's and mine. We were picking up the language faster, and so we became the interpreters and translators for our family dealings with American people. In the beginning, we just did it because it was easier and because we did not want to see them struggle over easy things. They were working hard for the more important things in our lives. Later, we realized so many other cousins and friends were doing the same.

I remember being at the grocery store with my father, buying diapers for Xue. They didn't have his size on the shelves. I hated to speak English outside the house. Even to my cousins I did not like speaking the language. My father was still looking on the shelves. A deep breath. I'm a big sister. It is the least I can do. I had started calling my father "Daddy."

"Daddy, I'll go ask them if they have any in the back."

"I'll go with you."

I put my hand in his, and we walked over to the clerk at the customer service counter. I was self-conscious that my father was going to hear me talk. I could barely see over the top of the counter. I stood on tiptoes, with one hand on the corner for balance. I tried to look brave. I was hesitant and quiet when the words came out.

"Do you have a box of number one Pampers? We didn't see any on the shelf."

I shook my head to support my words. I couldn't trust myself in English; my mother and father could barely trust me.

My father said in a louder voice, "Pampers number one."

He held up one finger. He didn't trust himself in English, either.

The fact that so few people trusted themselves in English was a big problem for my whole extended family. Over time, the kids were invited to the family meetings on how to improve our lives in America. We gathered at an aunt or uncle's house; they usually called the meetings because they were worried that their children were wasting opportunities to become educated people in America. All the young cousins were to learn not to become like the bad older cousins—bad usually because they had friends and went out with them and had started speaking English at home, and sometimes when they were angry with their parents, they would go into their rooms and slam the doors and say that their lives were horrible and that they wished they hadn't been born. The adults would point out the good role models for us to follow at these family meetings—good usually because they went to school every day and came home on time and spoke Hmong at home, and sometimes when they were happy with their mothers and fathers, they talked about how lucky they were to be in America and have opportunities to make a good life. High school was the highest educational level of the children in our family then. When we went to these family meetings, I usually sat with the cousins who were close to my age. The meetings were always the same. They began with the same words, in Hmong, by an uncle (they took turns):

"We almost died in the war. Many Hmong people died in the war. We are fortunate to have made it to America. Many died trying to get to this country of opportunity. Now we are in America. There are schools for children to go to. There are universities. Your mothers and fathers are not educated people. Maybe you go to school and you see that your classmates have parents who are doctors and lawyers and you wonder why your mother and father do not work and have disability checks and cannot help themselves, let alone you. We are not doctors and lawyers. We never had the chance. We do not speak English. You can."

They would say how much they loved us and hoped that we became great people in America. They said they understood that some of us may feel embarrassed at school because we got free lunches and our parents were on welfare. Sometimes they cried. At these meetings, I learned that what made our parents sad was not so much the hardness of the life they had to lead in America, or the hardness of the lives they had led to get to America, but the hardness of *our* lives in America. It was always about the children. And so the pressure built.

The children would sit and listen. I always thought the talks went on for a little too long and that they were much the same each time, but I enjoyed these gatherings because the family was together. Even then I knew that not many American families got together and tried to speak to each other about becoming better people in America. It was something special that my family did. Some of my cousins didn't enjoy the talks at all, especially the ones whose parents had called the meeting. They felt it was public ridicule. They complained about the comparisons among children.

We had one cousin, the one my family had lived with when we first came, who had graduated from high school. We were all proud of him. He looked older and wiser and more stylish to me than any other cousin because he carried a yellow notepad and a pen at the family meetings. Sometimes he wore a suit. He said he was going to go to college if the family would support him. Of course we all would—even children nodded. Then yes, he would go. He would go to a community college and then transfer to the University of Minnesota. He would blaze a trail for us in America toward education, so that when it was our turn, we could follow his lead. He had learned the term "role model" and used it with authority and a resounding eloquence that made the adults pause in pride. Dawb really listened to this part of the conversation. I could tell because she would nod her head as he said each word, her eyes following his pen on the paper as he marked each point he had made.

At home Dawb told me that we had to work hard so we could go to the University of Minnesota, too. It was a great school, she said. It was the University of Minnesota—smart Americans went there, like her teachers. Only the luckiest and smartest Hmong people could go. We had to work very hard so that we could make our father proud. Dawb said it was ambitious and that we shouldn't tell our parents or Grandma or anybody else that we wanted to go there. She understood how it was when people did not turn out as expected. I didn't contradict her. I wasn't even sure I wanted to go forward with the plans at all. Dawb said that people might laugh if we told them. That part, I agreed with. Dawb pressed on, said that we could remind each other if one of us forgot that the University of Minnesota was a great school. She said that maybe we could qualify and get in if we studied hard and really learned English. I knew there were no problems with her English. She was trying to be kind by saying "we." I saved my words: I didn't tell her that I didn't really care about the University of Minnesota or college. I wasn't even in junior high yet.

Kao Kalia Yang's riveting memoir parallels the stories of thousands of Hmong families who made the journey from war-torn Laos to overcrowded refugee camps in Thailand and onward to the United States. Available at your local bookstore for just $14.95.

DECEMBER

Photo © Cynthia Davidson Bend

Daphne Roberts and Cynthia Davidson Bend met again in 2006 when Daphne attended her fiftieth SPA Summit School reunion

FOREIGN STUDENTS IN SAINT PAUL

Cynthia Davidson Bend

"Walk together, talk together, all ye peoples of the earth. For then, and then only will we have peace."
—American Field Service

When the grim days of World War II had passed, American Field Service (AFS) ambulances were no longer needed by allied troops in Europe, so the AFS transformed its humanitarian mission into a student exchange program. Saint Paul's high schools were waiting with a warm red carpet despite Minnesota's plunging winter temperatures.

In 1955, my two youngest sisters, Patsy and Caroline, were in grades eight and eleven, so the time was right for my parents, Bill and Torry Davidson, to host an American Field Service student.

The American host families were interviewed in their homes, then matched with as compatible as possible a visiting student. Should a placement fail to work out, either the family or the student could contact the New York office. If advisable, the student could then be moved to a more suitable family.

My parents' involvement started when my sister Patsy saw an article in the Saint Paul paper explaining the program and requesting a host family for Daphne Roberts from New Zealand. The photograph of a tutu-clad girl—on point—caught Patsy's attention. At the time, she was taking ballet lessons, and the New Zealand girl with an interest in ballet (which turned out to be a past interest) intrigued Patsy. Her insistent requests prevailed. Mother, with her last two chicks soon to leave the nest for college, was ready to conclude her parenting career on an international note, and Dad agreed.

In 1956, Daphne set off our family's expansion as a worldwide welcome mat. In spite of jet lag, her wit was sharp. We pelted her with questions about the natural beauties of New Zealand, which she answered with more ease than she probably felt. One of the country's waterfalls, she said, "would be the highest in the world if it weren't for a little jut of rock halfway down."

"Why don't you blast it off?"

Smiling, Daphne retorted to Dad's facetious question: "Because we're not Americans."

Our enthusiastic laughter brought her firmly into our family.

Mother and co-director Betty Foster provided AFS with strong, nurturing leadership and activities that brought AFS students close to each other as well as to their host families. Here is part of the farewell letter from Daphne and her fellow AFSers:

"We are finding how hard it is to leave people you love. . . .You gave us unity. . . you gave us to love a country, the U.S.A., that most of us used to criticize. . . . through all the people we got to know, we found a true picture of America. . . . You made a family of us. . . .You helped to open for us the doors of an International and friendly world."

Djamal was from Palembang, Sumatra. The small, lightly-built olive-skinned boy of eighteen was an enigma to all of us. He came from the largest Muslim country in the world bearing gifts for everyone: batik fabric, a dress for Mother, shirts, small carvings from Bali—and very little English. As was usual with AFS students, he quickly acquired U.S. slang, soon followed by other essential phrases.

The morning after his arrival, he showed Mother his prayer rug. While with our family, he devoutly observed Muslim prayers, also Ramadan, despite his wispy frame, so ill-suited to a midwinter month's fast from sunrise to sunset.

Djamal gave us glimpses of an exotic culture: there was a leader in his town, Djamal told us, who was impervious to bullets and thus could never be killed. Another day we saw him leap onto a table when a dog entered the house, reminding us uncomfortably of "unclean" dogs, often a meat source in his country. But he did learn to pat dogs before he returned home.

Although Djamal arrived in balmy September, he was cold; the lowest temperature he had known was in the U. S. embassy in Jakarta. As Saint Paul's fifty-degree autumn breezes hit his skin, he shivered violently. This

Photo © Cynthia Davidson Bend

Djamal's Central High School graduation picture

continued until a fellow Indonesia AFS student took him in hand. Just as she had let him know that his appreciative belches after meals were not part of U.S. etiquette, she also set him straight on shivering. "Djamal, stop that," she commanded.

We never saw Djamal shiver again—well, perhaps once: on New Year's day he joined the Polar Bear Club with my sister, Patsy, and jumped through a hole in the ice of White Bear Lake. He emerged—quickly—into temperatures so cold that the water froze on his skin and the ice film cracked when he bent his arms. Onlookers quickly swathed him in blankets, so he suffered no ill effects. "I bet your Indonesian family will be impressed!" a bystander exclaimed. Djamal shook his head. "They won't know what cold feels like."

Patsy, a year older than Djamal, remembers his blunt curiosity about U.S. dating customs. He had been with our family about a week when Patsy returned from a date and was in bed when her door opened. Djamal walked in and sat on the bed beside her. Among other questions, he asked if her date had kissed her. Now that I've spent some time in Asia and seen how rare bedroom doors are, I can understand why he didn't think to knock.

Mother told us that he got along fine when he needed a date. "Mudder, I ask the cheerleaders." They always bounced to his aid with the right date, plus transportation.

When Djamal left Saint Paul the following spring, Mother told me she was not sure what he had gained from his U.S. experience. However, seventeen years after he left Saint Paul, Djamal wrote of his dream of be-

DECEMBER

ing in the kitchen with "Father" where he helped to wipe the dishes, not a man's job in his country.

Djamal postponed marriage in favor of education. His concerned brother wrote Mother and Dad, "Djamal is still single. I wonder why he would like to be a single man? Maybe Mr. and Mrs. could help me look for a miss for Djamal." Did he imagine a line of American girls waiting for an arranged marriage with an Indonesian? Djamal found his own bride: in 1981, thirty-nine-year-old Djamal wrote, "A Chinese girl, name Lie Hong Mei will become your daughter in law. MARRIAGE a Christmas present for Lie." He had not forgotten Christmas fun, nor had he given up internationalism. Their wedding photographs show his pretty wife and her attendants dressed in the gold-trimmed brilliance of Hindu traditional attire.

Three years later, Djamal and his wife, holding their eighteen-month-old son, welcomed Mother and me in Jakarta. The little boy in his sparkling native colors took "Mudder's" hand and ceremoniously kissed it. Djamal, now a forty-two-year-old man, wore heavy, dark-framed glasses that made his face look thinner than it was. He soon dispelled all doubts about the importance of his AFS year. Showing us letters we had sent, he patted his breast pocket. "I keep them here. I still eat Father's breakfast three mornings a week," he told Mother. Oatmeal instead of rice—in Asia! Djamal arranged a full day of sightseeing. "We have an American car," he said proudly, as he conducted us to the Ford he had borrowed from his employer. A delicious feast climaxed the day. The following morning, as we pulled apart and reluctantly approached the plane, we all wondered if this would be our last meeting.

Saint Paul Listings

JANUARY

Downtown Saint Paul Winter Farmers' Market

Through March
Saturdays, 9 a.m.–noon
290 East Fifth St.
651.227.8101
www.stpaulfarmersmarket.com
Local growers bring their fresh foods to sell directly to you.

Holiday Flower Show

Through mid-Jan.
Marjorie McNeely Conservatory, Como Park
651.487.8200
www.comozooconservatory.org

Urban Expedition

Jan.–May, 1–3 p.m., select Sundays
Landmark Center
651.292.3225
www.landmarkcenter.org
Travel the world without leaving Saint Paul. Each Sunday afternoon event features authentic cultural performances by area musicians and performers that celebrate the culture of the destination country with music and dance.

Land O' Lakes Kennel Club Dog Show

Jan. 2–4
Saint Paul RiverCentre
651.265.4800
www.rivercentre.org
Come watch over 2,000 dogs strut their stuff.

International Chamber Orchestra Festival

Jan. 8–30
Various locations and times
651.291.1144
www.thespco.org

Photo © Landmark Center

Urban Expedition, Ethiopia: Ethiopian Student Association (University of Minnesota) performing traditional dances of Ethiopia

Five chamber orchestras play in the first-ever International Chamber Orchestra Festival.

Orchid Show

Jan. 2–25
Marjorie McNeely
Conservatory, Como Park
651.487.8200
www.comozooconservatory.org

The Saint Paul Chamber Orchestra

Jan. 8, 9, 11, 16, 18, 22, 23, 24, 29, 30
Various locations and times
651.291.1144
www.thespco.org
From Mozart to Beethoven, the SPCO plays with the Chamber Orchestra of Europe and the London Sinfonietta in January.

Minnesota Boychoir Winter Concert

Jan. 11
Landmark Center
651.292.3225
www.landmarkcenter.org
Hear the lovely sounds of over 100 boys aged 7–18.

Saint Paul Winter Carnival

Jan. 22–Feb. 1
Downtown Saint Paul
651.223.4700
www.winter-carnival.com
Lots of winter events—parades, ice skating, ice sculpture, coronation, medallion hunt.

Historic Saint Paul Concert with the SPCO

Jan. 24
Saint Paul's United Church of Christ
651.291.1144
www.thespco.org
The Orchestra of the Age of Enlightenment plays baroque pieces on period instruments.

Fourth Friday at the Movies

January 23
Golden Thyme Coffee Café
651.645.1340
Social hour at 6:30 p.m. and film begins at 7 p.m.

Minnesota Opera
Faust

Jan. 24, 27, 29, 31, Feb. 1
Ordway Center for the
Performing Arts
612.333.6669
www.mnopera.org
Charles Gounod's version of the Goethe classic.

Winter Flower Show

Jan. 30–Mar. 16
Marjorie McNeely Conservatory,
Como Park
651.487.8200
www.comozooconservatory.org

Saintly City Cat Show

Jan. 31–Feb. 1
Saint Paul RiverCentre
651.265.4800
www.rivercentre.org
More than 300 felines compete to be crowned the Feline King and Queen of the Saint Paul Winter Carnival.

Photo © Patricia Bour-Schilla

Hilex bleach drops at the Winter Carnival

FEBRUARY

Saint Paul Winter Carnival

Jan. 22–Feb. 1
Downtown Saint Paul
651.223.4700
www.winter-carnival.com
Lots of winter events—parades, ice skating, ice sculpture, coronation, medallion hunt.

Winter Flower Show

Jan. 30–Mar. 15
Marjorie McNeely Conservatory, Como Park
651.487.8200
www.comozooconservatory.org

Saintly City Cat Show

Jan. 31–Feb. 1
Saint Paul RiverCentre
651.265.4800
www.rivercentre.org
More than 300 felines compete to be crowned the Feline King and Queen of the Saint Paul Winter Carnival.

Minnesota Opera, *Faust*

Feb. 1
Ordway Center for the Performing Arts
612.333.6669
www.mnopera.org
Charles Gounod's version of the Goethe classic.

World of Wheels

Feb. 6–8
Saint Paul RiverCentre
651.265.4800
www.rivercentre.org
Come view over 300 exhibits of hot rods, race cars, customized motorcycles, and antique vehicles.

Saint Paul Chamber Orchestra

Feb. 14, 19, 20, 21
Ordway Center for the Performing Arts
651.291.1144
www.thespco.org
This February the SPCO presents Beethoven's 1st and 2nd piano concertos and Haydn's The Creation.

Vietnamese Tet New Year Festival

Dates to be announced
Saint Paul RiverCentre
651.265.4800
www.vietnam-minnesota.org
Vietnamese music, dancing, contests, food, and celebration. Free admission.

Scottish Ramble

Feb. 14–15
Landmark Center
651.292.3225
www.landmarkcenter.org
Scottish music, dancing, food, and celebration.

Minnesota State High School League Girls' Hockey Tournament

Feb. 25–28
Xcel Energy Center
763.560.2262
www.mshsl.org

Historic Saint Paul Concert with the SPCO

Feb. 28
Saint Paul's United Church of Christ
651.291.1144
www.thespco.org
Douglas Boyd conducts Mozart's last symphonies.

MARCH

Winter Flower Show

Jan. 30–Mar. 15
Marjorie McNeely Conservatory, Como Park
651.487.8200
www.comozooconservatory.org

Minnesota Opera
The Adventures of Pinocchio

Feb. 28, Mar. 3, 5, 7, 8
Ordway Center for the Performing Arts
612.333.6669
www.mnopera.org
The storybook tale comes alive.

Minnesota State High School League Boys' Wrestling Tournament

Mar. 4–7
Xcel Energy Center
763.560.2262
www.mshsl.org

Minnesota State High School League Boys' Hockey Tournament

Mar. 11–14
Xcel Energy Center
763.560.2262
www.mshsl.org

Saint Paul Chamber Orchestra

Mar. 13–14
Ordway Center for the Performing Arts
651.291.1144
www.thespco.org
Fauré and Ravel.

Irish Celebration Dance

Mar. 15
Landmark Center
651.292.3225
www.landmarkcenter.org
Irish food, lively music, Irish dancing, and art vendors.

Saint Patrick's Day Parade
Mar. 17
Downtown Saint Paul
651.256.2155
www.stpatsassoc.org
Once the biggest parade in Saint Paul, and it's still very big.

Saint Patrick's Day Irish Ceili Dance
Mar. 17, 7–10 p.m.
CSPS Hall, 383 Michigan St.
651.290.0542
www.minnesotafolkfestival.org
Learn the steps of the Irish, for everyone is Irish on St. Paddy's day.

Spring Flower Show
Mar. 21–Apr. 26
Marjorie McNeely Conservatory, Como Park
651.487.8200
www.comozooconservatory.org

Donnie Smith Invitational Bike Show
Mar. 28–29
Saint Paul RiverCentre
651.265.4800
www.donniesmithbikeshow.com
Custom motorcycle builders pack River Centre, showing off their pride and joys.

APRIL

Spring Flower Show
Mar. 21–Apr. 26
Marjorie McNeely Conservatory, Como Park
651.487.8200
www.comozooconservatory.org

Saint Paul Chamber Orchestra
Apr. 4, 24, 25
Ordway Center for the Performing Arts
651.291.1144
www.thespco.org
The SPCO presents McGegan's Farewell Fireworks *and Abbado, Upshaw, and Haydn.*

Minnesota Opera
The Barber of Seville
Apr. 11, 14, 16, 18, 19
Ordway Center for the Performing Arts
612.333.6669
www.mnopera.org
The final revival of this opera classic.

Photo © Patricia Bour-Schilla

The Emerald Society of Minnesota at the Saint Patrick's Day Parade

27th Annual Minneapolis-Saint Paul International Film Festival

Mid-Apr.
612.331.7563
www.mspfilmfest.org
The largest film festival in the Upper Midwest. Over 150 films from more than 50 countries. Various locations.

Historic Saint Paul Concert with the SPCO

Apr. 18
Saint Paul's United Church of Christ
651.291.1144
www.thespco.org
Abbado conducts Haydn.

Saint Paul Art Crawl

Apr. 24–26
Downtown Saint Paul
651.292.4373
www.artcrawl.org
More than 200 artists open their studios to the public.

Downtown Saint Paul Farmers' Market

Through November
Saturdays, 6 a.m.–1 p.m.
and Sundays, 8 a.m.–1 p.m.
651.227.8101
www.stpaulfarmersmarket.com
Local growers bring their fresh produce to sell directly to you.

MAY

Festival of Nations

Apr. 30, May 1–3
Saint Paul RiverCentre
651.647.0191
www.festivalofnations.com
Over 90 ethnic groups share the foods, crafts, and traditions that form the mosaic of our American culture.

Como Memorial Japanese Garden

May 1–Sept. 30
Marjorie McNeely Conservatory, Como Park
651.487.8200
www.comozooconservatory.org

Cinco de Mayo Festival

May 1–2
District del Sol
651.222.6347
www.districtdelsol.com
Celebrate with live music, food, children's area, community wellness village, parade, vendors.

Living Green Expo

May 2–3
10 a.m.–5 p.m.
State Fairgrounds
651.215.0218
www.livinggreen.org
Environmental fair—workshops, live music, food, kids' activities.

Summer Flower Show

May 2–Oct. 4
Marjorie McNeely Conservatory, Como Park
651.487.8200
www.comozooconservatory.org
Roses, statice, geraniums, Asiatic lilies, heliotrope, New Guinea impatiens, petunias, and caladiums bloom throughout the season.

Historic Saint Paul Concert with the SPCO

May 2, 16, 30
Saint Paul's United Church of Christ
651.291.1144
www.thespco.org
Beethoven's 8th Symphony, *Mendelssohn's* Octet, *and Schumann's* Piano Concerto.

Saint Paul Civic Symphony Mother's Day Celebration

May 13
Landmark Center
651.292.3225
www.landmarkcenter.org
Bring your mother to enjoy music at the Landmark.

Sur Seine Music Festival

May 14–24
Black Dog Café and Wine Bar and other various locations
651.292.9746
www.surseine.org
International music festival. Jazz, rock, folk, and Celtic music.

Minnesota Dance Festival

May 16–18
Fitzgerald Theater
651.290.1221
www.balletminnesota.org
Variety of dance performances.

Saint Paul Chamber Orchestra

May 22, 23
Ordway Center for the Performing Arts
651.291.1144
www.thespco.org
Mendelssohn's Italian Symphony *fills the Ordway.*

Flint Hills International Children's Festival

May 26–31, first four days dedicated to school children and weekend open to the public
Ordway Center for the Performing Arts, Rice Park
651.224.4222
www.ordway.org
Parade, performances, dancing, international foods, and hands-on workshops for children.

JUNE

Summer Flower Show

May 2–Oct. 4
Marjorie McNeely Conservatory, Como Park
651.487.8200
www.comozooconservatory.org
Roses, statice, geraniums, Asiatic lilies, heliotrope, New Guinea impatiens, petunias, and caladiums bloom throughout the season.

Saint Paul (Seventh Place) Farmers' Market

June–Sept.
Tuesdays and Thursdays
Seventh Place, 10–2 p.m.
651.227.8101
www.stpaulfarmersmarket.com
Local growers bring their fresh produce to sell directly to you.

Photo © Patricia Bour-Schilla

On the porch at Grand Old Day

Music in Mears Park

Thursdays, 6–9 p.m.
June through Aug.
Mears Park
221 East Fifth St.
651.291.9128
www.stpaulafterhours.com
Enjoy the sounds of summer in the beautiful outdoors.

MMAA Patio Nights

June–Aug.
Thursdays
Minnesota Museum of American Art
50 West Kellogg Blvd.
www.mmaa.org
Music on the patio. Doors open at 7 p.m., $7. All ages are welcome—rain or shine.

Saint Paul Chamber Orchestra

June 4–6
Ordway Center for the Performing Arts
651.291.1144
www.thespco.org
The SPCO presents Mendelssohn's A Midsummer Night's Dream.

Grand Old Day

June 7
Grand Avenue,
Dale to Fairview
651.699.0029
www.grandave.com
Sporting events, parade, family fun area, teen battle of the bands, live music, festival gardens, and over 140 outdoor food and merchandise vendors.

Saint Paul Sommerfest

June 13–15
Downtown Saint Paul
651.489.9623
www.saintpaulsommerfest.org
A weekend of European splendor.

Sommerfest River Cruise

June 13
6–10 p.m., Harriet Island
"The best happy hour in town!" A fun-filled evening of dining and dancing on an elegant Mississippi River paddleboat with jazz, polka, and choral music. Casual dress. Purchase tickets at saintpaulsommerfest.org

Emperor's Ball
June 13
6 p.m.–12 a.m.
Landmark Center
651.489.9623
www.saintpaulsommerfest.org
A Viennese ball is recreated.

Sommerfest Promenade and Picnic
June 15
Saint Paul Cathedral parking lot, 2:30 p.m.
www.gai-mn.org
Horse-drawn wagons, carriages, and car show. Winners parade to Summit Avenue for music, food, and fun.

Twin Cities Jazz Festival
June 18–28
Mears Park
www.hotsummerjazz.com

Solstice Film Festival
Dates to be announced
Fitzgerald Theater
10 East Exchange St.
651.290.1496
www.solsticefilmfest.org
Get off the couch and experience a film festival unlike any other. Five days of film at downtown venues, with outdoor music and wrap parties at local restaurants.

Back to the 50s Car Show
June 19–21
Minnesota State Fairgrounds
651.641.1992
www.msra.com
Over 10,000 cars registered last year, over 300 vendors and crafters, over 350 swappers, plus 50s dances Friday and Saturday nights.

Music and Movies, *District del Sol*
Late June to first week in Aug.
Thursdays, 7 p.m.
Castillo Park
149 Cesar Chavez Rd.
651.222.6347
www.districtdelsol.com
Activities and music; movies at dusk. Beer, food, and gift vendors. Come and go as you please. No coolers, but bring your lawn chair.

JULY

Summer Flower Show
May 2–Oct. 4
Marjorie McNeely Conservatory, Como Park
651.487.8200
www.comozooconservatory.org
Roses, statice, geraniums, Asiatic lilies, heliotrope, New Guinea impatiens, petunias and caladiums bloom throughout the season.

MMAA Patio Nights
June–Aug.
Thursdays
50 W Kellogg Blvd.
Music on the patio. Doors open at 7 p.m., $7. All ages are welcome—rain or shine.

Music in Mears
Thursdays, 6–9 p.m.
June through Aug.
Mears Park
221 East Fifth St.
651.291.9128
www.stpaulafterhours.com.

Photo © Patricia Bour-Schilla

2007 Taste of Minnesota

Enjoy the sounds of summer in the beautiful outdoors.

Taste of Minnesota
July 2–5
Harriet Island and Downtown
651.772.9980
www.tasteofmn.org
Includes four music stages, multiple food vendors, and fireworks every night.

Hmong International Sports Tournament and Freedom Festival
July 4–5
Como Park
651.266.6400
www.hmongsportscenter.com
Largest Hmong community sporting event in the nation. Volleyball, soccer, kato, and tops tournaments; food, retail, and music.

Nine Nights of Music Series
July 7, 14, 21, and 28
Minnesota History Center Museum
345 West Kellogg Blvd.
651.259.3000
www.mnhs.org
Every Tuesday in July and August. Bring a lawn chair and pack a picnic or purchase food from the Café Minnesota terrace grill. In case of rain, concerts will be held inside the History Center.

Dragon Festival and Dragon Boat Races
July 11–12
Lake Phalen
651.646.7717
www.dragonfestival.org
Asian cultural festival with performances, food vendors, and dragon boat races in which paddlers follow the drumbeats.

Highland Fest
July 17–19
Highland Village
651.699.9042
www.highlandfest.com
Three-day outdoor festival. Food, art vendors, and live entertainment on two stages. Fireworks Friday and Saturday.

Rondo Days

July 17–18

www.rondoaveinc.org

Rondo Days are a central gathering time for celebrating the unique heritage of Saint Paul's historic Black community. The festival remembers Rondo with a senior citizens' dinner, one-day festival, famous drill team competition, parade, music, food, and art.

Rice Street Festival

July 22–25

651.285.4101

www.ricestreetfestival.org

Celebrate Rice Street. Parade begins around 5 p.m.

Car Craft Summer Nationals

July 24–26

Minnesota State Fairgrounds

877.413.6515

www.carcraft.com

Showcases over 4,000 street machines and muscle cars.

AUGUST

Summer Flower Show

May 2–Oct. 4

Marjorie McNeely Conservatory, Como Park

651.487.8200

www.comozooconservatory.org

Summer flowers throughout the season.

MMAA Patio Nights

June–Aug.

Thursdays

Minnesota Museum of American Art

50 West Kellogg Blvd.

Music on the patio. Doors open at 7 p.m., $7. All ages are welcome—rain or shine.

Music and Movies, *District del Sol*

Late June to first week in Aug.

Thursdays, 7 p.m.

Castillo Park

149 Cesar Chavez Rd.

651.222.6347

www.districtdelsol.com

Activities and music; movies at dusk.

Photo © Patricia Bour-Schilla

Rondo Days

Music in Mears Park

Thursdays, 6–9 p.m.
June through Aug.
Mears Park
221 East Fifth St.
651.291.9128
www.stpaulafterhours.com.
Enjoy the sounds of summer in the beautiful outdoors.

Circus Juventas

August (dates to be announced)
651.699.8229
www.circusjuventas.org
Youth performers create a spectacular Cirque du Soleil-like show. Afternoon and evening shows on select dates.

Nine Nights of Music Series

Aug. 4, 11, 18, and 25
Minnesota History
Center Museum
345 West Kellogg Blvd.
651.259.3000
www.mnhs.org
Every Tuesday in July and August. Bring a lawn chair and pack a picnic or purchase food from the Café Minnesota terrace grill. In case of rain, concerts will be held inside the History Center.

Irish Fair

August 7–9
Harriet Island
952.474.7411
www.irishfair.com
Upper Midwest's largest Irish festival. Lots of music, dance, history, food, and theater. Free.

Japanese Lantern Lighting Festival

Aug. 16
4 p.m.–dusk
Marjorie McNeely Conservatory,
Como Park
651.487.8200
www.comozooconservatory.org
Lanterns float in the Japanese garden ponds to celebrate Obon, the Japanese festival honoring one's ancestors. Japanese food and entertainment.

Minnesota State Fair

Aug. 27–Sept. 7
Minnesota State Fairgrounds
651.288.4400
www.mnstatefair.org
The biggest state fair in the Midwest. Lots of food on sticks.

SEPTEMBER

Minnesota State Fair

Aug. 27–Sept. 7
Minnesota State Fairgrounds
651.288.4400
www.mnstatefair.org
The biggest state fair in the Midwest. Lots of food on sticks.

Summer Flower Show

May 2–Oct. 4
Marjorie McNeely Conservatory,
Como Park
651.487.8200
www.comozooconservatory.org
Summer flowers bloom throughout the season.

Payne-Arcade International Harvest Festival

Sept. 10–13

Annual Torch Light Parade

Sept. 10

Parade runs on Payne between Rose and York streets

651.771.5477

Sponsored by the Payne-Arcade Avenue Business Association (PABA)

Selby Avenue JazzFest

Sept. 12

11 a.m. -7 p.m.

Corner of Selby and Milton

www.selbyareacdc.org

Outdoor festival celebrating jazz music. Bring the whole family. Delicious food, including lots of southern-style cuisine. Local artisans and businesses too.

Annual Twin Cities Black Film Festival

Sept. 18–20

Various locations in Saint Paul

www.tcbff.com

Opening and closing night premieres, panel discussions, festival parties, 25 independent film projects, plus much more.

OCTOBER

India Day

Oct. 4

Landmark Center

651.292.3225

www.landmarkcenter.org

Celebrate the culture of India.

Saint Paul Art Crawl

Oct. 9–11

Downtown Saint Paul

651.292.4373

www.artcrawl.org

More than 200 artists open their studios to the public.

Fall Flower Show

Oct. 10–Nov. 29

Marjorie McNeely Conservatory, Como Park

651.487.8200

www.comozooconservatory.org

Zoo Boo

Oct 17, 18, 23, 24, and 25

5–7:30 p.m.

Como Park Zoo

651.487.8200

www.comozooconservatory.org

Annual Halloween dress-up family festival.

Dia de los Muertos Family Fiesta

Oct. 25

Minnesota History Center Museum

345 West Kellogg Blvd.

651.259.3000

www.mnhs.org

Great Pumpkin Festival

Oct. 25

Landmark Center

651.292.3225

www.landmarkcenter.org

An autumn celebration for the whole family, including costume contests, music, and art projects.

NOVEMBER

Fall Flower Show

Oct. 10–Nov. 29

Marjorie McNeely Conservatory, Como Park

Photo © Landmark Center

Great Pumpkin Festival October 2007: Children's Home Society Choir performs in costume

651.487.8200
www.comozooconservatory.org

St. Martin's Day

Nov. 8
Landmark Center
651.292.3225
www.landmarkcenter.org

Minnesota State High School League Girls' Volleyball Tournament

Nov. 12–14
Xcel Energy Center
763.560.2262
www.mshsl.org

Capital City Lights

Mid-Nov.–Mar.
Downtown Saint Paul
651.291.5600
www.capitalcitypartnership.com
Come downtown and enjoy the holiday lights during winter.

Minnesota Hmong New Year

Nov. 27–29
Saint Paul RiverCentre
651.265.4800
www.rivercentre.org
Celebrate the Hmong New Year with dance, food, music, entertainment, and more.

DECEMBER

Holiday Bazaar

Dec. 3–5
Landmark Center
651.292.3225
www.landmarkcenter.org
More than 80 exhibits featuring local artists' work and gift items.

Bouquets Wine Tasting

Dec. 3
Marjorie McNeely Conservatory, Como Park
651.487.8200
www.comozooconservatory.org

Holiday Flower Show
Dec.-mid-Jan.
Marjorie McNeely
Conservatory, Como Park
651.487.8200
www.comozooconservatory.org

SKANDIA: Scandinavian Festival
Dec. 13
Landmark Center
651.292.3225
www.landmarkcenter.org
Celebrate Scandinavian traditions through music, dance, and food. Lutefisk available. Children's activities too.

Kwanzaa Celebration
Dec. 26
Minnesota History Center
651.259.3000
www.mnhs.org
Annual Kwanzaa celebration with crafts, stories, and music for all ages.

HEALTH AND FITNESS EVENTS

Teri J. Dwyer

Opportunities abound for outdoor recreation enthusiasts in Saint Paul, a city that offers the conveniences of an urban setting plus many hidden (and not-so-hidden) treasures. Paved paths along the river, bike lanes on major roads, parks and lakes, as well as sidewalks, paths, and trails throughout the city provide wonderful places to enjoy many different outdoor recreational activities. Through snow, ice, rain, heat, and humidity, Saint Paul's most active citizens can participate in events throughout the year.

Here's a month-by-month look at some of the health and fitness events that make this city a great place to live, work, and work out.

JANUARY

January 18—Frigid 5

If you ever wondered what goes on at the Minnesota State Fairgrounds in late January, participating in the **Frigid 5** is a great way to find out. The Frigid 5 is a 5K and 10K race circling the fairgrounds. There are also shorter races (¼ mile and ½ mile) for the kids. The permanent booths and wide-open roadway look quite different covered in snow with only hundreds of people around you instead of the thousands who attend the State Fair daily in August.
www.tslevents.com

January 24—Saint Paul Winter Carnival's Half Marathon and 5K

Nothing says Minnesota like winter—at least to folks in most of the rest of the United States. We heartily embrace winter by throwing a Winter Carnival each winter in Saint Paul. One of the many events of the Winter Carnival includes a health and fitness component—the "Coolest Race on Earth." **Saint Paul Winter Carnival's Half Marathon and 5K** starts and ends downtown. The courses follow the Mississippi River for the midportion of each race.
www.winter-carnival.com

People who participate in the events of the **Twin Cities Bicycling Club (TCBC)** are not willing to hang up their bikes just because of a little snow and cold. Join them for their **Winter Warm-up, Think Spring, We Don't Need No Stinkin' Winter,** and **Fridays on the Bike** events. They meet in various locations throughout the winter in Saint Paul.
www.mtn.org/tcbc

FEBRUARY

TCBC events (see January)

www.mtn.org/tcbc

MARCH

March 22—Saint Patrick's Day Human Race

For more than three decades, runners and walkers in the region have

Saint Patrick's Day Human Race

viewed the **Saint Patrick's Day Human Race** running and walking events as the start of the spring racing season in Saint Paul. The event offers an 8K run, a 5K run/walk, and youth runs from ¼ to ½ mile. www.tslevents.com

APRIL

April 4—Challenge Obesity 5K

Sponsored by Charities Challenge, **Run, Race Walk**, **Fitness Walk**, and **Walk by My Side** 2.5K are the first in a summer series of five events held at Como Lake. www.charitieschallenge.org

April 12—Running of the Pigs

If the name doesn't intrigue you, it should! This fun, festive 5K is on a loop course in front of Midway Stadium, home of the Saint Paul Saints, the event's sponsor (hint: their mascot is a large pink pig—makes for fun tee shirts!) The day's activities also include ¼-mile and ½-mile youth runs. Be sure to stay for the catered lunch afterward. www.tslevents.com

April date not yet scheduled—Saint Paul Parks' Annual Spring Parks Cleanup

You may not consider this a health-and-fitness event, but if you come out and participate, you can get a good workout. And you'll feel good about cleaning up the environment! Each year, **Saint Paul Parks and Recreation** hosts this event for families, groups, and individuals to help clean up the trash in Saint Paul's parks and recreation centers. The **Cleanup** is generally held on a Saturday in April. www.stpaul.gov/depts/parks

MAY

May 1—Menudo 5K

Saint Paul's West Side, with its large Hispanic/Latino population, hosts a **Cinco de Mayo celebration** each spring on the weekend closest to May 5. On the Saturday of this celebratory weekend, the business community also hosts the **Menudo 5K**. www.districtdelsol.com/cinco.html

May 2—Melpomene

If it's the first Saturday in May, it must be time for **Melpomene**! Cleverly dubbed the **Run Walk for Every Body**, this 5K run benefits the organization of the same name. The race offers separate women's and men's 5K runs, a co-ed 5K walk, a 3K family walk, and ½-mile and 1-mile kids' fun runs. This family-friendly event is run along the beautiful Mississippi River. www.melpomene.org

May 3—Walk for Animals

Hosted by the Humane Society, this event kicks off the national **Be Kind to Animals Week** at Como Park. www.animalhumanesociety.org

May 10—Mother's Day 5K

First in the series of four **Challenge RxExercise Holiday Events**, this 5K takes place at Como Lake. www.charitieschallenge.org

May 21—Challenge Hearts & Minds 5K

Sponsored by Charities Challenge, this is the second in the summer series of five events held at Como Lake. **Run, Race Walk**, **Fitness Walk**, and **Walk by My Side** 2½ K. www.charitieschallenge.org

May 24—Mississippi 10 Miler

Starts and ends at Summit Avenue and East Mississippi River Boulevard. This long-standing event is sponsored by the **Minnesota Distance Running Association**. The course is out and back along the Saint Paul side of the Mississippi River. www.runmdra.org

JUNE

June 6—Challenge Cancer 5K

Sponsored by Charities Challenge, this is the third in the summer series of five events held at Como Lake. **Run, Race Walk**, **Fitness Walk**, and **Walk by My Side** 2½ K. www.charitieschallenge.org

June 7—Grand Old Day on the Go!

Grand Old Day (the largest one-day music, food, and entertainment festival in the United States) kicks off the summer festival season in Saint Paul. What better way to kick off Grand Old Day than with the **Grand Old Day on the Go!** events—an 8K inline skate, 8K run, 5K run/walk, and ¼-mile and ½-mile youth runs. www.tslevents.com

June 7—Walk on the Wild Side

A 5K run/walk benefiting Dakota Communities, an organization providing services to people with disabilities. Event is held at Como Lake. www.dakotacommunities.org

Photo © Chris Fuller, *The Sporting Life*

Grand Old Day on the Go! Youth Run 2008

June 21—Father's Day 5K

Second in the series of four **Challenge RxExercise Holiday Events**, this 5K takes place at Como Lake.
www.charitieschallenge.org

June 27—Time to Fly 10K and 5K

Children's Cancer Research Fund hosts the **Time to Fly 10K** and **5K** at Harriet Island in Saint Paul. Besides the 10K and 5K races, there's a 2K and 1K kids' run.
www.childrenscancer.org/news _details_events_timetofly.html

JULY

July 4—Langford Park Races

These very low-key races (runners choose 2 or 4 miles) have had an entry fee of 50¢ since 1974. The course is a 2-mile loop on the streets of Saint Paul's picturesque Saint Anthony Park. Races begin and end at Langford Park. This race is a fun way to kick off your Fourth of July celebration.

July 11—Challenge Diabetes 5K

Sponsored by Charities Challenge, this is the fourth in the summer series of five events held at Como Lake. **Run, Race Walk**, **Fitness Walk**, and **Walk by My Side** 2½ K.
www.charitieschallenge.org

July 18—Highland Fest 5K

This low-key, family-friendly fun run is part of the annual **Highland Fest** celebration showcasing one of Saint Paul's many fine neighborhoods. The course is out and back along the Mississippi River.
www.highlandfest.com

July 22—Rice Street Mile

Race starts at the intersection of Rice Street and Front Avenue. The course is flat and point to point. Don't miss this opportunity to run one of the shortest road races offered in Saint Paul. The race kicks off the parade for the annual **Rice Street Festival**.
www.ricestreetfestival.org

AUGUST

August 5–26—MDRA Cross-Country Runs

Since 1974, MDRA has sponsored this series of cross-country races every Wednesday evening in August at Como Park in Saint Paul. The races are open to all ages and abilities.
www.runmdra.org

August 16—Saint Paul Inline Marathon

A chance for inline skaters from beginners to professionals to skate along the beautiful Mississippi River in Saint Paul. The race ends in downtown Saint Paul at Mears Park.
www.saintpaulinlinemarathon.com

August 23—Minnesota State Fair Milk Run 5K

Participants receive an admission ticket to the fair and a coupon for a free malt!
www.mnstatefair.org

Aug. 29—Challenge Arthritis 5K

Sponsored by **Charities Challenge**, this is the fifth in the summer series of five events held at Como Lake. **Run, Race Walk**, **Fitness Walk**, and **Walk by My Side** 2½K.
www.charitieschallenge.org

SEPTEMBER

September 6—Saint Paul Classic Bike Tour

A rare opportunity to bicycle around and through the City of Saint Paul on streets free of car traffic. This family-friendly event offers a 15-mile tour of Saint Paul or a 30-mile ride.
www.spnec.org

September 6—Sharing Life Walk/Run (3 miles)

This Lake Phalen all-ages event includes special races and games for the kids. Support organ donation education and raise money for families going through a transplant.
www.sharinglife.org

Photo © Chris Fuller, *The Sporting Life*

Paul Mausling Cross Country Meet 2007

September 18—West Fest Jalapeño Hustle 5K

Another race showcasing the city's West Side. This event is family-friendly and includes a **Chile Chase** that is free for runners ten years of age and younger.

September 20—MMRF Race for Research

The **MMRF Race for Research** raises awareness and funds for research on multiple myeloma, an incurable blood cancer. Multiple myeloma is the second most common blood cancer and the third most lethal cancer in people over 65. African Americans have the highest reported incidence of this disease. This **5K Walk/Run** is held at Lake Phalen.
www.mmrfrace.org

September 27—Dream Mile

Includes 10K and 5K runs plus 5K fun walk around Lake Phalen. **Dream Mile** is a national fundraiser to aid child welfare projects funded by Vibha in India and the United States; 10 percent of the proceeds are donated to the local chapter of **Big Brothers Big Sisters of the Greater Twin Cities**.
wiki.vibha.org

OCTOBER

October 4—Twin Cities Marathon

The Twin Cities Marathon (TCM), a Twin Cities tradition for over thirty years, traverses the Mississippi River. On the Saturday before Sunday's big marathon, TCM hosts its Saturday running events exclusively in Saint Paul. The **TCM 5K and Family Events** offer something for all ages and abilities. The races start and end near the state Capitol.
www.twincitiesmarathon.org

October 11—Paul Mausling Cross-Country Run (4K and 6K)

Named after Paul Mausling, former Saint Paul resident and graduate of Macalester College, this race offers another opportunity for runners of all ages and abilities to run a cross-country race at Saint Paul's Como Park.
www.tslevents.com

October 17—Halloween Hustle

The **5K Run/Walk** and **Kid's Fun Run** are sponsored by the Junior League of Saint Paul and takes place on Harriet Island.
www.jlsp.org

NOVEMBER

November 1—Rocky's Run

This cross-country race offers the public a rare opportunity to run on the same course as the University of Minnesota men's and women's cross-country teams at the Les Bolstad University Golf Course. The 8K and 5K races benefit a scholarship in Rocky Racette's name for the women's track and field and cross-country teams at the U of M.
www.tslevents.com

Photo © Chris Fuller, *The Sporting Life*

Frigid 5K 2008

November 22—Turkey Run

A tradition for the Sunday before Thanksgiving each year, this family-friendly fun run circles Como Lake, beginning and ending at the warm indoor headquarters of Como Elementary School.
www.tslevents.com

November 26—Giving Thanks 5K

Third in the series of four **Challenge RxExercise Holiday Events**, this 5K takes place on Thanksgiving Day at Como Lake. Get in your run before indulging in a big holiday meal.
www.charitieschallenge.org

TCBC events (see January.)
www.mtn.org/tcbc

DECEMBER

**December 25—
Joyful 5K Christmas Day**

Fourth in the series of four **Challenge RxExercise Holiday Events**, this 5K takes place on Christmas Day at Como Lake.
www.charitieschallenge.org

TCBC events (see January.)
www.mtn.org/tcbc

YEAR-ROUND SAINT PAUL ACTIVITIES

The Saint Paul Hiking Club

This group meets regularly at various locations throughout Saint Paul. Everyone is welcome. Visit www.stpaulhike.org for current hike locations and contact information.

WINTER ACTIVITIES

Cross-Country Skiing

Saint Paul grooms trails at three sites each winter: **Como Golf Course, Phalen Golf Course,** and **Highland 9-Hole Golf Course.**

Tuesday Night Lessons—

Lessons in classic and skate skiing are available through Saint Paul's Parks and Recreation.
www.stpaul.gov/depts/parks

Ice Skating Rinks

A number of outdoor ice-skating rinks located throughout the city. Amenities, including availability of rental skates, vary by location.
www.stpaul.gov/depts/parks
www.capitalcitypartnership.com

Key:

4K (2.5 miles)
5K (3.1 miles)
6K (3.75 miles)
8K (4.97 miles)
10K (6.2 miles)
Half Marathon (13.1 miles)
Marathon (26.2 miles)

Illustration © Andy Singer

Icycling

COFFEE HOUSES AND TEA SHOPS

A Fine Grind Coffeehouse
2038 Marshall Ave.
651.645.9700
www.afinegrind.com
A real, down-to-earth neighborhood coffee house where friends and neighbors gather. Lots of workspace, great music.

Amoré Coffee
917 Grand Ave.
651.222.6770
www.amorecoffee.com
Locally owned coffee house featuring award-winning coffee and authentic Italian gelato in a warm, friendly environment.

Artist's Grind
2399 University Ave. West
651.641.1656
A wifi coffee house run by artists. Organic fair-trade coffee, soups, sandwiches, and tamales.

Black Dog Coffee & Wine Bar
308 Prince St.
651.228.9274
www.blackdogstpaul.com
Sandwiches, soups, salads, pizza, exhibits, and events that celebrate the local arts community.

Blue Cat Coffee & Tea
151 Cesar Chavez St.
651.291.7676
Snappy drinks. Happy cats. Get your paws on a cup. Donations welcome.

Boiler Room Café
214 Fourth St. East
651.222.5727
Coffee. Pastries. Sandwiches. Charm.

Bread and Chocolate
867 Grand Ave.
651.228.1017
Coffee, sandwiches, and fresh-baked goods, including the best brownies in the city!

Brewberry's Coffee Place
475 Fairview Ave. South
651.699.1117
A neighborhood shop with a café-like setting where you can enjoy all-natural soups, sandwiches, frappes, ice cream, and free wifi.

Photo © Patricia Bour-Schilla

Featuring the world's largest collection of blue cats.

Certified Jamaican Blue Mountain and Kona coffee available daily.

Café Juliahna
879 Smith Ave. South
651.450.7070
www.cafejuliahna.com
Organic bakery and café that roasts its own fair-trade coffee. Family-friendly with free wifi.

Cahoots Coffee Bar
1562 Selby Ave.
651.644.6778

Coffee Bené
53 Cleveland Ave. South
651.698.2266
www.coffeebene.com
Organic fair-trade coffee.

The Coffee Grounds
1579 Hamline Ave. North
651.644.9959
www.thecoffeegrounds.net
Featuring free live music four days a week.

Coffee News Café
1662 Grand Ave.
651.698.3324
www.myspace.com/coffeenewscafe
A friendly neighborhood place serving liberal portions to liberal minds.

Cosmic's Coffee
189 Snelling Ave. North
651.645.0106
www.myspace.com/cosmicscoffee
Internet coffee shop. Check out the mural inside.

Executive Coffee & Tea
180 Fifth St. East
651.228.9820

Fresh Grounds
1362 West Seventh St.
651.224.2348
www.freshgroundscoffee.com
Coffee. Community. Conversation. Cause.

Ginkgo Coffeehouse
721 Snelling Ave. North
651.645.2647
www.ginkgocoffee.com
Serving only the highest-quality coffee, tea, smoothies, and food.

Ginkgo Coffee Bar
St. Joseph's Hospital
69 West Exchange St.
651.232.3084

Ginkgo Coffee Bar & Deli
Garden View Medical Building (next to Children's Hospital)
347 Smith Ave. North
651.220.6200
A coffee bar and deli with homemade sandwiches and other fresh, healthy food.

Golden Thyme Coffee Café
921 Selby Ave.
651.645.1340
A community hub offering special drinks named after jazz legends, fresh pastries, homemade soups, including a great gumbo, sandwiches, and entrees. Owners Stephanie and Mychael Wright serve up warm hospitality.

Grumpy Steve's Coffee
215 Wabasha St. South
651.224.8319

www.wabashastreetcaves.com
Coffee, tea, Italian sodas, beer and wine, fresh-made Belgium waffles, smoothies, and sandwiches. "You may come in grumpy, but you sure won't leave that way."

J & S Bean Factory
1342 Thomas Ave.
651.645.6466
"The good stuff."

J & S Bean Factory
1518 Randolph Ave.
651.699.7788
The first one.

Java Train
1341 Pascal St. North
651.646.9179
www.javatraincoffee.com
Family-friendly coffee house serving Izzy's ice cream. Play areas for kids, including a real train.

Jerabek's New Bohemian Coffeehouse
63 Winifred St. West
651.228.1245
www.jerabeks.com
Coffee house, bakery, deli, and gifts. Specializing in Old World pastries since 1906.

Kopplin's Coffee
490 Hamline Ave. South
651.698.0457
www.kopplinscoffee.com
For true brewing connoisseurs.

Lady Elegant's Tea Room
2230 Carter Ave.
651.645.6676
www.ladyelegantstea.com
Where the world waits while you have tea. Offering three-, four-, and six-course themed tea events all year 'round.

Madhatters Coffee Café & Tea House
945 West Seventh St.
651.227.2511
www.madhatterteahouse.com
Friends, food, and philosophy by the cup.

Nina's Coffee Café
165 Western Ave. North
651.292.9816
A café in a beautiful historic building made famous by F. Scott Fitzgerald.

Pat & Mike's Lobby Shoppe
85 Seventh Place East
651.292.8888
and
401 Robert St.
651.726.7777
Coffee bar, lunch, and gift shop.

Polly's Coffee Cove
1382 Payne Ave.
651.771.5531
Boxed lunches. Off-street parking. Delivery service available.

Rudies Coffeehouse

Rudies Coffeehouse

1169 West Seventh St.
651.291.1963
An edgy little coffee shop specializing in Thai coffee and online gaming.

Steep/Brew Coffee Shop

101 Fifth St. East, Suite 296
651.221.9859
store.sbcoffeeshop.com

The Tea Garden

1692 Grand Ave.
651.690.3495
www.teagardeninc.com
Specializing in bubble tea (a delightful drink with sweet, chewy tapioca bubbles in the bottom).

Trotter's Café and Bakery

232 Cleveland Ave. North
651.645.8950
Fair-trade Peace Coffee, organic grains from Minnesota farms, locally produced free-range eggs for breakfast, and real maple syrup!

White Rock Coffee Roasters

769 Cleveland Ave. South
651.699.5448
and
649 Snelling Ave. South
651.695.1960
www.whiterockcoffee.com
A legend since 5 a.m.

RESTAURANTS

128 Cafe
128 Cleveland Ave. North
651.645.4128
www.128cafe.net
It's cozy. $$

Abu Nader
2095 Como Ave.
651.647.5391
Small deli serves satisfying falafel sandwiches. $

Babani's
544 Saint Peter St.
651.602.9964
Saint Paul's first (maybe only) Kurdish restaurant. Friendly, warm place. $

Barbary Fig
720 Grand Ave.
651.290.2085
Great Mediterranean cooking. $$

Black Dog Coffee & Wine Bar
308 Prince St.
651.228.9274
www.blackdogstpaul.com
Nice digs and great Lowertown location. $

Black Sea
737 Snelling Ave. North
651.917.8832
www.blackseарestaurant.com
Turkish. Run by Ali and Sema. Neighborly, cozy, delicious, and comfortable. $

Blondies Café
454 Snelling Ave. South
651.204.0152
www.blondiescafe.com
Fun, cozy atmosphere. Nice place to sit with free wireless. $

Boca Chica Restaurante
11 Cesar Chavez St.
651.222.8499
www.bocachicarestaurant.com
Patio. Mariachi music every fourth Saturday of the month. $ *(lunch)* $$ *(dinner)*

Café BonXai
1613 University Ave. West
651.644.1444
Hmong-owned fusion restaurant. $

Café Juliahna
879 Smith Ave. South
651.450.7070
www.cafejulianhna.com
Vegetarian sandwiches and soups. Inexpensive. $

Cafe Latté
850 Grand Ave.
651.224.5687
www.cafelatte.com
Join the crowds at Cafe Latté. $

Café Minnesota
Minnesota History Center
345 West Kellogg Blvd.
651.297.4859
www.minnesotahistorycenter.org
Outdoor patio. Breakfast and lunch only. $

Photo © Patricia Bour-Schilla

Cossetta's Famous Italian Market and Pizzeria on West Seventh Street

Caffe Biaggio
2356 University Ave.
651.917.7997
www.cafebiaggio.com
Italian bistro. Delicious. $ *(lunch)* $$ *(dinner)*

Cecil's Delicatessen And Bakery
651 Cleveland Ave. South
651.341.0170
Best reubens in town. $

Cheng Heng
448 University Ave. West
651.222.5577
Cambodian. $

Cherokee Sirloin Room
886 Smith Ave. South
651.457.2729
www.cherokeesirloinroom.com
A Saint Paul classic. $$

Christo's
214 Fourth St. East
651.224.6000
www.christos.com
Greek food in the restored Union Depot. Lunch buffet. $

Coffee News Café
1662 Grand Ave.
651.698.3324
A real neighborhood place with great desserts. $

Cossetta Italian Market and Pizzeria
211 West Seventh St.
651.222.3476
A Saint Paul landmark. $

Dari-ette Drive In
1440 Minnehaha Ave. East
651.776.3470
Seasonal April–October
Car-hops who really, truly come out to your door! Homemade malts , cherry Cokes, burgers, fries, onion rings, and pizza burgers! The underlying flavor, though, is Italian. Owned and operated for over fifty years by an East Side Italian family, Dari-ette offers the traditional sauce, pasta, meatball sandwiches, hot

dago, even fried peppers! Topping it all off, the fresh banana malt! $

Dar's Double Scoop Ice Cream Shop
1046 Rice St.
No phone
One scoop for just $1.65. $

Day by Day Café
477 West Seventh St.
651.227.0654
www.daybyday.com
Good for breakfast, which is served all day. $

Degidio's
425 West Seventh St.
651.291.7398
Italian. Classic Saint Paul eatery. $

Dixie's on Grand
695 Grand Ave.
651.222.7345
www.dixiesongrand.com
Traditional Southern food. $$

Downtowner Woodfire Grill
253 West Seventh St.
651.228.9500
www.downtownerwoodfire.com
Cozy in winter. $$

East Side Thai
879½ Payne Ave.
651.776.6599
www.edenpizza.com
Tiny place, but best Thai and Pho. $

Eden Pizza
629 Aldine St.
651.646.7616
www.edenpizza.com
Saint Paul's newest pizza parlor, opened by lovers of cooking and poetry. $

Egg & I
2550 University Ave. West
651.647.1292
Breakfast and lunch. $

El Burrito Mercado
175 Cesar Chavez Blvd.
651.227.2192
www.elburritomercado.com
Satisfying, inexpensive Mexican taquería inside a West Side supermercado. $

El Patio Mexican Grill
242 West Seventh St.
651.209.9210
Authentic Mexican food with great service. $$

Everest on Grand
1276–78 Grand Ave.
651.696.1666
www.everestongrand.com
Nepalese. Terrific curries and momos (dumplings). $$

Fasika
510 Snelling Ave. North
651.646.4747
www.fasika.com
Ethiopian. If you like meat, you'll like Fasika. Prices vary. $

Flamingo
490 Syndicate Street North
651.917.9332
www.flamingorestaurantmn.com
East African-Eritrean cuisine. Fabulous. $

Forepaughs
276 Exchange St. South
651.224.5606
www.forepaughs.com
Victorian mansion built by its namesake in 1870. French. $$$

Photo © Patricia Bour-Schilla

Khyber Pass Café —great Afghani food

Fuji Ya
465 North Wabasha St.
651.310.0111
Authentic Japanese. $$

Grand Ole Creamery
750 Grand Ave.
651.293.1655
www.grandolecreamery.com
Yummy homemade ice cream. $

Grandview Grill
1818 Grand Ave.
651.698.2346
Gleaming '50s-decor malt shop. $

Great Waters Brewing Company
426 Saint Peter St.
651.224.2739
www.greatwatersbc.com
Brew pub and restaurant. $

Happy Gnome
498 Selby Ave.
651.287.2018
www.thehappygnome.com
Terrific pub food, over thirty taps, outdoor seating. $$

Highland Grill
771 Cleveland Ave. South
651.690.1173
www.highlandgrill.com
Good sweet potato fries and fun staff. $

Italian Pie Shoppe & Winery
1670 Grand Ave.
651.221.0093
www.italianpieshoppe.com
Established in 1976. $

Izzy's Ice Cream Cafe
2034 Marshall Ave.
651.603.1458
www.izzysicecream.com
Inspired, quirky flavors. $

Jay's Cafe
791 Raymond Ave.
651.641.1446
www.jays-café.com
Yum, yum. Attractive. (lunch) $
(dinner) $$

Jerabek's New Bohemian Coffeehouse and Bakery
63 Winifred St. West
651.228.1245
www.jerabeks.com
Best soups ever. Cozy. Saint Paul at its finest. Vegan options. $

Key's Café
767 Raymond Ave.
504 Robert Street North
651.646.5756
www.keyscafe.com
Great staff and food. Family restaurant since 1973. $

Khyber Pass Cafe
1571 Grand Ave.
651.690.0505
www.khyberpasscafe.com
Afghan. Delicious and friendly. $$

Kim Huoy Chor
1664 University Ave. West
651.642.1111
Cambodian-Chinese restaurant buffet. $

Krua Thailand
432 University Ave. West
651.224.4053
Thai. $

La Cucaracha
36 Dale St. South
651.221.9682
Mexican. Since the 1960s. $$

La Grolla
452 Selby Ave.
651.221.1061
www.lagrollastpaul.com
Great ambience and lovely food. $$$

Lee's & Dee's Bar-B-Que Express
161 North Victoria St.
651.225.9454
Good ribs. $

The Lexington
1096 Grand Ave.
651.222.5878
www.the-lexington.com
A classic. $$

The Liffey
Irish Pub
175 West Seventh St.
651.556.1416
www.theliffey.com
Outdoor patio. $$

The Little Oven
1786 Minnehaha Ave. East
651.735.4944
www.thelittleoven.com
Italian. Prices vary but very reasonable. $

Little Szechuan
422 University Ave. West
651.222.1333
www.littleszechaun.com
Authentic Szechuan cuisine. $

Loto
380 Jackson St., Galtier Plaza
651.209.7776
David Fhima's restaurant on Mears Park. Outdoor seating. $$

Luci Ancora
2060 Randolph Ave.
651.698.6889
www.ristoranteluci.com
Italian. $$

The M St. Café
Saint Paul Hotel
350 Market St.
651.228.3855
www.mstcafe.com
$$

Mai Village
394 University Ave. West
651.290.2585
A re-creation of a traditional Vietnamese restaurant. $, $$

Mancini's Char House
531 West Seventh St.
651.224.7345
www.mancinis.com
Saint Paul all the way. Great food and entertainment in a unique lounge. $$, $$$

Meritage
410 St. Peter St.
651.222.5670
www.meritage-stpaul.com
One of Saint Paul's newest restaurants. French influenced. $$

Mickey's Dining Car
36 West Seventh St.
651.222.5633
On National Register of Historic Places. Thirties art deco architecture. Open 24 hours a day, 365 days a year. $

Mirror of Korea
761 Snelling Ave. North
651.647.9004
A solid Korean restaurant. $

Moscow on the Hill
371 Selby Ave.
651.291.1236
www.moscowonthehill.com
Russian. Nice backyard patio. $$

Muddy Pig
162 Dale St. North
651.254.1030
www.muddypig.com
Neighborhood bar and grill. $

Muffuletta
2260 Como Ave.
651.644.9116
www.muffuletta.com
Outdoor seating. $ (lunch) $$ (dinner)

New Hong Kong Kitchen Chinese Palace
1192 Dale St.
651.489.8681
Chinese. $

Photo © Patricia Bour-Schilla

Moscow on the Hill

Nina's Coffee Café
165 Western Ave. North
651.292.9816
Great neighborhood hangout on Cathedral Hill. $

The Nook
492 Hamline Ave. South
651.698.4347
Classic neighborhood bar and grill. $

Obb's Sports Bar & Grill
1347 Burns Avenue
651.776.7010
Large portions of home-cooked meals, Friday night Lenten fish fries, quick, thoughtful service/servers, and roses on Valentine's Day. Top it off with an ice-cold beer. $

Pad Thai Grand Café
1659 Grand Ave.
651.690.1393
www.padthaigrand.
nv.switchboard.com
Thai. Friendly neighborhood restaurant.
$$

Padelford Packet Boat Co., Inc.
Harriet Island
651.227.1100
www.riverrides.com
Prime rib dinner cruises every Friday.
$$$

Pastor Hamilton's Bar-B-Que
1150 East Seventh St.
651.772.0279
www.pastorhamilton-bbq.com
One-of-a-kind Saint Paul eatery. Great ribs. $

Patrick McGovern's Pub
225 West Seventh St.
651.224.5821
$

Pazzaluna
360 Saint Peter St.
651.223.7000
www.pazzaluna.com
Dinner only. Complimentary valet parking. $$

Pizza Lucé
1183 Selby Ave.
651.288.0186
www.pizzaluce.com
Unusual, tasty pizzas; deliveries. Great taps. $

Porky's Drive-In
1890 University Ave. West
651.644.1790
The best onion rings. Classic car-watching hangout on summer weekends. $

Puerta Azul
1811 Selby Ave.
651.646.7033
www.puertaazulrestaurant.com
Excellent Puerto Rican cuisine. $$

Punch Neopolitan Pizza
704 Cleveland Ave. South
651.696.1066
Neighborhood bistro. $

Que Nha Vietnamese Restaurant
849 University Ave. West
651.290.8552
Vietnamese. $

Ray's Mediterranean Restaurant
1199 West Seventh St.
651.224.3883
www.raysmediterranean.com
$

Red's Savoy Inn and Pizza
421 East Seventh St.
651.227.1437
Close to police headquarters. $

Ristorante Luci
470 Cleveland Ave. South
651.699.8258
www.ristoranteluci.com
Italian. $$

River Boat Grill
Harriet Island riverfront
651.290.2363
www.riverboatgrill.com
$

Ruam Mit Thai Cafe
475 Saint Peter St.
651.290.0067
$

Saji-Ya
695 Grand Ave.
651.292.0444
www.sajiya.com
Japanese restaurant and bar. $$

St. Clair Broiler
1580 St. Clair Ave.
651.698.7055
www.stclairbroiler.com
$

St. Paul Grill
The Saint Paul Hotel
350 Market St.
651.292.9292
www.stpaulhotel.com
Classic Saint Paul eatery. $$$

Sakura
350 Saint Peter St.
651.224.0185
www.sakurastpaul.com
Japanese. $$

Serlin's Café
1124 Payne Ave.
651.776.90035
All-American. $

Shamrock Grill
995 West Seventh St.
651.228.9925
A real pub. Music too. $

The Strip Club
378 Maria Ave.
651.793.6247
Best flourless chocolate cake.
Great view of the downtown skyline. $$

Supatra's Thai Cuisine
967 West Seventh St.
651.222.5859
$

Photo © Patricia Bour-Schilla

Tin Cup's Place

Swede Hollow Café
725 East Seventh St.
651.776.8810
www.swedehollowcafe.com
Certified organic fair-trade coffees from around the world, incredible baked goods that melt in your mouth, soups, salads and sandwiches made to order on fresh breads. A lovely patio and a garden to linger in . . . $

Tanpopo Noodle Shop
308 Prince St.
651.209.6527
www.tanpoporestaurant.com
Simple and elegant Japanese food. Inexpensive. $

Taste of Thailand
1671 Selby Ave.
651.644.3997
www.tasteofthailand.net
$

Tavern on Grand
656 Grand Ave.
651.228.9030
www.tavernongrand.com
Famous for walleye. $$

Tavern on the Avenue
825 Jefferson Ave.
651.227.6315
www.tavontheavenue.com
Karaoke on Thursdays and Saturdays. $

Tay Ho Restaurant
302 University Ave. West
651.228.7216
Chinese, Vietnamese. $

Tin Cup's Place
1220 Rice St.
651.489.7585
Classic Saint Paul bar joint—chicken and ribs. Sunday brunch. Live music all weekend. $

Trieu Chau Restaurant
500 University Ave. West
651.222.6148
Outstanding soups and tasty sandwiches. Best egg rolls. $

Trattoria da Vinci
400 Sibley St.
651.222.4050
www.trattoriadavinci.com
Italian. Romantic. $$

Il Vesco Vino
579 Selby Ave.
651.222.7000
Nice patio. $$

W. A. Frost & Company
Dacotah Building
374 Selby Ave.
651.224.5715
www.wafrost.com
A favorite destination since 1975. Incomparable ambiance and Old World character. Fireplaces, charming bar, and European-style garden patio. $$, $$$

Yarusso's
637 Payne Ave.
651.776.4848
www.yarussos.com
Italian. Since 1933. Classic. Stop by for the sauce, stay for the bocce ball. $

THEATER

Actors Theater of Minnesota

350 St. Peter St., Suite 254
651.290.2290
www.actorsmn.org.
This professional theater company presents an annual season at the Lowry Lab Theater in downtown Saint Paul.

Anodyne Theatre

825 Carleton St.
651.646.8242
Anodyne Theatre produces conventional and unconventional works and continues community building by supporting emerging performing artists.

Commedia Beauregard

354 Warwick St.
651.797.4967
www.cbtheatre.org
"Theatre that is beautiful in expression." Commedia Beauregard presents theater in translation—classic and modern works from around the world translated into English and made accessible to a modern audience.

Dreamland Arts

677 Hamline Ave. North
651.645.5506
www.dreamlandarts.com
A gathering place for creative expression through the arts that builds a healthy community.

Gremlin Theatre

509 Sibley St.
651.228.7008
www.gremlin-theatre.org
This dynamic and exciting small professional theater focuses on a wide range of styles and works in an intimate, urban venue.

Great American History Theatre

30 East Tenth St.
651.292.4323
www.historytheatre.com
The Great American History Theatre is a nonprofit, professional theater in downtown Saint Paul devoted to creating and producing plays about Minnesota, the Midwest, and the diverse American experience.

The Historic Mounds Theatre

1029 Hudson Rd.
651.772.2253
www.moundstheatre.org
The Historic Mounds Theatre is home to Starting Gate Productions and provides Dayton's Bluff and Saint Paul's East Side, as well as the larger Twin Cities community, with engaging, live entertainment. The theatre itself is owned and operated by the Portage for Youth, a nonprofit, after-school and summer enrichment program for young women.

In the Basement Productions

P.O. Box 65861
www.itbp.org
Working out of the Fourth Street Theatre, this nonprofit company produces original, classic, and contemporary works, emphasizing the unique talents and contributions of each individual artist.

Lex-Ham Community Theater

1184 Portland Ave.
651.644.3366
www.LexHamArts.org
The Lex-Ham Community Theater offers a variety of ways for novice and experienced theater lovers and performers in the Saint Paul and Twin Cities area to become involved: Shakespeare Reading Series, acting classes, and main stage theater productions throughout the year.

Lowry Theater

16 West Fifth St.
651.227.2464
www.wegottabingo.com
Professional dinner theater presenting interactive comedies.

Lowry Lab Theater

350 St. Peter St.
651.644.1890

Minnesota Jewish Theatre Company

P.O. Box 16155
651.647.4315
www.mnjewishtheatre.org
Telling stories of our common search for identity in a multicultural world. Igniting your mind by touching your heart (even if you're not Jewish!). Performances located at Hillcrest Center Theater, 1978 Ford Parkway.

Nautilus Music-Theater

308 Prince St., Suite 250
651.298.9913
Nautilus supports the creation, development, and production of new operas and music theater pieces, working with writers, composers, performers, and directors. Works in progress are presented in a monthly rough-cuts program. Occasional full productions include world premieres and innovative presentations of existing works.

Skylark Opera

Landmark Center, Suite 414
75 West Fifth St.
651.292.4309
www.skylarkopera.org
Founded in 1980, Skylark Opera presents a wide-ranging repertoire of opera, operetta, and musical theater emphasizing strongly balanced musical and theatrical values. Skylark Opera stresses accessibility by performing works in English in intimate venues at moderate prices.

Park Square Theatre

20 West Seventh Place
651.291.7005
www.parksquaretheatre.org
This professional theater in downtown Saint Paul produces a perfect balance of familiar favorites and fresh new stories. 2009 productions include Dr. Jekyll and Mr. Hyde, Grey Gardens, I Have Before Me a Remarkable Document Given to Me by a Young Lady from Rwanda, *and* Spider's Web.

Penumbra Theatre Company

270 North Kent St.
651.224.3180
www.penumbratheatre.org
Penumbra Theatre Company is Minnesota's only professional African American theater company, performing at the Martin Luther King/Hallie Q. Brown Center in the heart of the Selby-Dale neighborhood. 2009 productions include The Whipping Man *and* Radio Golf.

Starting Gate Productions

P.O. Box 16392
651.645.3503
www.startinggate.org
Performing at the Mounds Theatre in the Dayton's Bluff neighborhood, this small professional theater group produces primarily classic and contemporary dramas and comedies.

SteppingStone Theatre for Youth Development
55 North Victoria St.
(corner of Portland and Victoria)
651.225.9265
www.steppingstonetheatre.org
SteppingStone Theatre is Saint Paul's premier youth-centered arts organization, creating high-quality, affordable family entertainment that feeds the mind.

Teatro del Pueblo
209 Page St. West, Suite 208
Saint Paul, MN 55107
651.224.8806
www.teatrodelpueblo.org
Teatro is a fun-loving, hard working theater company devoted to raising awareness of Latino issues, artists, and culture. Located on the West Side, Teatro serves many communities across the state with educational residencies, touring shows, and the Annual Political Theater Festival.

The Theatrical Music Company
152 Hurley Ave. East
651.554.7794
www.mnartists.org
The focus of this innovative, award-winning performance ensemble is on re-imagining how music tells stories.

Photo © Patricia Bour-Schilla

SteppingStone Theatre's new home

MUSIC

Arnellia's

1183 University Ave. West
651.642.5975
www.arnellias.com
Music almost every night; karaoke. The 'Legendary Club Apollo' of Minnesota.

Artists' Quarter

408 St. Peter St.
651.292.1359
www.artistsquarter.com
Jazz most nights.

Big V's Saloon

1567 University Ave. West
651.645.8472
www.bigvs.com
21+ experimental, indie, and punk shows.

Dubliner Pub

2162 University Ave. West
651.646.5551
Music nightly, except Mondays, starting at 9:30 p.m.

Ginkgo Coffeeshop

721 Snelling Ave. North
651.645.2647
www.ginkgocoffee.com
Jazz and folk.

Half Time Rec

1013 Front St.
651.488.8245
www.halftimerec.com
Irish, Celtic, and Cajun.

Hat Trick Lounge

134 East Fifth St.
651.228.1347
www.robincommunications.com/hat_trick_lounge.htm
Lots of music!

Minnesota Music Café

499 Payne Ave.
651.776.4699
www.minnesotamusiccafe.com
Fun place to dance.

O'Gara's Garage

164 Snelling Ave. North
651.644.3333
www.ogaras.com
Music every week.

Saint Paul Chamber Orchestra

408 Saint Peter St., Third Floor
651.291.1144
www.thespco.org
America's premier chamber orchestra.

Shamrock Grill

995 West Seventh St.
651.228.9925
Call for band schedule.

Station 4

201 Fourth St. East
651.298.0173
www.station-4.com
Many all-ages shows.

Tavern on the Avenue

825 Jefferson Ave.
651.227.6315
www.tavontheavenue.com
Music every Friday and Saturday night starting at 10 p.m. No cover.

Turf Club

1601 University Ave. West
651.647.0486
www.turfclub.net
One-of-a-kind music scene.

DANCE

Sunday Night Social Dances
Half Time Rec
1013 Front St.
651.488.8245
www.halftimerec.com
8–11 p.m. Band varies weekly. Usually couples dancing. Dance lesson before the dance. $5.

Swing Night on Thursdays
Wabasha Caves
215 Wabasha St. South
651.224.1191
www.wabashastreetcaves.com
Doors open at 6 p.m. Lesson at 6:15. Live music 7–9 p.m. Remember the password(s): Gus sent me. *All-ages event. $7.*

Third Saturdays Argentine Tango
Black Dog Coffee & Wine Bar
308 Prince St.
651.228.9274
www.blackdogstpaul.com
Lesson at 7:30, dance at 8 p.m. Beginners welcome.

Tuesdays Clogging
Oddfellows' Hall
(Corner of Hampden and Raymond avenues.)
651.644.9549
tanby@aol.com
Alcohol free. Dancing begins at 8 pm.

Wednesday Ceili Dancing and Lessons
The Dubliner
2162 University Ave. West
651.646.5551
7–9 p.m. Lesson at beginning of dance. Free.

Wednesday Ceili Dancing and Lessons
The Conway Recreation Center
2090 Conway St.
7–8:45 p.m. Alcohol free. Lesson at beginning of dance. Free.

ART GALLERIES

Art Resources Gallery
494 Jackson St.
651.292.8475

AZ Gallery
308 Prince St.
651.224.3757
www.theazgallery.org

Catherine G. Murphy Gallery
College of Saint Catherine
2004 Randolph Ave.
651.690.6637
www.stkate.edu/gallery/

Evoke Gallery
355 Wabasha St. North
Suite 140
651.224.6388
www.evokegallery.com

Grand Hand Gallery
619 Grand Ave.
651.312.1122
www.thegrandhand.com

9th Street Entry Gallery
Rossmor Building
500 North Robert St.
651.638.6527
www.bethel.edu/galleries

Olson Gallery
CLC Building, 2nd floor
3900 Bethel Drive
651.638.6527
www.bethel.edu/galleries

Raymond Avenue Gallery
761 Raymond Ave.
651.644.9200

Water and Oil Art Gallery
506 Kenny Rd.
651.774.2260
www.waterandoil.com

Photo © Patricia Bcur-Schilla

Raymond Avenue Gallery

Common Good Books
165 Western Ave. North
651.225.8989
www.commongoodbooks.com

Hmong ABC
298 University Ave. West
651.293.0019
hmongabc@hmongabc.com

Lee's Books
375 Wabasha St. North
651.225.9118

Micawber's Books
2238 Carter Ave.
651.646.5506
www.micawbers.com

Midway Books
1579 University Ave. West
651.644.7605
www.midwaybook.com

Red Balloon Bookstore
891 Grand Ave.
651.224.8320
www.redballoonbookshop.com

Sixth Chamber Used Books
1332 Grand Ave.
651.690.9463
www.sixthchamber.com

Photo © Patricia Bour-Schilla

Common Good Books

American Association of Woodturners Gallery of Wood Art
222 Landmark Center
75 West Fifth St.
651.484.9094
www.woodturner.org
Spectacular wood art.

Gibbs Museum
2097 West Larpenteur Ave.
651.646.8629
www.rchs.com
Experience the re-creation of pioneer and Dakotah life. Closed mid-Nov to mid-Apr.

The Goldstein Museum of Design
University of Minnesota
241 McNeal Hall
1985 Buford Ave.
612.624.7434
www.goldstein.che.umn.edu
Art in everyday life.

Jackson Street Roundhouse
193 East Pennsylvania Ave.
651.228.0263
www.mtmuseum.org
Working railroad museum

Minnesota Children's Museum
10 West Seventh St.
651.225.6000
www.mcm.org
Lots of fun for kids of all ages.

Minnesota History Center Museum
345 Kellogg Blvd. West
651.259.3000 or 800.657.3773
www.mnhs.org
Rotating exhibits. Extraordinary library.

Minnesota Museum of American Art
50 Kellogg Blvd. West, Suite 341
651.266.1030
www.mmaa.org
Small but stunning.

Raptor Center
University of Minnesota
1920 Fitch Ave.
612.624.4745
www.theraptorcenter.org
Check out the hawks, eagles, falcons, and owls.

Science Museum of Minnesota
120 Kellogg Blvd. West
651.221.9444
www.smm.org
Includes Omnimax Theater.

The Schubert Club's Museum of Musical Instruments
Lower level and second floor of Landmark Center
75 West Fifth St.
651.292.3267
www.schubert.org
Mon–Fri. 11 a.m.–3 p.m., Sun. 1–5 p.m. Free.

Twin City Railroad Museum
1021 East Bandana Blvd.
Suite 222
651.647.9628
www.tcmrm.org
State-of-the-art miniature railroad. Ages 5 and up: $4.

HISTORICAL SITES AND TOURS

Alexander Ramsey House
265 South Exchange St.
651.296.8760
www.mnhs.org/ramseyhouse
Home of Alexander Ramsey, completed in 1872. Guided hourly tours, 10 a.m.– 3 p.m., Fridays and Saturdays; noon–3 p.m. Sunday. Closed Jan. 2 to May 31.

Assumption Church
51 West Seventh St.
651.224.7536
Roman Catholic Church built in 1871. On National List of Historic Places. Guided or self-guided tours.

Cathedral of Saint Paul
239 Selby Ave.
651.228.1766
www.cathedralsaintpaul.org
Construction completed in 1915. Guided tours Mondays, Wednesdays, and Fridays, 1 p.m.

Governor's Residence
1006 Summit Ave.
651.297.2161
www.admin.state.mn.us/buildings/residence
Limited public tours.

Historic Fort Snelling
Highways 5 and 55
612.726.1171
www.mnhs.org/fortsnelling
Open May through October. Reconstructed 1820s military post. Costumed guides and demonstrations.

James J. Hill House
240 Summit Ave.
651.297.2555
www.mnhs.org/hillhouse
The red sandstone residence was completed in 1891. Art exhibit and tours. Tours $8 adults, $6 seniors.

Julian H. Sleeper House
66 Saint Albans St. South
651.225.1505
www.julianhsleeperhouse.com
Nine exhibition rooms of the Gilded Age. Includes President James A. Garfield's memorabilia. Tours by appointment.

Minnesota Korean War Veterans' Memorial
State Capitol Grounds
Dramatic sculpture honoring troops who fought in Korea.

Minnesota State Capitol
75 Rev. Dr. Martin Luther King Jr. Blvd.
651.296.2881 (tours)
www.mnhs.org/statecapitol
Cass Gilbert's masterpiece. Guided tours on the hour. Free.

Minnesota Vietnam Veterans' Memorial
State Capitol Grounds
www.mvvm.org
Granite memorial recognizes and honors the 68,000 Minnesotans who served in Vietnam, of whom 1,077 were killed and 40 are still missing.

Old Muskego Church
Luther Seminary
2375 Como Ave.
651.641.3456
www.luthersem.edu/events
First church built by Norse immigrants in America in 1844 in Wisconsin. Moved to Luther Seminary in 1904. Self-guided or guided tours upon request.

Ramsey County Courthouse and Saint Paul City Hall
15 Kellogg Blvd. West
651.266.8500
www.co.ramsey.mn.us
Built in 1932; art deco architecture. The "Vision of Peace" statue designed by Carl Milles is three stories high and sculpted from onyx.

Roy Wilkins Memorial
State Capitol Grounds
Honors Minnesota native and civil rights leader Roy Wilkins. Designed by Curtis Patterson.

Saint Paul Public Central Library
90 Fourth St. West
651.266.7000
www.stpaul.lib.mn.us
Italian Renaissance Revival building built in 1917.

Wabasha Street Caves
215 Wabasha St. South
651.224.1191
www.wabashastreetcaves.com
Swing dancing, tours. Cave tours 5 p.m. Thurs., 11 a.m. Sat. and Sun.

FOOD CO-OPS

Hampden Park Food Co-op
928 Raymond Ave.
651.646.6686
www.hampdenparkcoop.com
Working member discounts, friendly volunteer staff, great prices, strong neighborhood feel, terrific soups.

Mississippi Market Food Co-ops:
1810 Randolph Ave.
651.690.0507
www.msmarket.coop
Small and friendly.

Mississippi Market Food Co-ops:
622 Selby Ave.
651.310.9499
www.msmarket.coop
Superb deli and attractive layout. Café, tiny, exquisite outdoor park.

Photo © Patricia Bour-Schilla

Hampden Park Co-op

SPORTS

Bocce Ball
HalfTime Rec
1013 Front Ave.
651.488.8245
www.halftimerec.com
Also weekly dart and pool leagues.

Minnesota RollerGirls
Roy Wilkins Auditorium
175 Kellogg Blvd. West, Suite 501
Saint Paul
651.265.4899
www.theroy.org

Minnesota State High School League
2100 Freeway Blvd.
Brooklyn Center
763.560.2262
www.mshsl.org

Minnesota Swarm
317 Washington St.
888.MNS.WARM
www.mnswarm.com
Lacrosse

Minnesota Wild
317 Washington St.
651.222.WILD (box office)
www.wild.com
Hockey

Saint Paul Curling Club
470 Selby Ave.
651.224.7408
www.stpaulcurlingclub.org

Saint Paul Saints
1771 Energy Park Dr.
651.644.6659
www.saintsbaseball.com
Saint Paul's own minor league baseball team.

Saint Paul Bicycle Racing Club
www.spbrc.org
Bringing all levels of racers together.

CONTRIBUTORS' BIOGRAPHIES

Margaret Anzevino is the youngest of four daughters. She was actually born in the house on Beaumont Street. The first time she left it was when she went away to college. Margaret spent most of her thirty-nine years in education in the Roseville School District, first as a business teacher and then as a librarian. She loves traveling, reading, knitting, and politics. She left the house on Beaumont Street in 1995 when her mother died. She continued going back to the neighborhood until her church, St. Ambrose Church, closed. She still loves to drive down that street and relive the memories.

Sasha Aslanian is a lifelong Saint Paul resident, although she will admit to being born in Minneapolis. She now lives on Saint Paul's West Side with her husband and two daughters. She enjoys walking over the Wabasha Street Bridge to her job as a documentary radio producer at Minnesota Public Radio.

Mary Kay Bailey, part-time consultant and full-time mom, moved her family to Midway for the trains, parks, and yummy food. She is author of the blog live.eat.play.twincities.

Paul and Linda Bartlett moved from Green Bay to Eagan in 1996, discovered Lowertown a year later, and were hooked. They spent weekends frequenting the Farmers' Market and art galleries. Then epiphany struck: they dumped their suburban lifestyle and headed north. Look for them around Mears Park: they're the couple walking their Westie (Molly) and Scottie (Lucy).

Cynthia Davidson Bend is a budding young author of eighty-three years. Writing has enhanced her glamour, making her a three-time cover girl. Not since childhood, when she hit the front page of the *Saint Paul Dispatch* in the fond embrace of a circus boa constrictor, has she achieved such fame. So don't give up, you beauties: life begins at eighty. Read more: www.cynthiabend.dgi.bz.

Michelle Myers Berg is the fifth of eight children. She was raised by her parents, Paul and Arlene, and a whole host of fascinating people who roamed the streets of her Merriam Park neighborhood in the seventies. An actress, she has a BFA from the U of M-Minneapolis and completed her studies at American Conservatory Theatre. She lives in Saint Paul with her husband, Raymond, and their three children.

Gunilla Bjorkman-Bobb, who grew up in Finland and for some years called Denmark and Sweden home, moved to the United States in 1978. After being suburbanites, Gunilla, her husband, Gary, and their dog, Salla, now live on Saint Paul's Railroad Island. The gritty East Side neighborhood makes this family happy. The Bobbs can often be seen biking on Payne Avenue with Salla strapped in her basket, ears flapping in the wind. Or you'll see them in Swede Hollow Park, Salla optimistically in hot pursuit of deer or fox or hoping that the birds someday will forget how to fly.

Patricia Bour-Schilla has lived in Saint Paul all her life. She enjoys being with friends and family and spends her free time bicycling, hiking, and photographing. Her best friend is her partner, Larry.

Mary Legato Brownell, who grew up in Saint Paul, now lives just outside of Philadelphia and teaches in a nearby independent school. She's received study seminar grants from the National Endowment for the Humanities, the Leeway Foundation, Mid-Atlantic Arts Council, and Pennsylvania Council of the Arts. She has been published in *American Poetry Review, Pivot, Comstock Review, GSU, Margie, Wind, InkPot*, and other journals. She was awarded first honors by WB Yeats Society of NY, finalist and honorable mention by the *Comstock Review*, *"Discovery"/The Nation 2006*, and others.

Tom Conlon, a Macalester-Groveland native, has served on the Saint Paul School Board since 1992 and continues as its lone Republican member (and Saint Paul's only Republican elected official). He enjoys organizing authentic North Carolina barbecues at Gibb's Farm each spring and making near-annual trips to Germany each winter to ride and photograph railroad lines, a hobby since childhood. Each season, he is the announcer for Central High School's home basketball games and track meets. He loves local history and wants to see traditional Saint Paul landmarks and neighborhoods preserved. The *Saint Paul Almanac* gives him a way to capture those things he loves most about Saint Paul.

Carol Connolly, Saint Paul's first poet laureate, was appointed by Mayor Chris Coleman. Her family has lived in Saint Paul for six generations. She has been a political candidate, political and human rights activist, journalist, and poet. Her book of poems *Payments Due*, now in its fifth printing, was published by Minnesota Villages and Voices, a small press founded by poet Meridel LeSueur. Currently, Carol is a columnist for *Minnesota Law & Politics*, and for nine years, she has curated and hosted the monthly Readings by Writers series at University Club Saint Paul—one of a dozen venues in the Carol Connolly Reading Series named for her and now sponsored by Intermedia Arts. Each year, this series brings nearly 300 writers and poets to over 5,000 audience members.

Chelsea DeArmond lives in Saint Paul's historic Railroad Island neighborhood, where she loves to spend lots of time reading and writing on her front porch and walking in parks. She is studying to be a librarian at St. Kate's.

Anita Dualeh is a freelance writer and English as a Second Language consultant. She enjoys cooking food from around the world and has collected recipes from Korea, the Federated States of Micronesia, and Mongolia while living in each of these places. She is currently working on her repertoire of Somali cuisine.

Badeh Dualeh is a counselor. He is married and has a son. Though he has adjusted to winters in Minnesota, his favorite season is spring. Whenever he is in downtown Saint Paul, he likes to have a cup of coffee at Mickey's Dinner.

Teri J. Dwyer has been a fitness enthusiast all her life. She's been lucky enough to parlay her recreation passion into a great excuse to not grow up. As a freelance sports and health & fitness writer, she's made a career out of going outside to play.

Tina Dybvik boards the bus in Lowertown. Her work has appeared in *The Lake Country Journal* and *The Bear Deluxe Magazine*, and she occasionally sounds off in the *Downtown St. Paul Voice*. Visit her website at www.TinaDybvik.net.

Mahmoud El-Kati is a teacher and a writer. He is an active member of our Twin Cities community. He creates, works with, or supports a number of grassroots efforts, programs, and institutions throughout his immediate community. He finds it especially challenging as well as rewarding to work with and among the young. He believes that a clearer and more thoughtful understanding of history and an appreciation of the real meaning of culture make us wiser and mentally healthy human beings. He believes that the myth of "race" is at the core of American values and spoils nearly every virtue the nation claims. He believes an education that respects all human life is the key to a just society and that education is the enemy of the ignorance that springs from racism.

Abdulaziz Farah studies English at MORE Multicultural School in Saint Paul. He hales from Ethiopia.

Daniel Gabriel's new short story collection, *Tales from the Tinker's Dam*, has nothing to do with Saint Paul. Though he has worked for COMPAS for over 20 years—both as roster artist and as director for the Arts Education and Arts in Health Care programs—he denies any conflict of interest.

Tom Goldstein is a graduate of Carleton College and the William Mitchell College of Law. He grew up outside Washington, DC, but has called Saint Paul home since 1984. He is publisher and editor of the baseball journal *Elysian Fields Quarterly* and a member of the Saint Paul School Board. He also co-founded the annual Saint Paul Gus Macker Three-on-Three Tournament and spent five wonderful years coaching at Midway Little League. This past spring, twenty years after graduating from law school, he finally took—and passed—the Minnesota bar exam on his first try, showing that everybody gets lucky once in a while.

Heidi Grosch, as a new American immigrant to Norway, has renewed respect for the work of Neighborhood House. She performed as Constance Currie for public television and a Neighborhood House anniversary celebration and co-authored a script with EPOCH Productions about Constance Currie and her brother, Edward. She now writes for educational and children's markets.

Jan Zita Grover lives in the Tilsner Artists' Cooperative in Lowertown Saint Paul, where she spins, knits, writes, and works at Mississippi Market on Selby.

Patricia Hampl is a true daughter of Saint Paul—born here, resident here, fed by the place. She is the author of several critically acclaimed memoirs, including the recent *The Florist's Daughter* (2007), and is the recipient of a MacArthur Fellowship. You can learn more about her at www.patriciahampl.com.

Phebe Hanson has been keeping a diary since she was ten, writing poems since she was forty-seven, and e-mailing since she was sixty-nine. She is a Bush Literary Fellow who has published two books of poetry (*Sacred Hearts* and *Why Still Dance*), and co-authored a travel-friendship memoir, *Not So Fast*, with Joan Murphy Pride. Currently she is working on a book of poems about her mother, who died at age thirty-one, when Phebe was eight. Phebe is the proud mother of three grown children, nine grandchildren, and the great-grandmother of two.

Barbara Haselbeck grew up in Saint Paul and returned to live here about eight years ago, after her children were grown. She works as an editor in Minneapolis.

Margaret Hasse, winner of a National Endowment for the Arts Poetry Fellowship, among other literary honors, lives with her husband and two sons in the Tangletown area of Saint Paul. Her latest collection of poems is *Milk and Tides* (Nodin Press, 2008). Margaret's poems have been set to music and put in concrete in Saint Paul sidewalks. She hopes her poems will also appear on billboards, as skywriting, and stamped on the back of bowling shirts.

Mike Hazard is a multimedia artist who lives in Lowertown near the Farmers' Market. The poems here are from his series *Cornucopia*.

Donal Heffernan, a Saint Paulite for many years, figures the city takes planning to get lost in, which makes it one of his favorite places. A poet and writer as well as a baseball fan, he has written for the Tampa Bay Devil Rays, *FAN Magazine NYC*, and the Saint Paul Saints.

Dwight Hobbes has written for *Essence*, *Reader's Digest*, *Washington Post*, *Saint Paul Pioneer Press*, *Mpls/St. Paul*, *MN Law & Politics*, *Twin Cities Daily Planet*, and *Insight News*, where he writes the opinion column "Something I Said" and is lead arts critic. His plays are *Shelter*, *Dues*, *You Can't Always Sometimes Never Tell*, and *In the Midst*.

Jennifer Holder is a freelance writer regularly contributing to the *Minnesota Spokesman-Recorder* and the *Twin Cities Daily Planet*. Born in Jamaica, she lived in New York and California before settling in Saint Paul. Her book *A Black American in China: My Year of Teaching English in Zhejiang Province* is available.

Snow Htoo came to Saint Paul in June 2007 after living in a refugee camp in Thailand. She doesn't know how her parents chose her name, but certainly they never expected she would one day play in the snow with her children during the winter. Snow would like to get a job and continue studying English. She studies Functional Work English with the Minnesota Literacy Council.

Matt Jackson is thirty and has lived in Saint Paul his whole life. He owns rental property and so has a lot of free time. He spends it eating pho on University, drinking beer on Selby, and reading in the sun on Grand Avenue, accompanied by a cup of Earl Grey. Drop by and say hello.

Drew Johnson is a software engineer, homebrewer, and roller derby fan. Under the name "Garrison Killer," Drew writes the game recaps for the MNRG. He lives on Dayton's Bluff with his wife, Sherry, and their son.

Pat Kahnke is a freelance writer, an international slow-pitch softball instructor, and the pastor of Saint Paul Fellowship Church in Frogtown.

Deborah Keenan is the author of seven collections of poetry, including *Good Heart* and *Willow Room, Green Door*. She is the co-editor, with Roseann Lloyd, of *Looking for Home: Women Writing about Exile*, which won an American Book Award in 1991. Among other awards, Keenan has received two Bush Foundation Fellowships, an NEA Fellowship, and the Loft-McKnight Poet of Distinction Award. She has four children and is a professor and faculty advisor in the Graduate Liberal Studies School at Hamline University. Keenan lives and works in Saint Paul.

Garrison Keillor is the host and writer of *A Prairie Home Companion*, the author of many books, including the Lake Wobegon novels and *Daddy's Girl*, and the editor of *Good Poems* and *Good Poems for Hard Times*. His most recent publications are *Pontoon* and *Liberty*. His syndicated column, "The Old Scout," is seen in papers coast to coast. A member of the Academy of American Arts and Letters, he lives in Saint Paul.

Bob Knutson is an eater: Serlin's pies; trail lunches in the Boundary Waters Canoe Area Wilderness with bug juice (o.j.), raisins, and peanut butter on crackers; shore lunches with just-caught walleye; red velvet chocolate cake; ribs at Cherokee Steak House; and, a little out of the way, Sachertorte in Vienna.

T. R. Lacy was born in Minneapolis, 1943; BA, St. Olaf College. Retired English, speech, and journalism teacher. Editor, graphic artist, photojournalist, and poet. Founding editor of the *Elliot Park Surveyor* (Minneapolis) and the *Community Development Review* for the City of Minneapolis. Primary concerns/interests: *all* arts; "contemporary" liberté, égalité, fraternité; the commonweal and environmental sustainability; lifelong learning and serenity, etc. Currently residing in Minneapolis, focusing on poetry, photography, reading, and on *Jan*, his dear companion for sixteen years.

Andrea Taylor Langworthy admits she's not above stealing words from her husband's mouth for her *Rosemount Town Pages* newspaper column. One, about having lunch with her former husband, placed first in the *Chicken Soup for the Divorced Soul* contest. She also writes a monthly profile for *Minnesota Good Age* newspaper. Find her at andrealangworthy@frontiernet.net.

Tiffany Lee is a fourteen-year-old freshman. She loves to text on her phone and talk for hours after nine. She does nothing but sit around, babysit her little brother and her niece, and do chores. When possible, she writes poems and daydreams about one day flying with birds and tracking people down like a hawk. Otherwise, she's home being a complete bum.

Michelle Leon is finishing her degree in creative writing at Metropolitan State University. She loves writing, animals, cooking, gardening, things that are fun, *and* living in Saint Paul! Back in the day, she played in the band Babes in Toyland—yes, she will tell all about it, if you buy her a beer.

Kathryn Lindaas's family settled in West Saint Paul after nine months of hotel luxury on United Airlines' dime. Despite a fierce loyalty to United and Saint Paul, Kathy went over to the other side when she moved to Minneapolis and her career path put her on Northwest Airlines' payroll.

Charles Locks has written and lectured on Cass Gilbert. He is the author of the novel *Greater Trouble in the Lesser Antilles*.

Saul Lu was born in Burma but because of government oppression fled to the refugee camps in Thailand and then came to the United States He studies English at MORE Multicultural School in Saint Paul. Both he and his wife are employed at BIX Produce, alternating first and second shifts so they can also care for their children. His family likes going to Lake McCarron and other parks to swim, play soccer, and go sliding in winter. His favorite foods are his wife's home-cooked meals of pork or chicken with rice and vegetables. He loves bananas, grapes, and a variety of other fruits.

Najla M. is from Yemen. She's a student at Hubbs Center and is preparing for college. She has been living in Saint Paul for two years, and this is her second writing submission for the *Saint Paul Almanac*. She's so happy to join all the other writers in this beautiful book, which has many interesting subjects. Thanks for giving her the chance to join all of you again.

William S. McDowell II describes himself as a Black, thirty-six-year-old father of five, born in Kankakee, Illinois. He moved to Saint Paul in July 2000 and attended school at the MLC Learning Center in Rondo Library in 2008. He doesn't have his GED yet, but he still writes about his lifestyle in order to encourage those who are in the same boat he's rowing in.

Ronee McHendrik is mother/grandmother of ten—all of whom are, of course, fabulous. In addition to past publications as a biomedical research scientist, Ronee is currently writing a self-help book, *Don't Change, Just Bitch!* She is bogged down in the chapter "How to Relax and Enjoy Being a Procrastinator."

James McKenzie, after thirty-four years in the University of North Dakota English Department, eight of them directing UND's annual Writers Conference, volunteers at the Center for Victims of Torture and wears out shoes at an alarming pace in Saint Paul's Mac-Groveland, Merriam Park, and Highland Park neighborhoods.

Arthur C. McWatt taught for thirty-three years in the secondary schools of Saint Paul. He received his MA from the University of Minnesota in 1969. He has been writing about African American history for more than thirty years. He hopes to have his manuscript, *Crusaders for Justice: 1885 to 1985*, published in the future. Arthur and his wife, Katie, are the parents of four adult children and seven grandchildren. He's a lifelong resident of Saint Paul.

Lou "The Photo Guy" Michaels dreams of taking the perfect shot. He lives in Saint Paul and runs around each day taking photos. He's been photographing professionally for forty years. Contact Lou at lou@louthephotoguy.com or at www.louthephotoguy.com.

R. Allen Miner lives west of the river and has been getting lost trying to find his way around Saint Paul for over thirty years. He's done somewhat better since his daughter and her family moved to the Highland Park area three years ago. Grandchildren are a great learning experience.

Jim Moore is the author of six collections of poetry, including *Lightning at Dinner, The Freedom of History*, and *The Long Experience of Love*. His poems have appeared in many magazines and anthologies, including *American Poetry Review*, *The Nation*, *The New Yorker*, *Paris Review*, *Threepenny Review*, and *Pushcart Prize Anthology*. Moore has received many awards and fellowships. He teaches at Hamline University, the Colorado College, and online through the University of Minnesota Split Rock Arts Program. He is married to the photographer JoAnn Verburg. They live in Saint Paul and Spoleto, Italy.

Phyllis Moore, soon to be a world-famous science fiction and fantasy novelist, is the official biographer of precocious Danny Kress. Phyllis also writes for an online publication, www.triond.com.

José Moreno is a custodian in a Saint Paul middle school. He is licensed as a boiler engineer. Recently he started a small cleaning business with his wife. He has been involved in the Minnesota Community developing prevention programs for tobacco, HIV, and arthritis. He is part of a team making a thirty-minute Spanish video on HIV prevention that will be aired on Minnesota Public Television. Jose is very involved in the Episcopal Church, where he teaches classes on baptism and first communion. He loves spending time with his wife and daughter at Harriet Island, feeding the ducks and eating on the boat restaurant.

Nora Murphy lives in Saint Paul, the river town where she was born. She is the author of several children's history books, co-author of *Twelve Branches: Stories from Saint Paul* (Coffee House Press, 2003) and the forthcoming *Knitting the Threads of Time* (New World Library, 2009).

Su mya Naing is a Saint Paul Public School student. She is in ninth grade.

Suzanne Nielsen has never had an address outside of Minnesota a day in her life. It wasn't until recently, when phone numbers advanced to ten digits, that she thought of herself as an important contributor to a system held accountable. This is when she became a notary public. She carries her stamp with her at all times, with the Boy Scout motto on the tip of her tongue: *Be Prepared.*

Judith Niemi is an Iron Ranger by birth (Eveleth) and habit, and a long-time freelance editor, writer, and wilderness guide. She'll edit anything, writes mostly about travel and wilderness places. When not home in Saint Paul, she is probably teaching writing, canoeing, or animal tracking in northern Minnesota, Iceland, or the Peruvian Amazon. judith@womeninthewilderness.org.

Kimberly Nightingale has been accused of telling stories. She fantasizes about a Saint Paul with streetcars once again running down Grand, Selby, St. Clair, Payne, Maryland, Snelling, West Seventh, and more. The streetcars gleam. There's no diesel exhaust. Everybody is meeting everybody. Kimberly gets crabby if she doesn't hear live music regularly. You can find her at a concert near you.

Patrick O'Dougherty is a Carlson Heritage Wall author at the University of Minnesota. In the fall season, he works in the haunted houses where he plays lead coffin. Is that you, coffin? He is also a writer leader in Progressive causes.

Sandra Opokua is a Saint Paul Public School student in ninth grade. She is originally from Ghana, West Africa.

Eva Palma-Zuniga is a Chilean journalist and a freelance writer. She was the Spanish acquisitions editor at Llewellyn Worldwide, editor of *La Prensa de Minnesota*, and writer for *Viceversa Magazine*. She also worked for the Resource Center of the Americas. She has received the "Chile con mis ojos" award twice for her short stories, which have been shown on a Chilean TV station.

Gordon Parks (1912–2006) was a photographer, filmmaker, writer, and poet who blazed an incredible path of artistic brilliance. He was born in Kansas and moved to Saint Paul when he was fifteen years old. After working as a porter, against all odds he made a name for himself as a fashion photographer in Saint Paul and later became a photographer and reporter for *Life* magazine, famous for his gritty photo essays about the grinding effects of poverty in the United States and abroad. He wrote several books, poetry, and screenplays. He wrote and directed *The Learning Tree* (1969) and *Shaft* (1971). His work won many awards.

Alexs Pate's debut novel, *Losing Absalom*, received a Minnesota Book Award and was named Best First Novel by the Black Caucus of the American Library Association. Other novels include the *New York Times* bestseller *Amistad*, *Finding Makeba*, *The Multicultiboho Sideshow* (winner of a 2000 Minnesota Book Award), and *West of Rehoboth*. Pate is assistant professor of African-American and African Studies at the University of Minnesota. He taught creative writing and literature in Saint Paul at Macalester College in the 1990s. Pate lives in Minneapolis.

Melinda Pha is a Saint Paul Public School student. She is in ninth grade.

Mary Jean Port teaches writing at The Loft Literary Center. A late bloomer, she wed in her forties and likes to say she married her first and second husband at the same time. She lives in that other city with her husband, stepdaughter, and the idea of someday getting a Golden Retriever.

Kristine Price is a writing major at Metro State University and a frequent contributor to *Wright County Journal Press* and *Drummer* as a features writer. When not fighting for computer time with her teen at home, she is working on a memoir of her life in Saint Paul.

Brad Richason exhibits his unbalanced mental state by running vast distances for no rational justification and engaging in even greater lunacy as a Twin Cities-based freelance author. He can often be seen running along the Mississippi with his two chief collaborators, his wonderful wife, Missy, and Roscoe, the mischievous Golden Retriever.

Tou SaiKo Lee is a Spoken Word Poet born from a refugee camp in Thailand; he reflects his experiences, struggles, and vibrant Hmong culture through his writing. He creates an ICE box where creativity melts off the sides and adapts into the shapes of whatever surface it lands on.

Abram Sauer is not Jewish. He only mentions this as once, or sixty-two times, he has been assumed to be, which he isn't. His first novel, *Madison Zaftig*, will be available later. Its first word is *The*. Abram lives in a tri-state area and welcomes writing projects. Contact him at abesauer@yahoo.com. Check out his website at www.madisonzaftig.com.

Larry Schilla was born on the levee and played on the Mississippi River and bluffs most of his childhood and still does by hiking and biking. He plans on living on the West End of Saint Paul for a long time to come.

Andy Singer is a four-armed, six-eyed alien with large horns and powerful jaws. In 1965, he came from the planet Neptor to observe the earth and make small drawings of everything he saw. His multiple arms have enabled him to be very prolific and his multiple eyes have enabled him to see things that most humans are unaware of. If you see him riding his bicycle around Saint Paul, don't be intimidated by his appearance. He's really quite friendly. You can see more of his drawings and cartoons at www.andysinger.com.

Linda Straley grew up on the East Side of Saint Paul. After college, she moved to Arizona and for a time lived in Indiana and Florida. Minnesota is her home now. Growing up, she loved spending time with her grandparents because they always made her feel special. She would constantly pick their brains about family history, which led her maternal grandfather to give her a Scandinavian nickname that translated means "question box"—still fits to this day.

Michael Teffera was born and raised in Addis Ababa, Ethiopia. He's been here in Minnesota for two years. He graduated in Business Management from Addis Ababa University and worked in the Commercial Bank of Ethiopia for five years. Now he works at Wells Fargo Bank. He has three hobbies: writing short stories and poems, watching movies, and riding his bicycle.

See Thao is a Saint Paul Public Schools student. He is in ninth grade.

David Tilsen is still living in a rich fantasy world surrounded by family, friends, dogs, and squirrels. He doesn't particularly like the squirrels.

Drew Tilsen is the ultimate grease monkey doctor. You can almost always find Drew at his automotive repair shop Magics Automotive located at 237 Richmond, one block from West Seventh and St. Clair. He says a doctor has it easy with only one make and two models.

Ken Tilsen (aka Mandamus) Can be found at a protest or at one of his seventeen (and counting) great-grandchildren's birthday parties. Ken believes in *habeas corpus* for all people, including Americans and non-Americans, native peoples, immigrants, activists, farmers, children, grandchildren, and great-grandchildren.

Steve Trimble lives in the Dayton's Bluff neighborhood near Indian Mounds Park. He has taught at the college level and specializes in researching and writing the story of the Twin Cities and Minnesota. He serves on the editorial board of the Ramsey County Historical Society and the St. Paul Heritage Preservation Commission. This year he has a new book—*Historic Photos of St. Paul*—and a back yard full of heirloom tomatoes.

Gaoiaong Vang, Gao for short, is fourteen years old. Regular, hilarious teenage Hmong girl hoping one day she can roam the word with the dinosaurs. Yeah . . . She loves long walks on the beach and bogo dancing, *not*. She enjoys herself and she enjoys hanging out with the world. That's all.

Diego Vázquez, Jr. writes poems to flowers, birds, rocks, rivers, salmon, and people too! Vázquez wrote stories in *Twelve Branches*, and his novels include *Growing through the Ugly* and *The Fat-Brush Painter*. You might meet him in your school through a COMPAS residency. He is proud to have his poem stuck in cement.

Julian Welna is a thirteen-year-old Saint Paul native in eighth grade at Highland Junior High School. He loves the outdoors and enjoys fly fishing, writing, poetry, hunting, boating, swimming, and shooting clay target sports.

Lia Yang moved from Vietnam to the U.S. in 1993. After spending five years in San Diego, where it's nice and warm, she moved to Saint Paul where, she says, "it is not." Despite the weather, she loves to spend time outdoors in her big vegetable garden, and really enjoys walking everywhere she can. With five children and many, many grandchildren to visit, she puts in a lot of miles. Lia studies English at the Hmong American Partnership.

Kao Kalia Yang was born in Thailand's Ban Vinai Refugee Camp in 1980, and she immigrated to Saint Paul when she was six years old. A graduate of Carleton College and Columbia University, Yang is the co-founder of Words Wanted, an agency dedicated to helping immigrants with writing, translating, and business services. Visit her web site at www.kaokaliayang.com.

Nhia Xiong is a Saint Paul Public School student. She is in ninth grade.

PERMISSIONS

"Woman on Laurel Street Reports That Her Neighbor Has Stolen Nine Pairs of Her Shoes and Left a Pile of Honey and Flour by Her Car" from *Willow Room, Green Door* © 2007 by Deborah Keenan, reprinted with the permission of Milkweed Press.

"The Funeral" reprinted with the permission of ATRIA Books, a division of Simon & Schuster Adult Publishing Group from *Eyes with Winged Thoughts* by Gordon Parks. Copyright © 2005 by Gordon Parks.

Miscellaneous limericks © 2007/2008 by Garrison Keillor. Used with permission. All rights reserved.

Excerpt from *The Past Is Perfect: Memoir of a Father/Son Reunion*, "Seeing Willie Mays" © 2008 by Alexs Pate. Used with permission. All rights reserved.

"Trying to Leave Saint Paul" by Jim Moore, reprinted from *Pleiades*, 2008. Copyright © 2008 by Jim Moore. Used with permission.

Excerpt from *The Florist's Daughter*, copyright © 2007 by Patricia Hampl, reprinted by permission of Houghton Mifflin Harcourt Publishing Company.

Excerpt from *The Homecomer: A Hmong Family Memoir* © 2007 by Kao Kalia Yang, reprinted with the permission of Coffee House Press.

"Brand Names" from *Why Still Dance* © 2005 by Phebe Hanson, reprinted by permission of Nodin Press.

An excerpt from "Down St. Albans Hill in a Wooden Coaster" © 1996 by Arthur C. McWatt, reprinted by permission of the Ramsey County Historical Society, from vol. 30, no. 4 (Winter 1996), 1922 of *Ramsey County History*, published by the Ramsey County Historical Society.

"First Day of Kindergarten" and "In Response to the Evangelist Door-Knocking Who Asked: *What Saves You?*" from *Milk and Tides* © 2008 by Margaret Hasse, reprinted by permission of Nodin Press.

2009 YEAR PLANNER

	JANUARY	FEBRUARY	MARCH
1	TH NEW YEAR'S DAY	SU	SU
2	F	M GROUNDHOG DAY	M
3	SA	T	T
4	SU	W	W
5	M	TH	TH
6	T	F	F
7	W	SA	SA
8	TH	SU	SU INTERNATIONAL WOMEN'S DAY DAYLIGHT SAVING TIME BEGINS
9	F	M	M MAWLID AL-NABI
10	SA	T	T PURIM
11	SU	W	W
12	M	TH	TH
13	T	F	F
14	W	SA VALENTINE'S DAY	SA
15	TH	SU	SU
16	F	M PRESIDENTS' DAY	M
17	SA	T	T ST. PATRICK'S DAY
18	SU	W	W
19	M MARTIN LUTHER KING JR. DAY	TH	TH
20	T	F	F SPRING EQUINOX
21	W	SA	SA
22	TH	SU	SU
23	F	M	M
24	SA	T MARDI GRAS/SHROVE TUESDAY	T
25	SU	W ASH WEDNESDAY	W
26	M CHINESE NEW YEAR	TH	TH
27	T	F	F
28	W	SA	SA
29	TH		SU
30	F		M
31	SA		T

2009 YEAR PLANNER

	APRIL		MAY		JUNE	
1	W	APRIL FOOLS' DAY	F		M	
2	TH		SA		T	
3	F		SU		W	
4	SA		M		TH	
5	SU	PALM SUNDAY	T	CINCO DE MAYO	F	
6	M		W		SA	
7	T		TH		SU	
8	W		F		M	
9	TH	PASSOVER BEGINS	SA		T	
10	F	GOOD FRIDAY	SU	MOTHER'S DAY	W	
11	SA		M		TH	
12	SU	EASTER	T		F	
13	M		W		SA	
14	T		TH		SU	FLAG DAY
15	W		F		M	
16	TH		SA		T	
17	F		SU		W	
18	SA		M		TH	
19	SU		T		F	JUNETEENTH
20	M		W		SA	
21	T		TH		SU	FATHER'S DAY
22	W	EARTH DAY	F		M	SUMMER SOLSTICE
23	TH		SA		T	
24	F		SU		W	
25	SA		M	MEMORIAL DAY	TH	
26	SU		T		F	
27	M		W		SA	
28	T		TH		SU	
29	W		F	SHAVUOT	M	
30	TH		SA		T	
31			SU			

2009 YEAR PLANNER

	JULY	AUGUST	SEPTEMBER
1	W	SA	T
2	TH	SU	W
3	F	M	TH
4	SA INDEPENDENCE DAY	T	F
5	SU	W	SA
6	M	TH	SU
7	T	F	M LABOR DAY
8	W	SA	T
9	TH	SU	W
10	F	M	TH
11	SA	T	F
12	SU	W	SA
13	M	TH	SU
14	T	F	M
15	W	SA	T
16	TH	SU	W
17	F	M	TH
18	SA	T	F
19	SU	W	SA ROSH HASHANAH
20	M	TH	SU INTERNATIONAL DAY OF PEACE
21	T	F	M EID AL-FITR
22	W	SA RAMADAN BEGINS	T FALL EQUINOX
23	TH	SU	W
24	F	M	TH
25	SA	T	F
26	SU	W	SA
27	M	TH	SU
28	T	F	M YOM KIPPUR
29	W	SA	T
30	TH	SU	W
31	F	M	

2009 YEAR PLANNER

	OCTOBER		NOVEMBER		DECEMBER	
1	TH		SU	DAYLIGHT SAVING TIME ENDS ALL SAINTS DAY	T	
2	F		M	DAY OF THE DEAD	W	
3	SA		T		TH	
4	SU		W		F	
5	M		TH		SA	
6	T		F		SU	
7	W		SA		M	
8	TH		SU		T	
9	F		M		W	
10	SA		T		TH	INTERNATIONAL HUMAN RIGHTS DAY
11	SU		W	VETERANS DAY	F	
12	M	INDIGENOUS PEOPLE DAY	TH		SA	HANUKKAH BEGINS
13	T		F		SU	
14	W		SA		M	
15	TH		SU		T	
16	F		M		W	
17	SA		T		TH	
18	SU		W		F	MUHARRAM
19	M		TH		SA	
20	T		F		SU	
21	W		SA		M	WINTER SOLSTICE
22	TH		SU		T	
23	F		M		W	
24	SA	UNITED NATIONS DAY	T		TH	
25	SU		W		F	CHRISTMAS
26	M		TH	THANKSGIVING DAY	SA	KWANZAA BEGINS
27	T		F		SU	
28	W		SA	EID AL-ADHA	M	
29	TH		SU		T	
30	F		M		W	
31	SA	HALLOWEEN			TH	NEW YEAR'S EVE

Notes

Got a Saint Paul story? Send it to editor@saintpaulalmanac.com

The Saint Paul Almanac

Subscribe to it

Three annual issues for $30

(price includes tax, shipping, and handling)

To order

online: www.saintpaulalmanac.com

mail: Subscriptions
Saint Paul Almanac
PO Box 16243
Saint Paul, MN 55116

If mailing, please fill out and send the info below.

Begin with *2008 Saint Paul Almanac*

Begin with *2009 Saint Paul Almanac*

Check or money order enclosed

Charge: __ Visa __ MasterCard

CARD NUMBER

EXPIRATION DATE

SIGNATURE OF CARDHOLDER

MAILING ADDRESS

E-MAIL

For gift orders

SHIP TO NAME

MAILING ADDRESS